Learner biographies and learning cultures:
identity and apprenticeship in England and Germany

the Tufnell Press,
London,
United Kingdom

www.tufnellpress.co.uk

email contact@tufnellpress.co.uk

British Library Cataloguing-in-Publication Data
A catalogue record for this book is
available from the British Library

| *paperback* | *ISBN* | *1872767389* |
| | *ISBN-13* | *978-1-872767-38-3* |

Copyright © 2012 Michaela Brockmann
Database right the Tufnell Press (maker).

Printed in England and U.S.A. by Lightning Source

Learner biographies and learning cultures: identity and apprenticeship in England and Germany

Michaela Brockmann

ETHNOGRAPHY AND EDUCATION

The *Ethnography and Education* book series aims to publish a range of authored and edited collections including both substantive research projects and methodological texts and in particular we hope to include recent PhDs. Our priority is for ethnographies that prioritise the experiences and perspectives of those involved and that also reflect a sociological perspective with international significance. We are particularly interested in those ethnographies that explicate and challenge the effects of educational policies and practices and interrogate and develop theories about educational structures, policies and experiences. We value ethnographic methodology that involves long-term engagement with those studied in order to understand their cultures, that use multiple methods of generating data and that recognise the centrality of the researcher in the research process.

www.ethnographyandeducation.org

The editors welcome substantive proposals that seek to:
>   explicate and challenge the effects of educational policies and practices and
>   interrogate and develop theories about educational structures, policies and
>   experiences,
>   highlight the agency of educational actors,
>   provide accounts of how the everyday practices of those engaged in education are
>   instrumental in social reproduction.

The editors are
>   Professor Dennis Beach, University College of Borås, Sweden,
>   Bob Jeffrey, (Commissioning Editor), The Open University,
>   Professor Geoff Troman, Roehampton University, London and
>   Professor Geoffrey Walford, University of Oxford.

Titles in the series include,

Creative learning: European experiences, edited by Bob Jeffrey;

Researching education policy: Ethnographic experiences, Geoff Troman, Bob Jeffrey and Dennis Beach;

The commodification of teaching and learning, Dennis Beach and Marianne Dovemark;

Performing English with a postcolonial accent: Ethnographic narratives from Mexico, Angeles Clemente and Michael J. Higgins.

How to do Educational Ethnography edited by Geoffrey Walford

Ritual and Identity; The staging and performing of rituals in the lives of young people, Christoph Wulf et al.

Young people's influence and democratic education: Ethnographic studies in upper secondary schools, edited by Elisabet Öhrn, Lisbeth Lundahl and Dennis Beach

Contents

Acknowledgements

I am deeply indebted to the colleges and firms who agreed to take part in this study, and, above all, to the young people who let me into their worlds and from whose personal stories I learnt so much and without whom the study could not have happened. Equally, I would like to thank everyone who provided support by opening up avenues and setting up contacts. In particular, I am grateful to colleagues at Paderborn University, who kindly offered me a base for my research in Germany.

I am grateful to the editor of this book series, Dennis Beach, and the team at Tufnell Press for making this book happen.

I would like to thank Lorna Unwin, who, as my supervisor at the Institute of Education, provided expert guidance and continual support and encouragement throughout the writing of my thesis. I am also grateful to David Guile and Natasha Kersh for their helpful advice and valuable comments on earlier drafts, and to Karen Evans and Alison Taylor, who examined my thesis and who encouraged me to write this book.

Finally, a big thank-you goes to my family and friends for their emotional support and for the opportunity to explore ideas.

Chapter 1

Introduction

Background and research focus

The school-to-work transition has been described as a crucial phase in the life course, one in which young people make choices and decisions with may be critical in setting the direction of their future lives (for example, Ball, Maguire and Macrae, 2000a). With the de-standardisation of the life course and young people having to cope with discontinuities in their education and work careers, transitions are said to have become increasingly complex (Heinz and Krüger, 2001). Vocational education and training is an important arena within which young people make decisions, and one which has been undergoing substantial reform, in terms of both structure and content, involving a vast array of possible and sometimes uncertain outcomes.

While the interplay of structure and agency is a prevailing theme in the existing literature on school-to-work transition, studies have commonly emphasised the role of one over the other. Thus, outcomes concerning post-compulsory pathways are typically explained in terms of individualisation (for example, Heinz, 2002; Witzel and Kühn, 1999), or, more commonly, socialisation theory (for example, Banks et al., 1992; Bloomer and Hodkinson, 1997). The latter studies have demonstrated the continued relevance of structural factors, above all social class, in determining the distribution of resources and choice of transition pathways. Similarly, research on young people's experiences of work-based learning has focused on the reproduction of social class and, in particular, the role of organisational and occupational identity (for example, Colley et al., 2003).

On the whole, these studies have tended to neglect the rich biographical experiences of young people, and hence the complex nature of identity construction. As the studies lack an adequate conceptualisation of identity, biographical events and experiences are often drawn upon superficially and selectively. While many are longitudinal in design, they typically follow young people only over a relatively short period of time. Also, drawing on the dominant discourse of the academic-vocational divide (Pring, 1995) and neglecting young people's perspectives and experiences, much research dismisses vocational choices and constructs young people as failures and second-chance learners.

Working class students are commonly viewed as constituting a homogenous whole of 'practical' learners with enduring identities. The challenge for me in my own research was to take a more holistic approach to the study of school-to-work transitions.

This book is based on my doctoral thesis which I undertook, on a part-time basis, from October 2007 to September 2011. It examines the school-to-work transitions of young people in contrasting national policy and vocational education contexts—the apprenticeship systems in England and Germany. Adopting a comparative, multi-method ethnographic approach, combining biographic-interpretive interviews with participant observation, it explores the construction of learner biographies as temporal and context-specific; how young people negotiate their learner identities over time and in the context of particular learning environments. Distinguishing it from existing research, it is particularly concerned with young people's situated subjectivities, including their changing perspectives, over time and in different contexts: how they experience and act upon their environments, particular situations and events. Rather than using evidence selectively, the biographical approach allows for the reconstruction of young people's biographies, how certain dispositions and identities of learning were formed over time, in particular situations and environments, and how these led to further experiences of learning and hence processes of identity formation to the point where young people begin their apprenticeship, which constitutes a new arena for identity construction with its own rules and discursive framework.

A particular concern of the study is with the relationship between learners and the social identities (Goffman, 1968a) of occupations and pathways (and the norms and values that underpin them); the ways in which young people actively negotiate their self-identities; and the co-construction (production and re-production) of social structures and particular 'learning cultures' (James and Biesta, 2007). The concept of a learning culture serves to explore the ways in which learning environments are shaped by social contexts and the actors, such as tutors and learners, within them. The study goes beyond narrow conceptions of occupational or organisational identity by exploring the processes of identity construction as young people negotiate multiple identities, moving in a variety of social contexts. It is built on the work of Judith Butler (1990) on performativity which offers a valuable framework for understanding identities as discursively constructed, rather than as 'given' or natural, combined with the biographical approach of Alheit (2002, 2003), which emphasises the need for understanding meaning-making within the unique biographical experiences of individuals.

The book looks at apprenticeship as a 'universally understood model of learning' (Fuller and Unwin, 2009: 414), which involves the acquisition of skills, knowledge and values of a particular occupation, coupled with a 'process of maturation' that enables the individual to 'grow into the behaviours and understandings associated with being a useful citizen and a sense of self' (ibid.: 405). By comparing retail and motor vehicle apprentices in England and Germany, the study looked at different institutional contexts as constituted by contrasting apprenticeship programmes (one in the traditional craft sector, the other in the service sector) and contrasting vocational education and labour market systems (Germany and England) and their impact on transitions and young people's perspectives in relation to learning. While the German model famously centres on the notion of *Beruf*, or vocation (Deissinger, 2008), and involves apprenticeship as the continuation of education and development of the person, the English system has traditionally focused on skill formation in the workplace (for example, Ryan, 1999).

Apprenticeship presents an interesting and timely case because of its current prominence in the UK government's approach to raising post-compulsory participation in education and its comparatively low status (Fuller and Unwin, 2008) in a country which has privileged higher education. In the current climate of high youth unemployment and a contracting university sector with rising fees, expanding the apprenticeship system has been of heightened concern for the coalition government. At the same time, there has been growing criticism of low quality schemes, raising questions about the government's aim of making apprenticeship a genuine alternative to higher education. This contrasts with the high-status German dual system of apprenticeship, which increasingly attracts school leavers with higher educational qualifications (Hanf, 2011).

In this book, I will argue that young people actively perform socially recognised identities, which they interpret in the contexts of their biographical experience. Learner identities are not natural or abiding, but are formed through concrete experiences of learning and constituted in institutional settings and learning cultures with discursive frameworks that prioritise certain forms of knowledge. Thus, young people may reject certain types of learning and may develop alternative learning careers which they reflexively negotiate. Apprenticeship, therefore, may be a positive choice. However, while apprenticeships in Germany centre on the integration of theory and practice, vocational education in England is based on the academic-vocational dichotomy and assumptions that vocational learners reject all classroom learning. The learner identities of young people in the two countries reflect these different discourses. Apprenticeship is an important framework for identity construction and the school-to-work transition. In Germany, this constitutes a highly regarded route, which is promoted through the institutional system. By contrast, in England, in its current form, apprenticeship may present a diminished opportunity for young people, undermined by low quality and predominantly practical content, offering limited perspectives in terms of work careers and civic participation.

Overview of the structure of the book

The book is organised in eight chapters. Chapter 2 examines the wider institutional and political context of apprenticeship in England and Germany. The German dual system is well established and based on politics of consensus, leading to comprehensively defined competence in particular occupations. It leads to recognised social positions and is generally associated with relatively smooth transitions. Vocational education is seen as the continuation of general education. By contrast, in England, apprenticeships have historically been weakly regulated and the structure and content vary by sector and by individual employer. In addition, apprenticeship has become an instrument of government policy to increase participation in post-compulsory education. This has led to a lowering of standards and the status as a post-16 educational pathway remains fragile. Recent developments have reinforced the dichotomy of academic and practical learning and raise important issues of social justice.

Chapter 3 reviews some of the key research literature on school-to-work transition in England and Germany. While much of the research is extremely valuable, improving our understanding of the factors shaping transitions, it will be shown that studies tend to lack a proper conceptualisation of identity construction. They have focused on either structuralist or individualist perspectives, while ignoring young people's biographical experiences and thus the complex processes of identity formation.

Chapter 4 begins by outlining the theoretical framework which problematises the concept of identity. It centres on Judith Butler's theory of performativity (1990). Young people's identities are not a given, but are discursively produced as they cite social norms and discourses in order to be recognised as subjects by others. The theory stresses the role of individual agency at the same time as the power of social norms in the discursive production of identities. In addition, the biographical approach, based on writers such as Ricoeur (1992) and Alheit (2002, 2003), emphasises the need to understand meaning-making within the unique biographical experiences of individuals. As individuals seek to make sense of their lives, they constantly interpret and re-interpret their past and present experience, shaping their anticipation for the future and guiding their action.

These theoretical premises underpin the methodological framework of the research. The study uses a multi-method ethnographic approach, combining in-depth biographical interviews with multi-site participant observation. It centres on biographical interviews (Wengraf 2001) so as to explore an individual's learner identity as it is constructed over time and in multiple social contexts. This is complemented by participant observation in the young people's workplaces and colleges to provide an insight into the learning cultures of sites which are assumed to be an essential part of apprenticeships and hence of the young people's construction of identity.

Chapter 5 introduces the different learning sites and draws on the findings from the participant observations. It provides the context and thus sets the scene for the discussion in Chapters 6 and 7. However, it goes beyond this and seeks to capture the overall learning cultures of the workplaces and colleges and gain an understanding of the ways in which learner identities were being constructed. This includes an exploration of the institutional context of the content and structure of apprenticeships and how this was interpreted by apprentices, their tutors and co-workers in interaction with each other. The analysis considers tutor discourses, the ways in which the young people were expected to learn, and the values afforded to occupations, apprenticeships and learning. While certain dominant identities were identified, it became clear that a range of identities co-existed, as the discursive framework of sites intercepted with the young people's biographical backgrounds.

Chapters 6 and 7 present the comparative analysis of individual case studies, based on the biographical interviews and fieldwork notes. A major finding is the role of apprenticeship as a means for identification in the transition to adulthood. In relation to retail (Chapter 6), the analysis explores the ways in which the young people construct 'secure' and 'fragile' identities and the extent to which retail apprenticeships offered a means of identification. It highlights the difference in status and quality of the German and English schemes. However, other factors, notably family background and the experience of discontinuities, play a role. The identity of motor vehicle maintenance apprentices in both

England and Germany centred first and foremost on the practical know-how associated with the occupation (Chapter 7). While the German young people valued the apprenticeship as a comprehensive training occupation, based on the integration of theory and practice, for three of the English apprentices it pivoted on mechanics as a predominantly practical craft. However, detailed analysis revealed a much more nuanced picture of identity formation, calling into question previous studies which present vocational education students as a homogenous group of 'practical' learners.

In Chapter 8, some of the key findings are discussed with particular reference to the conceptual and methodological framework developed in this study. First, based on participant observation in the colleges, the construction of learning cultures is explored and attention is drawn once more to the ways in which identities are constituted through the discursive frameworks of institutional settings. Following this, it is shown how the young people's biographies reveal a more nuanced picture of identity construction. A further section draws out the implications for policy and, in particular, the importance of providing quality apprenticeships as a framework for identity construction and for the transition from school to work. The chapter concludes by revisiting the literature while outlining the key contribution of the new conceptual and methodological framework to the study of school-to-work transition and the (discursive) construction of learner identities.

Chapter 2

Setting the Scene: Vocational Education and Apprenticeship in England and Germany

Introduction

In this chapter, I set out the broader context of the vocational education and apprenticeships systems in England and Germany. In both countries, the apprenticeship system originated in the craft-based system of the middle ages. However, these systems have evolved into distinct 'apprenticeship cultures' each with their own characteristics (Deissinger, 2008). For example, while England has privileged mass higher education (Mayhew, Deer and Dua, 2004), Germany has relied on producing a skilled, intermediate workforce, primarily through its dual system of apprenticeship (Deissinger, 2008). Germany and England provide an illuminating contrast because of their divergent vocational education systems and traditions. The comparison therefore serves to highlight differences in young people's transition and the way in which they negotiate the different contexts, including the institutional structures as well as values, beliefs and expectations. The chapter explores the two apprenticeship systems in turn and thus sets the scene for the individual case studies. It starts by giving an overview of the historical development and policy landscapes, before looking at the contexts of the motor vehicle maintenance and retailing apprenticeships.

The context of the German Dual System

Development and key characteristics
In Germany, the dual system has enjoyed a relatively high status, in large part owing to its roots in the guild system of the late nineteenth century. It was then that, as part of privileges granted to protect the old *Mittelstand* against increasing competition from industrial capitalism, the craft guilds became self-governing public bodies, responsible for the administration of apprenticeships. This entailed the restructuring of the apprenticeship system, soon to include compulsory part-time education at vocational schools—a combined outcome of progressive school reforms and policies that sought to bind the working classes to the bourgeois state (Greinert, 2007). These developments therefore saw the institutionalisation of the dual system: vocational training, located largely in the

workplace, complemented by college-based technical and general education, and underpinned by the notion of *Beruf*, literally meaning vocation.

The regulation for each training occupation is based on two parts: the Training Ordinance, which covers the workplace element; and the Framework Curriculum for vocational education in colleges. The Training Ordinances are regulated by federal law and list the content (that is, the scope of activities) for the apprenticeship in relation to the workplace as well as the assessment specifications. The Vocational Training Act 2005 enshrined the principle of *berufliche Handlungskompetenz* (occupational competence of action-taking), which is defined as 'the vocational skills, knowledge and competences necessary to engage in a form of skilled occupational activity in a changing working world' (Vocational Training Act, 2005: 15). The Training Ordinance lists the knowledge, skills and competences for the relevant occupation. However, they are broadly defined and not spelled out in detail, nor are they each assessed on their own. Assessment is based on a set of exemplary activities which are held to be indicative of a broader competence. In pedagogical terms, it is based on the principle of 'complete action', that is, a critical aim of vocational education is for apprentices to carry out entire work processes (to autonomously plan, carry out and monitor particular activities). As Heinz and Taylor (2005) have noted, vocational education in Germany is regarded as a 'collective good' by employers and civic society. It benefits employers by providing the intermediate skilled workforce for the occupational labour market (Marsden, 2007) as well as society through the social integration of young people (Müller and Gangl, 2003; Heinz and Taylor, 2005).

The defining principle of the college element is that of *Handlungskompetenz* (competence of action-taking), defined as: 'the willingness and ability of individuals to act responsibly and in a manner appropriate to the situation in social, private and work situations' (for example, KMK, 2003: 4). *Handlungskompetenz* encompasses occupational, personal and social competence. Thus, *Handlungskompetenz* relies on individuals being able to draw on multiple resources, including theoretical knowledge and social and personal competences, to deal with complex and increasingly unpredictable tasks (Erpenbeck, 2005). The educational mandate goes therefore far beyond the occupational training of the young person and is intended 'to further the general education previously acquired', thus enabling young people to participate in and 'co-create the world of work and society' (for example, KMK, 2003: 3).

So as to better integrate theory and practice, the 1990s saw the reconfiguration of knowledge from subjects into so-called 'learning fields' (*Lernfelder*), which relate to authentic activities in the workplace. Since then, 'action-oriented' teaching and learning has become the key didactic principle, based on the idea that it promotes the relevance of what is taught, encouraging reflection and thus facilitating learning through work. The integration of theory and practice is further promoted through the college workshop, in which students apply theoretical knowledge in practical activities. The Framework Curriculum states the aims and broad content of each learning field, while leaving the detailed content and particular teaching methods aimed at developing *Handlungskompetenz* to the individual college and/or teacher, stating that action oriented teaching and learning can be achieved through a variety of methods (ibid.: 5).

Occupational identity is an integral part of the literature on German vocational education. Underlying this identity is the notion of the *Beruf* and the particular conception of competence. The *Beruf* constitutes a powerful social identity with a recognised societal status (Harney, 1998; Streeck, 1996). It is founded upon a distinct set of characteristics, such as a particular scope of activities and a code of conduct. Transition studies in Germany have demonstrated the extent to which social identities of occupations and the associated images and activities guide young people's construction of self-identity (Scherr, 1995), including their choice of occupation (Ulrich, 2006; Puhlmann, 2006). For example, young people choose training occupations which they perceive to be in line with their own abilities or to promote a particular self-image (Ulrich, 2006).

German commentators have referred to 'occupational socialisation' as the process through which the social identity of a *Beruf* becomes part of an individual's self-identity (Heinz, 1995; Lempert, 2006). A learner's occupational identity is seen as developing in line with his or her growing competence (Rauner, 2007). This is recognised by the dual system and, building on the multi-dimensional notion of competence, vocational programmes are specifically designed so as to promote identification with the occupation (for example, Paulini-Schlottau, 2006, for the retail occupations). Thus, rather than promoting uncritical conformance to institutional norms, programmes seek to develop learners who are able to take part in the creation of their work environments and in innovative processes in modern work organisations (Harney, 1998). Unger (2008) refers to occupational identity as 'self-referential knowledge', which is produced through the experience and reflection of everyday practice. Put succinctly by a BIBB (Federal Institute for Vocational Education and Training) expert, 'identification with the occupation is not a job requirement, it grows over time' (Hanf, 2010).

On the other hand, the vocational education system as a whole and the dual system in particular are highly segregated. The vocational education system is comprised of the dual system of apprenticeship, full-time vocational schools, and the so-called 'transition system', of which the first is the most prestigious by far. The transition system is comprised of vocational and pre-vocational programmes, including vocational schools, occupational preparatory schemes, and vocational colleges for students without a contract with an employer. It was designed in view of increasing numbers of school leavers who were unable to obtain an apprenticeship place.

The stratifying nature of the vocational education system is reflective of social inequalities stemming from the tripartite secondary education system, divided into general secondary, intermediate and grammar schools (although other forms of schools, such as comprehensives, exist). Thus, young people with general secondary school certificates are much more likely to enter transitional schemes than those with intermediate or grammar school certificates (Beicht, Friedrich and Ulrich, 2007a). The dual system also discriminates against women, reflecting the dominance of craft-based occupations, and young people from migrant families. In the context of a tight training market, social inequalities have become more pronounced.

Traditionally the stronghold of young people with general school leaving certificates, the dual system has been dominated by intermediate school graduates since the early 1990s (Educational Reporting Consortium, 2010). Indeed, the dual system divides into a hierarchy of segments, from the lower status occupations, (including bricklaying, gardening and retail assistance) with nearly sixty per cent of trainees from general secondary schools, to high status occupations (including IT, accountancy and banking), where over half of trainees have university entry qualifications. Women are over-represented in the full-time vocational colleges, training for comparatively lower status occupations.

School-to-work transitions

The dual system constitutes a major alternative route to academic education and has been associated with relatively smooth transitions from school to skilled and stable employment and low rates of youth unemployment, compared to other industrialised countries, including Britain and Canada (Müller and Gangl, 2003; Heinz and Taylor, 2005). It is an institution which is highly valued by young people and their parents, and the transition process is facilitated by providing expert guidance during the final years at school as well as the practice of compulsory placements with an employer. Increasingly, school leavers with university entry qualifications opt to do apprenticeships before embarking on a degree course as employers value practice-relevant skills (Behrens, Pilz and Greuling, 2008). However, the situation in the training market has become increasingly difficult in recent years due to a sharp decrease in places in 2001/2, and a growth in school leaver cohorts. Despite an increase in training places since 2006, there is a continued shortfall due partly to an increasing backlog in the number of applicants from previous cohorts (Eberhard, Krewerth and Ulrich, 2005; Ulrich and Krekel, 2007). This has led to the expansion of the transition system, which has absorbed much of the increased demand for vocational schemes. The increase in its importance is problematic as the programmes do not lead to recognised vocational qualifications, but serve as a waiting loop for young people to enter the dual system or the (less prestigious) full-time vocational schools. A survey of young people entering the transition system found that for most of the young people these alternatives represented stop gap solutions while they were planning to enter the dual system at a later stage (Ministry of Education and Research, 2008).

As a result, transition from school to work has become increasingly difficult and extended. This is reflected in the rising proportion of applicants aged twenty or over (33.2% in 2006) (Beicht, Friedrich and Ulrich, 2007b). A study on school-to-work transition shows that the likelihood of entering the dual system immediately on leaving school declined considerably from 2002, paralleled by an increase in the proportion entering the transitional system (ibid.). Of all new entrants to the vocational system in 2008, 47.9% were in the dual system, 18.1% in full-time vocational colleges, and 34.1% in the transitional system (Educational Reporting Consortium, 2010). However, the vast majority (70-80%) of young people in the transition system eventually enter either the dual system or full-time vocational schools (Hanf, 2011).

While remaining the first choice for many school leavers, access to the dual system is strongly dependent on socio-demographic characteristics and social background, such as educational attainment (level of school and grades), sex, education of parents, and whether young people are from a migrant community (Beicht, Friedrich and Ulrich, 2007b; Ulrich and Krekel, 2007). Partly due to more complex skills demands, entry criteria for training places have been tightened, with many employers expecting higher school level certificates. Commentators have pointed to the difficult situation of students from general secondary schools, traditionally the main target group of the dual system (Reissig and Gaupp, 2007).

The increased complexity of school-to-work transition is also evident in the proportions of young people unable to realise their occupation of choice, with many having to adjust their expectations to reality. A survey of school leavers found that among those who were successful in obtaining a place in the dual system, one-third said that their place did not match or only partially matched their choice, reflecting the narrowness of opportunities (Ministry of Education and Research, 2008). Girls were far less likely to obtain a place of their choice, reflecting the concentration of women in fewer occupations.

The context of motor vehicle maintenance and retailing apprenticeships in Germany

Table 2.1 shows the number of new starts in the relevant frameworks for 2009. While the car mechatronic/service mechanic occupations are clearly male-dominated, women slightly outweigh men in the retail occupations[1]. The apprenticeship programmes differ in status. Whereas the mechatronic and retail salesman/woman enjoy a relatively high status, the car service mechanic and the retail assistant are considered low status in the hierarchy of dual system occupations (Educational Reporting Consortium, 2010). This is most evident in the higher proportion of students with qualifications above general secondary school in the case of the mechatronic and retail salesman/woman, as well as their higher success rates and lower rates of termination of contract.

Table 2.1 Apprenticeship starts, Germany, 2009

	All starts	Of which women	General secondary School	Intermed. School	Grammar school	Success rate (%)	Termination of contract (%)
Car mechatronic	18,141	555	7,626	8,937	1,275	91.8	20.8
Car service mechanic	1,776	54	1,242	348	21	76.5	24.7
Retail salesman/ woman	33,087	18,864	11,232	15,936	4,170	92.4	21.1
Retail assistant	26,196	16,686	14,502	8,670	1,101	86.1	26.0

Source: BIBB Database of Trainees 2009   footnote 1 see over

The duration of the car mechatronic apprenticeship is forty-two months (three and a half years). While in the past, car mechanics attracted in the main students from lower general school, the increasing numbers of students with intermediate and grammar school qualifications (8,937 and 1,275 respectively against 7,626 from lower general school, see Table 2.1), reflect the growing educational demands on the part of employers and the increased status of the new occupation. As a result of a concern over the lack of training places, particularly for students from general secondary school, the occupation of car service mechanic was introduced in 2004. It can be obtained after two years of the car mechatronics programme. An evaluation study (Musekamp, Spöttl and Becker, 2008) found that while the new occupation had led to more training places and enhanced access for students from lower general school and those with a disadvantaged background, there remained questions over the long-term employment of skilled car service mechanics in the face of a lack of employer demand for a relatively narrow skill range.

The training occupations retail assistant and retail salesman/woman were substantially reformed in 2004. Recognising the growing diversification of the sector in terms of structures and forms of companies, notably the rise of 'discount' establishments, a product of the fierce price competition in the German retail market, and those with a constantly changing range of products, the regulations broke with aspects of the *Beruf* principle and for the first time incorporated a number of optional elements (Paulini-Schlottau, 2007). The duration for the occupation of retail salesman/woman is three years and the qualification of retail assistant can be obtained after the first two. Retail apprenticeships are available in two sub-sectors: clothing and food, of which the former is generally more prestigious and popular with young people. This is partly due to its association with fashion and design, but also because clothing has in the past been associated with more traditional stores and hence more favourable conditions and opportunities for progression, although discount outlets (commonly associated with less favourable conditions) are no longer restricted to the food sector.

1   In Germany, in 2003, the occupation of 'car mechanic' was replaced by the training occupation of the 'car mechatronic' — a compound term linking the mechanical and electronic skills required — to reflect the technological advances in engineering. In later chapters, the German and English apprenticeship programmes will be referred to generically as 'motor vehicle maintenance', except where a distinction is being made between the German mechatronic and the car service mechanic

Retail salesman/woman and retail assistant feature as numbers one and two in the ranking list of training occupations in terms of intake of apprentices (the car mechatronic comes fourth). However, the picture painted in the research literature of the retail sector and the training environment is often negative. For example, a study of first-year apprentices on both programmes suggested that retail is often second choice—two-thirds viewed their apprenticeship as a stop-gap in the face of a lack of opportunities (Deuer, 2007). A study into the experience of retail apprentices during the initial phase identified a number of factors associated with a difficult experience, which may contribute to young people considering dropping out (Kutscha, 2007). Apprentices were commonly faced with demanding situations while lacking the required occupational knowledge, with little support from senior colleagues, notably in interaction with customers. There seems little doubt that the image of retailing has to some extent been tainted by poor practices in the discount sub-sector, with frequent reports on the pressurised environments, long working hours, restricted opportunities for learning, and a lack of internal training courses (common in more traditional retail firms) (Knoppik, 2009).

The English context of apprenticeship

Development and key characteristics
Contrary to developments in Germany, vocational education in England has been dominated by the state's historical preference for voluntarism and a general belief that skills are best acquired on the job, without compulsory formal vocational education (Ainley and Rainbird, 1999; Deissinger, 2008). Ryan (1999) describes the learning paradigm as one of labour market training rather than vocational education. The Victorian age saw the institutionalisation of the divide between education and training, with apprenticeships geared towards acquiring narrow sets of skills through on-the-job training, and apprentices regarding themselves as production workers rather than students. It was as late as 1964 that the British government intervened in vocational training by passing the Industrial Training Act and establishing the sector-based Industrial Training Boards (ITBs). The ITBs took some interest in apprenticeship, and the ITB for the engineering sector made significant reforms to the design and content of apprenticeship programmes. The apprenticeship system was at its height following World War Two, but began to decline in the late 1960s and 1970s due to the decline of the manufacturing industry. All but two of the ITBs were abolished in 1981 (Clarke, 1999).

Historically, participation in full-time education post-16 has been low—until the mid-1980s most young people left school aged sixteen in order to enter employment (Ball, Maguire and Macrae, 2000a). However, the steep rise in youth unemployment which followed the collapse of the manufacturing industry triggered a major government intervention in vocational education when the Youth Training Scheme (YTS) was introduced in 1983. YTS was of variable quality and ultimately reinforced the image of vocational education as low status and undesirable, in many ways still overshadowing current attempts to upgrade it. YTS was divided into Mode A, in which trainees had employed status, and Mode B, in which they received a training allowance from the state. Weak regulation meant that employers were able to draw on YTS participants as a pool of cheap labour, a practice that for many young people led to serial placements rather than skilled employment (Unwin and Wellington, 2001).

In the late 1970s, in the context of increasing concerns over the country's low skills levels, the then Department of Employment and the Manpower Services Commission (MSC) began arguing that vocational qualifications should be reformed so as to reflect more closely the needs of industry (see Raggatt and Williams, 1999 for a detailed analysis). Existing (provider-led) qualifications were seen as failing to do that, while apprenticeships were seen as time-serving (Unwin et al., 2004). In 1981, the MSC published a report ('A New Training Initiative') calling for apprenticeship to be based on the achievement of a set of competences derived from national occupational standards rather than on a specified number of years (MSC, 1981). As a result, a new form of vocational qualification was devised—competence-based National Vocational Qualifications (NVQs). Introduced in 1986, they represented a lasting change to the vocational education landscape.

NVQs are assessment led, that is, they are based on the ability to demonstrate competence and are not necessarily tied to a programme of learning. Indeed, underpinning knowledge is not separately assessed, but is assumed to be shown through the performance of tasks. NVQs have been widely criticised for the narrowness of skills and the lack of theoretical content (see inter alia, Wolf, 1995; Raggatt and Williams, 1999).

At the same time as the introduction of NVQs, the MSC also introduced the concept of 'Core Skills' to provide the so-called generic skills (for example, problem solving, communication, application of number) that YTS trainees should achieve alongside the job-specific NVQs. This concept has also been critiqued for its failure to match the type of general and civic education that forms part of the curriculum studied by vocational students and apprentices in some other European countries (Green, 1998). Since then, successive governments have been concerned with establishing a vocational route that could fulfil the twin goals of enhancing the UK's skills base and improve post-16 participation. However, a series of White Papers reaffirmed GCSE and A-levels as the cornerstones of mainstream education, while vocational routes failed to gain parity of esteem (Richardson, 1998; Jephcote and Abbott, 2005).

Apprenticeships

The desire to produce qualifications that would meet the nation's skills needs underpinned the launch of the 'Modern' Apprenticeship in 1994. It was to be distinct from previous government-sponsored schemes, notably YTS, and so was set up at a minimum level 3. Apprentices were to be employed, with apprenticeships available in a wider range of sectors than in the past, and available to both men and women. However, the aim to provide intermediate level skills has arguably been compromised as apprenticeships came to serve as a tool for social inclusion of so-called low achievers (Fuller and Unwin, 2003a; Fuller, 2004). The Labour government expanded the Modern Apprenticeship to include previous youth training schemes (at level 2), and since 1997, the expansion in terms of numbers of apprentices has largely been at level 2. There have been concerns over low standards and low completion rates (Fuller, 2004). Funding for apprenticeships is linked to the completion of its key components: NVQs as the practical element located in the workplace, the Technical Certificate (introduced first in 2001, but subsequently made optional in response to employer criticism) designed to provide the theoretical underpinning in classroom education in colleges, and key (now 'functional') skills. Key Skills are aimed at young people who have not achieved a certain level of English and maths in their GCSEs (usually a minimum level of grades A-C). They continue to be criticised by educationalists for being purely remedial and falling short of a general education component (Canning, 2007).

The generally low standards have also resulted in apprenticeships having a low status among young people and their parents as an educational route, though it must be noted that some apprenticeships (for example, with leading companies such as Rolls Royce and BT) are vastly oversubscribed. While in Germany, commonly around 50% of each cohort enter the dual system (Hanf, 2011), in England a mere 5.6% of young people aged 16-18 started apprenticeships in 2010 (The Data Service, 2011). Often reminiscent of YTS, it has been suggested that the perceived low status may deter young people from entering apprenticeship, deciding instead to remain in full-time education (Beck, Fuller and Unwin, 2006; Roberts, 2004).

Indeed, a host of factors combined to encourage students to stay in full-time education, not least Labour government policy to increase participation in higher education to fifty per cent of 18-30 year-olds, school funding regimes, and, crucially, the poor quality of information and guidance on vocational education pathways, particularly in schools, where few teachers have adequate knowledge of vocational routes (Foskett and Hemsley-Brown, 2001). This has commonly resulted in all but the lowest-attaining students continuing to A-levels. Thus, the historic distinction between academic and practical knowledge has been reinforced in recent developments and has led to the stigmatisation of vocational education. This has not only undermined the goal of producing an intermediate skills workforce but also raises serious questions about social justice (Raffe, 1994). Similar developments have been observed in other countries with voluntarist traditions, such as Canada (Taylor, 2010).

The academic-vocational divide reflects wider social inequalities, with the lower socio-economic classes over-represented in the apprenticeship scheme (Fuller, 2004). Not unlike the situation in Germany, apprenticeships are marked by continued gender segregation and under-representation of minority groups which triggered a major investigation by the Equal Opportunities Commission (Miller, 2005; Fuller, Beck and Unwin, 2005; Beck, Fuller and Unwin, 2006). Gendered expectations within the informal networks of family, friends and schools guide young people's decision-making on career choice. These are further promoted and reinforced by the stereo-typical views of major stakeholders, notably careers advisors and employers. This has detrimental effects on women, who are more likely to end up in lower status, lower paid sectors (Fuller, Beck and Unwin, 2005). In addition, taking up an apprenticeship traditionally held by the opposite sex, may be viewed as particularly risky, given the uncertainty associated with vocational qualifications more generally (Beck, Fuller and Unwin, 2006).

A key problem in England has been the lack of a robust framework for the provision of vocational education and apprenticeships in particular. A major reason for this is that, unlike in Germany, there is no established mechanism in the English system for the systematic involvement of all interests in the development of qualifications. It is essentially state-led, with vocational education as a tool to address skill needs, and the government able to introduce changes at will, what has been referred to as 'leaflet law' (Ryan and Unwin, 2001; Fuller and Unwin, 2008). Thus, rather than being demand-led, it has been the responsibility of quangos, such as the now disbanded Learning and Skills Council (LSC), to fulfil government-imposed targets concerning the number of vocational qualifications, including apprenticeships, with training providers commonly left with the task of recruiting apprentices, irrespective of demand. In recent changes, and in response to criticism, the National Apprenticeship Service has been tasked with promoting apprenticeships, particularly among employers, providing a service matching apprentices to employers, and working closely with local authorities.

Thus, a key criticism has been directed at the system of governance for leaving employers in a passive role (Steedman, 2010; House of Lords, 2007). While Sector Skills Councils (SSCs), working with Awarding Bodies, are responsible for the development of vocational qualifications, they consult only with a minority of employers, while trade unions are particularly marginalised. Qualifications thus reflect only the interest of a few employers with many more feeling that their voice is not being heard. One of the outcomes of this process has been that, with successive vocational education reforms, myriad qualifications have been introduced with little labour market currency and confusion over their value. At the same time, in an effort to entice employers, government specifications for apprenticeships have allowed for a great deal of flexibility. In 2009, the Apprenticeship, Skills, Children and Learning (ASCL) Act for the first time since 1814 (when the Statue of Artificers, introduced in 1568, was repealed) provided a statutory basis for apprenticeship. It sets out minimum requirements (Specification of Apprenticeship Standards for England (SASE)) for the provision. However, and particularly in comparison with other European countries, this is still rather weak, with minimal requirements for off-the-job learning and no provision for collective interest representation. In her government-commissioned Review of Vocational Education, Wolf (2011) articulated many of these criticisms. In particular, she pinpointed the need for better provision that enables young people to progress, both, horizontally across employers and vertically to more advanced education including higher education. The Review called for broader qualifications and a general education element, as well as a system that facilitates wider employer involvement.

In the absence of a robust statutory framework, quality has been variable, with some good provision in certain sectors, and schemes resembling little more than work experience in others (Ryan, Gospel and Lewis, 2006). Research into the organisation of apprenticeships in large employers in different sectors revealed the variability of programmes particularly in relation to the technical certificates, with some good provision on and off the job in sectors such as engineering and IT, and poor provision in retailing and construction, where employers showed a lack of interest in the educational elements (ibid.).

It appears that apprenticeship is often marked by low commitment on the part of both employers and apprentices. Research found high levels of dissatisfaction with both the technical certificate and key skills elements, which were found to be irrelevant, not meeting employer skill needs, and not integrated with on-the-job training. Key skills have been cited as a major reason for non-completion (Unwin and Wellington, 2001). On the other hand, where employers have a clear interest in running apprenticeships, for example, where they are motivated to secure the future of the organisation, apprenticeship programmes may go well beyond government requirements, in both traditional sectors, such as engineering, and non-traditional, such as business administration (Fuller and Unwin, 2007). Criterion-based assessment was introduced in order to make qualifications more transparent and accessible (Torrance, 2007). However, critics have commented that this assessment-led system may neglect learning processes and promote an instrumental approach, focusing on 'assessment as learning' rather than assessment of and for learning and promoting a culture of low expectations whereby students and apprentices are guided through the various assessment elements through detailed coaching (Torrance, 2007: 291; Unwin et al., 2008).

In recent years, both the Labour and the Conservative-Liberal Democrat coalition governments have given priority to improve the status and the provision of apprenticeships. Under Labour, apprenticeships (together with the new vocational diplomas, introduced as an alternative to A-levels in 2008) were to become the key element in the planned expansion of post-16 education, as the leaving age for compulsory education was raised to eighteen from 2015 (to seventeen from 2013). The current government has, like the previous one, pledged to increase the number of apprenticeships (by 75,000 by 2015 [Murray, 2011]). The expansion has become all the more urgent in the wake of funding cuts in the higher education sector, sharply increased university fees and growing youth unemployment, as apprenticeships are being promoted as an alternative to higher education (Shepherd, 2010).

The context of motor vehicle maintenance and retailing apprenticeships in England[2]
As in Germany, the vehicle maintenance and repair programme is clearly
dominated by male apprentices, while the distribution of men and women is
fairly even in retailing (see Table 2.2). While a majority of vehicle maintenance
apprentices go on to level 3, the dominant qualification in retail is level 2. The
majority of entrants to the vehicle maintenance programme are aged 16-17,
with GCSE-level qualifications. In retailing, it can be assumed that the average
age of entrants is higher, as many retailers provide apprenticeships for their
existing workforce.

It is notable that the expansion in apprenticeships has been most pronounced
in the 'non-traditional' sectors, with 'Business, Administration and Law' and
'Retail and Commercial Enterprise' by far the most popular (76,590 and 61,620
starts respectively in 2009) ('Engineering and Manufacturing Technologies'
ranking fourth, at 37,680 starts) (The Data Service, 2011). However, the quality
and status of programmes certainly in Retail and Commercial Enterprise is
often low, with level 2 commonly the highest qualification, and high drop-out
rates. For Retailing, though lower than for Vehicle Maintenance, success rates
have almost doubled over recent years, from 35% in 2004/5 to nearly 70% in
2009/10 (ibid.).

Table 2.2 Apprenticeship starts, England, 2009/10

	All starts	Of which women	Level 2	Level 3 and above	Success rate (%)
Vehicle Maintenance and Repair	9,660	190	5,690	3,970	76.0%
Retail	16,910	9,300	15,020	1,900	68.7%

Source: The Data Service, 2011

The apprenticeship framework 'Vehicle Maintenance and Repair' at Level 2
consists of four elements: a work-based element (the NVQ Level 2), a college-
based element (the Technical Certificate Level 2), Key Skills (Communication;
Application of Number; ICT) at Level 1, and an induction into 'Employment
Rights and Responsibilities' (IMI, 2011). The Level 2 apprenticeship takes
two years to complete (the Level 3 apprenticeship takes a further year). The
Institute of the Motor Industry (IMI) is the Sector Skills Council for the

2   Since this study was conducted, the English qualifications system has been overhauled
once more. All qualifications have been mapped onto the Qualifications and Credit
Framework to further enhance flexibility by allowing for the combination of different units,
each with their own credit value.

automotive industry. The IMI develops the constituent qualifications of the framework and is also the awarding body for the NVQ, Technical Certificate and key skills elements.

The Retail Apprenticeship framework (Issue 5, Version 3) was implemented in January 2008 (Skillsmart Retail, 2008). It consists of the following mandatory elements: NVQ Retail Skills at Level 2, the Technical Certificate in Retailing at Level 2, Key Skills at Level 1 (Application of Number, Communication). The unit 'Employment Rights and Responsibilities' is included in the Technical Certificate. The framework is the result of a major review and overhaul, led by the Sector Skills Council Skillsmart Retail. The aim was to 'develop a model of delivery of the programme that would help to re-engage large retailers in the programme' in the context of a decline in employer demand for retail apprenticeships (Skillsmart Retail, 2008: 8). Reasons for the lack of employer engagement included the introduction of the Technical Certificate, seen as an unnecessary component (although it was reinstated after consultation with the Employers' Apprenticeship Advisory Group as part of the review), and the considerable pressure on providers to improve completion rates in the face of the poor image of the retail sector which was seen as a 'career of last resort' with trainees lacking motivation and prone to drop out (ibid.: 11-12). The approach taken was to make the framework more flexible so as to meet employer skill needs, in part by reducing the number of units required, leaving greater scope for employers to reflect specific job roles. Crucially, according to the new framework employers may use their own internal training programmes mapped against the NVQ, Technical Certificate and Key Skills element of the framework, subject to approval by the awarding bodies, and, as a result, the apprenticeships may be entirely work-based. The take-up of retail apprenticeships has since recovered considerably (from 8,950 in 2004/5 to 16,910 in 2009/10). The improved numbers and success rates are likely to be due to the increased government efforts to promote apprenticeship within large retailers.

Several studies identified the lack of employer commitment as being particularly visible in retailing, with authors questioning the prospects for apprenticeship in the sector. Lewis, Ryan and Gospel (2008) found that large retailers in particular saw little benefit in running apprenticeships but preferred instead to upskill their existing workforce. Both the NVQ and theoretical elements were seen as not reflecting employer skill needs, with Key Skills particularly unpopular. Employers resented having to remedy what they perceived as the responsibility of the failing school system.

In a study of key stakeholders in the sector, Spielhofer and Sims (2004) found that owing to commercial pressures of meeting profit targets, the training element was often minimal, with typically no off-the-job element and a focus on assessment of existing skills. Completion rates were particularly low, with reasons including the lack of employer support, high work pressures, uncertainty over the value of qualifications, and the opportunity of (better paid) low skill employment. There was also a widespread attitude among employers that young people in retail are not looking for a career and that they look for practical work, rejecting any educational element.

Echoing these findings, a comparison of skills in the English and German retail sectors (food and electrical) (Mason, Osborne and Voss-Dahm, 2008) revealed that German employers placed much greater importance on formal qualifications, with seventy per cent of staff in the case study companies having completed apprenticeships, while firms in England relied predominantly on short-term in-company training. This also reflected the low-skilled nature of the work in English retailing, with staff carrying out routine work, receiving supervision and instructions from managers. By contrast, German staff had greater autonomy over a larger range of responsibilities, with a focus on team work rather than hierarchical relationships.

Conclusions

It appears that the key problem of apprenticeships in England is the low standards, not withstanding the high-quality provision in certain sectors and firms. This means that, not only does the scheme as a whole fail to attract a higher level of school leavers, it also reinforces the academic-vocational divide as well as wider social inequalities. As Avis (2004) has argued, because of the scant importance attached to knowledge in much provision and hence young people's ability to transcend contexts, the vocational education system reproduces existing patterns of class differentiation. Similarly, Unwin (2004) has called for the abandoning of the 'deficit approach' to vocational education in England, according to which vocational education is for young people deemed not able to achieve at an academic level. Unwin (2004) has singled out the separation between vocational and general education, while others have pointed to the mental/manual divide (Clarke and Winch, 2004).

The German dual system has become increasingly segregated, with high status schemes attracting young people with higher qualifications and squeezing out those from general secondary schools. However, it is the case that all dual system schemes constitute the continuation of education (with a compulsory education leaving age of eighteen) and hence the basis for competence development and development of the person. It would appear that if apprenticeships in England were to become a genuine alternative to higher education, they would need to encompass an educational element as well as an occupational profile based on the integration of theory and practice that allows for the development of occupational identity (something not raised by the 2011 Wolf Review). Current government initiatives which celebrate the virtues of practical activity and romanticise craftsmanship run the risk of further reinforcing the academic-vocational divide (Gove, 2010).

Chapter 3

School-to-Work Transitions: A Review of the Literature

Introduction

The study of transitions is part of the lifecourse research tradition, where 'the lifecourse is understood as a sequence of stages or status-configurations and transitions in life which are culturally and institutionally framed from birth to death' (Heinz and Krüger, 2001: 33). Thus, lifecourse research stresses the normalising role of institutions and values which lead individuals to reach particular life stages and follow institutional pathways according to established patterns and expectations, in relation to, for example, educational pathways (Elder, 1985; Elder, Kirkpatrick Johnson and Crosnoe, 2003).

Over the past few decades, with the de-standardisation of the lifecourse and more unpredictable and non-linear transitions, processes of school-to-work transition are said to have become all the more critical, with young people having to cope increasingly with discontinuities in their education and work careers (Heinz and Krüger, 2001; Alheit, 2002). In Britain, up until the 1980s, it was common for working class young people to seek early labour market entry without any or few prior qualifications. With the collapse of the youth labour market, the increase in the numbers of young people participating in post-16 education, and a diversified institutional landscape, there has been a heightened interest by researchers in young people's decision-making, choice of pathways and transition patterns (see Ecclestone, Biesta and Hughes, 2010). In the context of liberal education policies in 1980s Britain, one set of literature has challenged assumptions underlying much government policy that posit young people as rational human beings navigating different pathways for optimal gain, ignoring the effect of opportunity structures on young people's decision-making as well as the role of wider social influences and the intertwining of life domains (for example, Hodkinson, Sparkes and Hodkinson, 1996).

In this chapter, I begin by reviewing some of the key research on school-to-work transitions in England and Germany. As the book is concerned with young people's identity construction in particular learning sites, a further section looks at the literature in relation to identity and learning environments, such as those of education, training and work. This includes a discussion of research on particular teaching and learning arrangements and assessment methods.

While there has been a large body of research since the 1960s, few studies are concerned with the social and psychological processes involved in young people's decision-making, the lived experience of young people and the meanings they attach to their experiences. All studies grapple with the respective roles of structure and agency and most tend to emphasise the importance of one over the other. Much research focuses on the outcomes of transitions and analysis is shaped by the researchers' own understandings of, for example, socialisation processes, rather than by the young people's lived reality. Furthermore, studies are commonly influenced by the researchers' value framework of so-called good and bad jobs and a dismissal of vocational pathways as positive choices. Finally, whilst many view identity or perception of the self as crucial and integral elements of transition to work and to adulthood, these concepts are rarely theorised or problematised. It will be argued that the biographical approach, by reconstructing identity formation through successive and linked experiences, is ideally suited to exploring young people's subjectivities over time and how these are embedded in institutional and ideological contexts.

Identity and the study of transition

School-to-work transitions: An overview of definitions, perspectives
and conceptual frameworks from the 1960s to the present
Studies on school-to-work transition are plentiful. One important strand of research concerns the cross-national comparison of transitions. Criticising the restrictiveness of some of the research, Raffe (2008) highlights the importance of using a broad definition of a transition system, including a range of contextual factors, such as the vocational education system, the labour market, social welfare systems and family backgrounds. He defines a transition system as 'the relatively enduring features of a country's institutional and structural arrangements which shape transition processes and outcomes' (ibid.: 278).

The concept of transition came to be contested by academics who argued that the notion, underpinned by assumptions of linear, standardised transitions and often measured in terms of narrow economic indicators, was inadequate to describe what are complex processes, and that 'youth' and 'adulthood' cannot be thought of as distinct phases (for example, Cohen and Ainley, 2000). However, the concept has become increasingly broadened over the past two decades to encompass the non-linear and non-sequential nature of transitions, the complex intertwining of a range of life domains, including family and leisure, as well as the impact on transition patterns of a range of aspects, including health, sexuality and disability. Research on youth transitions in some of Britain's poorest neighbourhoods (Johnston et al., 2000; MacDonald and Marsh, 2005) found that the young people's transitions were effected by numerous disruptive events, ranging from those related to health and bereavement to drug consumption and criminal activity. The researchers conclude that such an expanded conceptualisation is of continued value in the study of transitions today (Shildrick and Macdonald, 2007).

The theoretical framework for studying transitions has shifted over time. Developmental perspectives informed early studies, but the focus on 'growth tasks' which young people were assumed to have achieved by certain stages was dismissed as normative and outdated as unemployment rose (see Evans and Furlong, 1997). Nevertheless, the impact of early life experiences and psychological factors on transition processes is widely accepted today. Hemsley-Brown (1999) in her study on young people's post-16 choices in England highlights the important role of self-image and group identity. Young people tended to choose programmes in line with their self-image (for example, a course for 'people like me'), and matched their choice to that of friends, thus gaining acceptance by the peer group, and, following Erikson (1968), protecting their own identity.

Researchers in the 1960s and 1970s were primarily concerned with social reproduction and the role of structural factors, such as socio-economic attributes. They suggested that young people experienced continuous and smooth transitions as they had been socialised into accepting particular social positions through socialisation processes in the family home, neighbourhoods and school contexts (Ashton and Field, 1976; Willis, 1977). For example, Paul Willis (1977) in his influential work *Learning to labour—How working class kids get working class jobs*, sought to demonstrate how the rejection of academic schooling and the perceived superiority of manual work by the young men he studied was directly related to the culture of their social class background. Similarly, Ashton and Field (1976) identified clearly demarcated trajectories whereby a person's family background determined school level and subsequent position in the labour market. Their analysis suggested continuous identities and transitions as young people's self-image, including their orientation to learning and to work, was shaped by the type of upbringing they experienced in the family, and was reinforced at school and in the workplace.

More recent authors have challenged this work, maintaining that transitions to work were never unproblematic, even in times of full employment (Vickerstaff,

2003; Goodwin and O'Connor, 2007). Based on further work on Elias et al.'s research, including a follow-up study, Goodwin and O'Connor (2007, 2005, 2003) rejected Ashton and Field's (1976) findings of smooth transitions. Their analysis showed that the majority of young people experienced very difficult and complex patterns of transition, in which they had to adjust their expectations to the realities of the labour market. While social class reproduction did occur, this was as a result of structural constraints, notably a lack of opportunities. Rather than following their predetermined paths, many young people aspired to jobs different from those of their parents. However, many did not achieve their occupational aspirations and ended up in jobs they perceived as undesirable (Goodwin and O'Connor 2005; O'Connor and Goodwin, 2004).

The early focus on social reproduction contrasts with individualist perspectives which have become more prevalent since the 1990s and are based on assumptions that transitions have become more complex and less predictable as a result of increased unemployment, the diversification of educational pathways and the onus being on individuals to improve their 'employability' (Heinz, 2009). The traditional concept of the lifecourse, according to which education and training, employment, marriage and parenthood were linked in sequence, is seen to have become increasingly 'destandardised' and non-sequential (Nagel and Wallace, 1997; Heinz and Krüger, 2001).

The individualist perspective draws on sociologists such as Giddens (1991) and Beck (1992) who refer to 'late modernity' as an era in which traditional structures and certainties have been replaced by a 'risk society'. Individuals are forced to make choices amidst a 'puzzling diversity of options and possibilities' on the basis of a wealth of information often through mediated experiences. Giddens (1991) views the self as a 'reflexive project', where the need to sustain a coherent self becomes crucial, and people face the task of reflexively shaping and continuously revising their self-identities.

The greater prominence given to individual agency is reflected in a shift of theoretical perspective and terminology from the study of 'transitions' to that of individual 'biographies' as life projects (Heinz, 2009). This emphasis on individual decision-making and life planning is illustrated by, for example, the work on 'choice biographies' of young people in the Netherlands and Britain (du Bois Reymond, 1998) and in Australia (Wyn and Dwyer, 1999), who were found to defer their commitment to the labour market in favour of a range of other life experiences, such as travel and voluntary work. Similarly, a study by researchers at the University of Bremen concerning the transition from school to work by German apprentices focuses on the reflexive negotiation of 'strategies' for dealing with discontinuities (Heinz, 2002; Witzel and Kühn, 1999).

While there can be no doubting the tremendous changes in social and economic conditions over recent decades, some commentators have criticised these writers for neglecting the role of social structure and the embeddedness of people's actions in social relations while overstating individual agency (Furlong, 2009; Roberts, 2009; Smith, 2009). According to Furlong and Cartmel (2007) the differentiation of education and labour market opportunities has led to new class-based inequalities. Also, as a result of the dominance of individualist values and the rhetoric of choice, people feel a heightened sense of responsibility for dealing with risk at an individual level (and hold themselves responsible for failure).

Furlong and Cartmel's research on transitions in Scotland found that children from poorer backgrounds were experiencing similar processes to those described by Ashton and Field in the 1970s, with school experience reinforcing class-based differences of orientation to education, for example, by teachers focusing on the academically able (Furlong et al., 2003; Furlong, 2004). Studies based on large-scale and longitudinal data have confirmed the continued effect of structure, such as parental social class, on choice of educational pathways (see, for example, Schoon and Parsons, 2002, for the UK, and Heckhausen and Tomasik, 2002, for Germany).

In the 1980s and 1990s there emerged a body of research specifically concerned with the respective roles of structure and agency, with young people's subjectivities and their ability to negotiate 'learning careers' and to 'become somebody' (for example, Banks et al., 1992; Bates and Riseborough, 1993a, b; Hodkinson, Sparkes and Hodkinson, 1996; Bloomer and Hodkinson, 1997; Ball, Maguire and Macrae, 2000a). These have examined school-to-work transitions in the context of young people's lives as a whole and their interrelation with other life domains. Underlying this research have been more sophisticated conceptualisations of the relationship between structure and agency.

Ken Roberts and colleagues (1994) coined the term 'structured individualism' to denote that, while young people have always exercised agency, their decision-making and career choices are mediated by structural factors. In response to the pervasive rhetoric of a poverty of aspiration among young people from disadvantaged backgrounds, Roberts (2009) insisted that far from a lack of aspiration, young people's choice of educational pathway is influenced by social background, thus pointing to the importance of 'opportunity structures' in determining transition outcomes. In a similar vein, Karen Evans' notion of 'bounded agency' denotes the ways in which contextual factors, and in particular institutional frameworks of vocational education, shape young people's subjectivities and may support or hinder their agency (Evans, 2007; Evans, 2002; Evans et al., 2001; Rudd and Evans, 1998; Evans and Heinz, 1994a, b). In their Anglo-German comparison of school-to-work transitions, Evans and Heinz (1994a, b) found that young people's approaches and attitudes towards transition were shaped by the differentially regulated systems in England and Germany.

Echoing Evans and Heinz' work and their concern with the influence of institutions on young people's subjectivities, Andreas Walther (2006) in Germany identified 'regimes of youth transitions' based on studies on the social integration of youth in several European countries. These regimes not only encompass the institutional features of countries, but also the ideological and cultural values that underpin them as well as other structuring mechanisms, such as gender and ethnicity. They therefore represent the different realities within which youth transitions are embedded, that is, the taken-for-granted opportunity structures that inform young people's orientations and decisions, and hence serve as 'interpretative backgrounds' for differences and similarities in comparative transition studies (Walther, 2006: 136).

Broadly based on Esping-Andersen's (1990) typology of welfare regimes, Walther distinguishes between 'universalistic' (Denmark, Sweden), 'employment-centred' (Germany, France, Netherlands), 'liberal' (UK, Ireland) and 'sub-protective' (Italy, Spain, Portugal) transition regimes. Besides identifying differing institutional features and policies concerning education, social welfare and employment, the author pinpoints particular values underlying the 'concept of youth' (ibid.: 126). Thus, in relation to the UK, it is suggested that the focus has historically been and still is on young people gaining economic independence through early labour market entry. By contrast, in the highly regulated vocational education and employment systems in Germany, young people are under pressure to adapt to privileged social positions, and, failing this, end up in stigmatised training schemes and/or in the peripheral labour market.

Transition studies since the 1980s

Since the 1980s, there has been a raft of studies concerned with the respective roles of structure and agency, often stressing the importance of one over the other. Outcomes of transitions in terms of post-compulsory pathways are commonly explained in terms of individualisation (for example, Heinz, 2002; Witzel and Kühn, 1999) or socialisation (for example, Banks et al., 1992; Hodkinson, Sparkes and Hodkinson, 1996; Bloomer and Hodkinson, 1997). In what follows, some of these studies will be discussed in more detail. It will be argued that, while they have offered a more sophisticated approach to understanding the interplay of structure and agency, the studies have tended to neglect the biographical experiences of young people and hence the complex nature of identity construction. Past events are considered only superficially and selectively, ignoring wider social contexts and relationships, and working class students are commonly presented as a homogenous whole. Drawing on the discourse of the academic-vocational divide (for example, Pring, 1995), young people in vocational training are commonly constructed as failures and second chance learners, thereby dismissing the possibility of vocational education as a positive choice (for example, Archer and Yamashita, 2003).

In England, studies of the 1980s and 1990s are set in the context of the free market approach to education introduced in the 1980s, stressing individual responsibility and 'choice', an approach which assumes that resources are equally distributed, and that careers are linear and subject to rational decision-making. To some extent, therefore, these studies set out to emphasise the continued effect of structure and appear to overemphasise structural factors. Conceptualisations of identity are closely linked to class background, processes of socialisation and outcomes of selection and self-selection. Thus, as part of the ESRC 16-19 Initiative, a study examining young people's decision-making and transition patterns in four labour market regions in Britain (Banks et al., 1992; Bates and Riseborough, 1993a, b) pointed to inequalities of access to resources and differential patterns of participation. The authors distinguished between accelerated and protracted transitions (Banks et al., 1992: 9).

These authors paint a bleak picture of the ability of 16 to 19 year-olds to exercise agency and control. Many aspects of identity are deemed to have been formed by the age of sixteen, being subsequently merely reinforced through post-16 education. As transitions are the result of processes of selection and self-selection, their analysis is reminiscent of that of Ashton and Field (1976), suggesting smooth transitions in which young people select careers according to their socialised selves, where the reflexive agency of working class young people serves merely to reconcile them with their predetermined paths and careers in what are considered low status jobs (Bates, 1993; Bates and Riseborough, 1993a, b).

In an ethnographic study of young women on a Youth Training Scheme in adult health and social care, Bates (1993) explains the processes involved in what she describes as the young women's initial resistance and gradual acceptance of their new careers in terms of an adaptation facilitated by the girls' social background. Bates describes the occupation as carer as an extended domestic career, which draws heavily on the resources and qualities the girls were presumed to have acquired through their family background and upbringing, including attitudes and skills that allowed them to cope with stressful tasks and violence. Thus, one young woman is reported to have reached a point when she felt she had chosen a career that was 'right for her', a process Bates refers to as 'reconstructing fate as choice' (Bates, 1993: 23). It is tempting to deny these young people any meaningful form of agency, given that their actions are highly circumscribed by social structures. However, Bates' analysis exemplifies the bias of what are commonly middle-class researchers, dismissing the possibility of vocational education as a positive choice. Furthermore, her reference to the girls' upbringing and her assertion that structural factors serve to explain 'why working class girls get working class jobs', seems, at best, a blatant over-generalisation and stereotyping of working class young women.

Since Willis' research (1977), there have been numerous studies seeking to demonstrate the ways in which working class young people are 'socialised' into vocational education pathways. As in the earlier work, the young people are commonly reported to reject academic learning and ascribe superior value to manual labour as real work, while many authors portray vocational education as 'second chance'. For instance, based on their research on disadvantaged youth in Northeast England, Shildrick and MacDonald (2007) conclude that the young people had no interest in academic learning, apparently taking at face-value the young people's assertions. Similarly, in his study of the school-to-work transitions of apprentices in Germany and Canada, Lehmann (2005) drew on Bourdieu (1993) to demonstrate the social reproduction of inequalities and the similarities in the two countries. Echoing Willis' (1977) analysis, Lehmann dismissed the young people's assertions that their trades were their preferred choice, suggesting that their valuing of manual work was the outcome of their working class upbringing. He further explained that the young people had to justify their choices in the face of a dominant discourse that privileges academic education. While this may be so, it appears that the author, by drawing on the same discourse, dismissed vocational education as a positive choice. Similarly, in their studies on decision-making by students in secondary schools in the

South of England, Hemsley-Brown (1999) and Foskett and Hemsley-Brown (2001) found that work-based programmes were commonly perceived as the route for poorly attaining students and viewed as 'dropping out of education' by young people and their parents, teachers and careers advisors. Post-16 choices were strongly influenced by social background, with middle class students not considering vocational education, while those from working class backgrounds were found to opt for work-based learning because of their rejection of school and a desire to earn a living. This contrasts with Unwin and Wellington's (2001) finding that apprentices on a Modern Apprenticeship programme felt they had made a positive choice, which reflected their preferred mode of learning. They did not feel they had dropped out of education.

Bloomer and Hodkinson and colleagues' (Hodkinson, Sparkes and Hodkinson, 1996; Bloomer and Hodkinson, 1997, 2000a, b) highly influential work on career decision-making casts doubt on government policies based on assumption of rationality and individual choice. In their study *Triumph and Tears*, Hodkinson et al. (1996) examined the career decision-making and transitions of young people through the first eighteen months of a government-funded training scheme. The work is a powerful illustration that transitions are not linear or predictable processes, but rather are subject to serendipitous events and false starts. The transition from school to work is closely intertwined with other life domains. Decision-making is seen as the result of social background and *habitus*—a set of dispositions of how to act in everyday situations—(Bourdieu, 1993) and young people are seen to make choices within 'horizons for action', that is, their choices are defined by both, objectively available opportunities and their subjective perceptions of these.

In a further longitudinal study on young people's transitions from Year 11 into further education, the authors developed the concept of a 'learning career' (Bloomer and Hodkinson, 2000a, b; 1997) to explore the ways in which young people's dispositions to learning change over time and as a result of changing circumstances in different domains of life. The concept posits the individual as an agentic human being, acting on events, experiences and changing circumstances and it illustrates how learning dispositions change as people manage changing circumstances and attach different meanings to learning (Bloomer and Hodkinson, 2000b). For example, one young woman, Amanda, dropped her A-level studies in favour of a vocational qualification as she perceived the need to earn an income to maintain her flat and care for her sick boyfriend. Echoing Furlong and Cartmel (2007) and others, this suggests the continued bearing structural factors have on young people's careers, in particular, class and gender.

Nevertheless, drawing on the notion of *habitus*, the authors appear to overemphasise the role of structure as actions are seen as closely bound by social background. The concept of *habitus* appears inadequate to account for change and young people's agency; how young people experience and act upon social situations, and how dispositions may change over time. Furthermore, the work lacks a theory of identity, which is rather vaguely linked to processes of socialisation, which remain equally unexamined.

The authors cite the example of Helen who experienced a difficult transition, starting as a trainee in car body repair shop and eventually switching to retail assistant in a record shop (Hodkinson, Sparkes and Hodkinson, 1996). The research illustrates the role of important structural factors, notably the lack of opportunities and the constraint posed by local social networks of working class families. The authors establish that in the record shop 'Helen was gradually socialised into accepting that this might be her career'. However, little insight is offered into the processes of what is portrayed as passive socialisation. While she 'always liked that shop' and 'always liked music', the authors offer no explanation as to the motivating factors and the processes that led her to regard the new career as a positive choice. As the data are not located in the young woman's biographical experience, we gain no insight into the meaning she attaches to either retail work or car body repair. The notion of socialisation fails to explain the young woman's reflexive agency. For example, Helen's determination to work in the repair shop went against established social norms and would have required her to resist cultural expectations. The origins and development of this career path and her emerging identity are not explored.

The concept of learning careers has subsequently been used and developed within different contexts of further education (for example, Lawy, 2006; Vaughan and Roberts, 2007; Gibson, 2004). Re-analysing data from Bloomer and Hodkinson's (1997) study, Lawy (2006) emphasises the contextual and relational nature of learning and the reflexive relationship between learning, knowledge and identity. He shows that young people actively construct their learning careers according to their perception of knowledge and of themselves as learners. By engaging with different pathways, identities become confirmed, transformed or gradually evolve in subsequent learning environments.

Crossan et al.'s (2003) analysis of the learning careers of non-traditional learners is among the few studies using a biographical, life history approach.

They demonstrate that learning careers evolve throughout the lifecourse and may change according to situations and events in the wider social contexts of people's lives, for example, triggered by the end of a relationship of caring for an older relative. Importantly, the study shows that transformation of identity is a gradual process and may be fragile and reversible. Learner identities built upon a rejection of schooling are deeply rooted and low self-confidence has to be continually overcome.

Adopting the model of career-decision making developed by Hodkinson, Sparkes, and Hodkinson (1996), Ball and colleagues (Ball, Maguire and Macrae, 2000a, b; Maguire, Ball and Macrae, 2001) gave greater prominence to the agentic potential of young people in their study of the transition patterns of a group of young people in South London over a four-year period (1995-99) from the ages of sixteen to twenty years-old. The study illustrates the close intertwining of social contexts as young people develop their multiple identities through their work and learning careers. However, in contrast to Hodkinson, Sparkes and Hodkinson (1996), Ball and colleagues focused less on social reproduction and examined young people's ability to construct reflexive identities. Drawing on the concept of 'structured individualism' (Roberts, Clarke and Wallace, 1994), they conclude that the extent to which young people are able to 'formulate and realise goals' is dependent on their structural position (Ball, Maguire and Macrae, 2000a: 145), in that whilst new economies offer opportunities for the reflexive construction of identity, they also produce new inequalities, leading to 'secure' as well as 'fragile' identities.

Secure identities are part of relatively stable transitions, often with long-term goals, and 'few doubts about becoming somebody' (ibid.: 150). Echoing previous studies, young people from privileged backgrounds are more likely to construct these 'choice biographies' (Wyn and Dwyer, 1999), within extended transitions, combining and switching between several identities, as they are able to take risks without penalty. Young people from less privileged backgrounds are more likely to experience 'fractured' transitions, as they 'struggle to become somebody' (Ball, Maguire and Macrae, 2000a: 150). For these young people the priority is often to respond to and negotiate difficult circumstances and events.

Ball and colleagues powerfully illustrate the enormous resourcefulness of young people. One of the crucial findings is that life domains beyond education and training may be more important for the construction of identity and highlights the interrelatedness of a range of 'careers' embedded in people's lives. This is illustrated by one young woman who resists the stereotypical black (anti-learning) culture in her college and who redefines her own black identity and her sense of self as a 'C and D kind of person' (ibid.: 26). She overcomes what might have been her 'expected' learning career based on her structural position in what is described by the authors as a 'triumph over adversity' (ibid.: 31).

Important experiences may lie outside the domain of education and training. For example, one boy renegotiates his learner identity as a result of a positive learning experience of acquiring skills working in the twilight economy with his DJ father. The experience restores his 'sense of purpose' (Erikson, 1968), enabling him to rebuild a self-esteem that has been undermined by school and enabling him to re-negotiate his learner identity. Finally, identity formation takes place within a complex network of relationships, including relationships of dependence and social obligation (Irwin, 1995). For example, Rena is caught between her Indian family's expectations for a traditional domestic life and her own aspirations for a career in Hair and Beauty.

While the study illustrates the resourcefulness of young people, the idea of combining and switching identities with apparent ease needs to be treated with caution. Indeed, it is doubtful whether identities can ever be 'secure'. Importantly, the assertion that young people from more privileged backgrounds are more likely to become 'individualised' in terms of developing and achieving aims needs to be problematised. For instance, young people's horizon for action may be restrictive in other respects, such as family expectations concerning advanced education and careers. Conversely, young people from working class backgrounds may be able to construct reflexive identities and identify and achieve long-term goals. In addition, while traditional norms have declined, there are new regulatory regimes in their place which are no less powerful, as exemplified by the new femininities and masculinities and other identities available through popular consumption (Nayak and Kehily, 2008). Also, in the context of an expanding array of pathways there are new cultural expectations of young people with, as an illustration, the gap year becoming the norm (ibid.). Finally, as with the other studies discussed in this section, the research lacks a theory of identity.

The notion of individualisation is even more pronounced in Heinz and colleagues' longitudinal study tracing young people in Germany over eight years after completing their apprenticeship (Heinz, 2002; Witzel and Kühn, 1999). Their notion of 'self-socialisation' theorises agency and the ways in which individuals develop strategies through a reflexive dealing with their situation. The work identifies 'modes of biographical action', that is, over-arching dispositions that describe the strategies they had taken as a result of self-socialisation.

However, the concept of 'self-socialisation' appears problematic as it posits individuals as constantly reflexive and rational beings. By overemphasising individual agency the study neglects the role of unreflected disposition and of structural factors. The term 'strategy' seems misleading as decisions may not always be 'strategic' but may result from other factors, such as a lack of confidence or an unreflected horizon for action. This compares with Scherr's (1995) study of transitions of vocational and higher education students in Germany which found that, far from apprentices being individualised, their decision-making was seen as pragmatic in the context of limited opportunities. The study also powerfully illustrates the continued role of standardised biographies in guiding young people's decision-making, as well as the role of social identities of occupations (see also Chapter 2).

Comparative studies

To date, there have been few Anglo-German comparative studies on school-to-work transitions. One exception is the ESRC 16-19 Initiative study (Banks et al., 1992) that was extended to include a cross-national study comparing youth transition patterns in expanding and contracting labour markets in England and Germany (Bynner and Roberts, 1991; Evans and Heinz, 1991, 1994a, b).

These studies point to the salience of different vocational education and labour market contexts in shaping young people's attitudes and transition patterns and show that the different transition patterns and attitudes of young people reflect the contrasting institutional and labour market contexts within the two countries (Evans and Heinz, 1991). Whereas in Germany the route to skilled employment was through the dual system, in England the system consisted of a variety of routes, and often meant employment with a 'significant training element'. These differing contexts were strongly mirrored in young people's attitudes towards education, training and work. The authors assert that the main distinction is between the 'apprentice' status of German young people, and 'employee' status of their British counterparts.

Drawing on the concept of structured individualism (Roberts, Clarke and Wallace, 1994), the authors found that the extended transition within the highly regulated vocational education system in Germany allowed for more individualised pathways, providing opportunities to try out different vocational routes, compensating for false starts and setbacks as it provided 'stepping stones for career repair'. According to the authors, the longer transition in German vocational education promoted 'active individualisation' and 'strategic' and 'risk-taking' career decision-making. In contrast, accelerated transitions in England were the result of a weakly defined progression route and closer proximity to the labour market, favouring 'passive individualisation', weakly defined goals and uncertain strategies defined by 'step-by-step' and 'wait-and-see' approaches (Evans and Heinz, 1994b: 210).

The idea that young people's subjectivities and decision-making are shaped by the institutional context was further confirmed in a comparative study which examined the experience of a sense of control and the exercise of personal agency among three groups of young adults (those in higher education, in employment, and those experiencing unemployment) in different regions in Eastern and Western Germany and in Britain (Evans et al., 2001; Behrens and Evans, 2002). In the highly structured German transition system, many people felt that their chances were limited and thus their sense of control reduced, whereas in the weakly regulated English context, people generally felt that opportunities were open to all.

Biographical approaches

Studies in the biographical research tradition have been particularly sensitive to exploring individual subjective experience. Biographical research is based on a unique methodological approach, the biographic-interpretive method (Wengraf, 2001), which seeks to reconstruct individual biography: that is, the actual lived experience of situations and events over time and the ways in which these experiences are acted upon and shape individuals' anticipation of the future. Biographies thus provide insight into the meanings of events and experiences to individuals, how they form particular dispositions over time, and how they make sense of and integrate a range of often contradictory experiences (Dausien, 1998).

Biographical research thus highlights the many ways in which subjectivities are shaped by contextual factors. In contrast to other research, it is not primarily concerned with the outcomes of transitions but with the processes of experiencing and decision-making young people find themselves in, and is regarded as a uniquely sensitive tool for exploring the complex interaction between individuals and their social environment. It has been used in studies on youth and social disadvantage, including those on youth unemployment (Alheit, 1994); school-to-work transitions of migrant women (Schittenhelm, 2005); disadvantaged youth (Rosenthal et al., 2006); and unqualified youth (SOSTRIS, 1999).

The biographical approach seems essential if we are to gain an understanding of transitions as shaped through lived experience. Rosenthal et al. (2006) in their study on barriers to reintegration of disadvantaged youth found that lack of qualifications and unemployment were not the primary concerns of many young people who were trying to cope with problems originating from adverse circumstances experienced in childhood.

Schittenhelm (2005), in her study of young migrant women in Germany, distinguishes between *habitus*-conforming and reflexive transitions. Her notion of 'orientation knowledge' denotes the knowledge that people gain through their ongoing life experiences and which provides the basis for their agency. While the *habitus* transmitted through upbringing provides one set of resources, including patterns of interpretation, individuals generate new meanings in interaction with others as they move within multiple social contexts of home, school and peer group (including learning from the experiences of significant others). Young people may reflect on and re-interpret their status as migrants, as ethnic minorities and as women where the new perspectives clash with existing cultural norms. Indeed, the reproduction of social division was often a result of a lack of opportunities rather than a *habitus*-conforming strategy, where young women had failed to access high-status dual system apprenticeships.

Another example is a study on the social re-integration of 'disaffected' youth through participatory approaches in nine European countries (Stauber, Pohl and Walther, 2007; Walther, 2006; Stauber, 2007, 2006). The research was based on case studies of training schemes and on biographical interviews with young people who were facing difficulties in their school-to-work transition and who attended these schemes designed to re-engage them with education and training based on participation. Crucially, the starting point of the study was an overriding concern with subjectivity. This was deemed all the more important in the context of the destandardisation of the lifecourse and increasing demands on young people in terms of making decisions concerning their future lives. Being concerned with increasing young people's motivation, the study sought to understand young people's orientations and aspirations and the structural factors that were influencing these. Barbara Stauber maintained that 'transitions have to be considered much more from the perspective of motivational careers, which demands a contextualised understanding of structural and biographical (de-) motivators' (2007: 44). It was found that active participation and interactive relationships were critical in motivating young people. Thus, the projects acknowledged the young people's biographical pasts and the difficulties they might have encountered, while providing experiences to develop particular interests and building self-esteem and a sense of self-efficacy (Bandura, 1997).

Identity and learning environments in education and work

Situated learning theory

Much research concerned with school-to-work transition in relation to particular learning environments, including those of vocational education and training pathways and, notably, apprenticeship, draws on situated learning theory as put forward by Lave and Wenger (1991; Lave, 1991). These authors emphasise learning as participation in a social 'community of practice' where a particular 'culture' of values, norms and beliefs is constituted through the practice of its members. Learning is a transformative process which involves the construction of identities and 'implies becoming a different person' (Lave and Wenger, 1991: 53). Apprenticeship is seen as one such community of practice where newcomers, through 'legitimate peripheral participation' are initiated into a trade by experienced crafts people. This goes far beyond the acquisition of skills and knowledge and involves a process of identification with the cultural values, customs and practices associated with a particular occupation.

A wealth of studies has drawn on situated learning theory to analyse work-based learning and the relationship between learning and identity formation. Drawing on Lave and Wenger (1991) and Engeström (2001), Fuller and Unwin (2003b) identified expansive and restrictive learning environments in their analysis of apprenticeship learning in English companies. These differed in the quality and scale of opportunities for participation in terms of on and off-the-job learning and the breadth of experience. A further influential body of work, emanating from the ESRC's Teaching and Learning Research Programme (TLRP), examined the dynamics of so-called 'learning cultures' and their influence on students and tutors in environments of learning in further education (James and Biesta, 2007). These will be discussed in the next section.

Nevertheless, situated learning theory has several shortcomings. While Lave and Wenger assert that learning occurs naturally through participation, unstructured learning without a formal input may not be compatible with the demands of modern society (Fuller and Unwin, 1998). Engeström (2004) argues that the lack of formal knowledge and learning-by-doing promotes an uncritical approach to knowledge and precludes change. His theory of 'expansive' learning combines formal knowledge and interaction with others in authentic situations in order to enable critical analysis of accepted practice. 'Adaptive' learning, on the other hand, occurs where learners readily imitate behaviours in an unreflective way.

In addition, Lave and Wenger (1991) fail to distinguish between the social identity of the craft and the self identities constructed by individuals and suggest that moving from novice to expert is a smooth process. While for Yukatec Mayan midwives, born into a community of practice, identity formation may be relatively smooth and homogenous, in the Western world it is a highly complex and individuated process, shaped by events and situations within and beyond the world of education and work. Unwin and Wellington's (2001) study of apprentices' perspectives on learning illustrated this through the worries and unease felt by young people starting off on their apprenticeships. Similarly, Handley et al.'s (2007) findings among young management consultants highlight the stress of adapting to a community of practice and negotiating individual identities within the context of a strongly normative corporate identity and strong power relationships between employer and employee (Alvesson and Willmot, 2002; Handley et al., 2007).

Learning cultures
Part of the ESRC's TLRP programme, a major longitudinal study of students on Further Education courses (childcare; health studies; electronic and telecoms engineering) in England aimed at gaining a better understanding of and improving opportunities for learning in further education (James and Biesta, 2007; Hodkinson, Biesta and James, 2007, 2008). Drawing on Lave and Wenger (1991), the authors developed the concept of a 'learning culture', which has proved highly influential for exploring how particular learning environments and opportunities are shaped by social contexts and by the actors, such as tutors and learners, within them. The concept emphasises the contextual and relational nature of learning 'as social practice constituted by the actions, dispositions and interpretations of participants' which serve to continually produce and reproduce the culture (Hodkinson, Biesta and James, 2007: 419). Learning cultures constitute distinct systems of meanings, which are simultaneously structuring and are being structured by the dispositions, beliefs and values of social actors within them. Individual learning sites are governed by the values, expectations and beliefs by a variety of actors and institutions, including tutors, students, and employers, in relation to what constitutes good learning and teaching. However, again drawing on *habitus* (Bourdieu, 1985), young people's agency is perceived as restricted and predetermined by their social background as they

seek to conform to desired forms of behaviour. It ignores learners' continual negotiation and renegotiation of identities as they try to make sense of their lives, and in particular the negotiation of multiple identities within divergent social contexts. Thus, the study tends to over-emphasise the role of organisational or occupational identity.

Colley et al. (2003) explored the ways in which learner identities are transformed within different learning environments. Drawing on Bourdieu, the authors introduce the concept of 'vocational *habitus*' to describe the ways in which students' identities are transformed by learning cultures. The vocational *habitus* defines the (highly normative) set of dispositions with which students are expected to respond to the demands within the vocational culture. The authors emphasise that students entering the community of practice, rather than passively absorbing the vocational culture, orient themselves to the vocational *habitus*, that 'operates in disciplinary ways to dictate how one should properly feel, look and act, as well as the values, attitudes and beliefs that one should espouse' (Colley et al., 2003: 488).

Examining the transformative nature of learning cultures, the authors found that the three courses they researched were associated with distinct cultures and ways in which students constructed their identity (James, Davies and Biesta, 2007). The childcare course was deemed highly socialising, conditioning conforming students into adopting expected behaviours and attitudes, including accepting their position in the social and professional hierarchy. Students who were already 'pre-disposed' to the particular culture because of their social background and prior life experience (for example, of caring for children or relatives) come to develop what are regarded as 'suitable dispositions', including a 'nice' demeanour and conveying a sense of moral propriety in their quest to establish 'a sense of their proper place'.

As indicated in the previous section, the concept of *habitus* is not conducive to the study of identity formation. The scope for individual agency is limited and only extends to co-constructing and reproducing existing learning cultures, and to strategies that enable learners to cope with an idealised notion of vocational *habitus*. For example, the health workers learned forms of detachment to deal with the emotional demands of their work. Importantly, the social reproduction obscures the individual experiences of students and the processes of identity formation. The authors' analysis generates a sense that transitions are smooth processes, echoing earlier studies of social reproduction (for example, Ashton and Field, 1976). It ignores learners' continual negotiation and renegotiation of identities as they try to make sense of their lives, and in particular the negotiation of multiple identities within divergent social contexts. Also, it ignores the uniqueness of learner experience, depending on their backgrounds and their positioning within the learning environment (James and Biesta, 2007). Most importantly, it denies the possibility for change, either in the learning environment or in individual learners. This rests on and reinforces stereotypical views held by academics and practitioners of students' abilities and preferences, and belies evidence that young people can and do have different learning experiences, and that learner identities may be transformed.

Despite stressing the importance of (pre-) disposition, the data provided by the authors is de-contextualised and provides no information on the social background and previous experiences of students, apart from social class or gender variables. Rather than exploring individual experience, working class students are treated as a homogenous whole, socialised into accepting what are regarded low skilled jobs, a perspective reminiscent of the ESRC 16-19 Initiative studies (for example, Bates, 1993).

In a related paper, the authors argue that young people value vocational courses only if they are 'significantly different from the "normal" school experience' (Davies and Biesta, 2007: 36), where 'different' is defined as 'practical', involving 'real work' and a particular pedagogical approach. Again apparently taking young people's accounts at face value, this finding is highly misleading. Drawing on the discourse of the academic-vocational divide, it again implicitly assumes that these young people reject academic learning (rather than a particular experience of it), an assumption that seems to have underpinned the lowering of standards of so much vocational education in England.

The co-construction of learning environments

Work by Bloomer and Hodkinson (1997) and Bloomer (1997) highlighted the interaction between students and tutors in co-constructing learning opportunities. In their study of young people moving into post-16 education (Bloomer and Hodkinson, 1997), the authors found that learning opportunities were shaped by both, the tutors' interpretation of the curriculum (including the perceived aims and constraints, their perception of student needs and expectations of learning), and the students' dispositions to learning and knowledge (for example, their perceptions of the purpose of learning). Thus, they found that the teaching and learning arrangements varied considerably between different classes. In addition, young people's post-16 choices strongly depended on their sense of themselves as learners and their perceptions of learning and knowledge, that is, the value they attached to the knowledge and the perceived purpose of learning. There was a close relationship between choice of further education and how young people perceived their career development. As the young people entered further education they adopted different types of 'studentship', ranging from 'conforming' and 'innovatory' to 'strategic compliance' and outright 'retreatism', reflecting young people's dispositions as they made sense of the new environment (Bloomer, 1997). Many held an instrumental view of learning, wanting to get a qualification as a necessary prerequisite for their planned careers.

Crucially, their dispositions to learning and knowledge were found to change over time as a result of experiences of different learning environments and courses, including experiences of interactive learning and a recognition of their role in generating knowledge. Often, these experiences were accompanied by a rise in self-confidence and were reported to be transformative in the sense that the young people reported becoming different people. This demonstrates the close intertwining of learning and identity formation. However, while the research draws attention to the different dispositions towards learning, based on the students' differing perceptions, values and experiences, often linked to domains outside the learning environment, these are merely described while their origins remain unexplored. This runs the risk of taking at face value certain 'dispositions' such as instrumental approaches to learning and thus stereotyping certain groups of young people.

The co-construction of learning opportunities and learning cultures was explored in a further set of studies (Evans et al., 2006, Evans, Kersh and Kontiainen, 2004; Hodkinson and Hodkinson, 2003), which also took account of the significance of individual biographies in workplace learning. Thus, in a study on adults returning to work after extended career breaks (Evans, Kersh and Kontiainen, 2004) their biographies were held to be important in terms of the prior knowledge and skills learners brought to the workplace and in the ways in which they took advantage of learning opportunities. Learning dispositions were seen to be shaped by life experience and social background and subsequently by work environments, for example, through the development of particular skills and hence confidence.

These studies highlight the complexity of learning environments and improve our understanding of 'situated' learning in vocational education and in work organisations. Importantly, they avoid the dualism of structure and agency, as the interaction between learners is seen as contributing to the overall structure or learning culture, which in turn informs the individuals' dispositions and identities.

A holistic model of learning

Many studies have examined the ways in which learning environments (in general or vocational education or in work organisations) contribute to young people's identity formation. In relation to vocational education, authors have highlighted apprenticeship as a holistic model of learning and its importance in young people's identity formation, not merely in terms of occupational identity but also in terms of personal development and citizenship (Fuller and Unwin, 2009). Parker (2006) in his research on young people on apprenticeship schemes in English professional football in the 1990s, explores how the learning environment served to shape identities and reproduced forms of hyper-masculinity.

In a general education setting, several authors have illustrated the ways in which gender identities are constructed in primary and secondary schools (Renold, 2005; Paechter, 2006, 2010; Paechter and Clark, 2007). Pollard and Filer's (1999, 2007) influential study of English school children demonstrates how learning is an integral part of the construction of self as pupils attempt to make personal meanings of their lives. While pupils actively constructed their learning and overall identity, this process was subject to powerful social influences from different social contexts as pupils struggled 'to attain and maintain a viable social identity in changing settings over time' which involved having to straddle multiple and often divergent social contexts, including those of family home, school and peer group. Echoing biographical research, the active negotiation of identities was particularly important in the context of discontinuities, such as the initial transfer to secondary school, and with the broadening of social influences later on in adolescence, with many developing differentiated social and academic identities. In line with Bloomer and Hodkinson's study (1997), changes in attitudes to learning occurred in the approach to GCSE exams, as pupils oriented their learning towards career plans and anticipated futures. The study suggested differential patterns of identity formation by social class as students in comprehensive school contexts experienced greater fragmentation of identities than their more affluent counterparts in independent schools. Working class pupils experienced the widest gap between the values and expectations dominating in the different social contexts of school, family home, and peer group.

Different approaches to teaching and learning

Following the previous discussions in this chapter, different approaches to teaching and learning can be expected to impact on the learning culture, reflecting dominant discourses of vocational education, and assumptions concerning how and what students are expected to learn.

Over the past couple of decades new approaches to teaching and learning have been developed to increase the effectiveness of vocational education in the light of changing occupational conditions. Accelerating technological and socio-economic change and more complex work processes have highlighted the need for improved knowledge transfer, understanding of work processes, and for students to direct their own learning in order to deal with fast changing work environments (Stender, 2006). In Germany, self-directed or action-oriented teaching and learning arrangements were introduced in the mid-1990s (Mulder and Sloane, 2004). The approach is based on constructivist learning theory according to which learning occurs through experience and the learner generates knowledge through his or her interpretation of that experience. This is in contrast to approaches where learning consists of the passive intake of objectively defined knowledge and skills through a process of teacher-directed transmission. The new teaching and learning approaches are designed to promote a particular type of learner-worker with high levels of autonomy and motivation. Regardless of whether these aims are achieved, the approach will have an impact on the learner's sense of self and their approach to learning and knowledge, and provides an interesting context or type of 'learning culture' for exploring the construction of identity. The finding that the approach promotes the learning and participation of low attaining students suggests its potential for transforming established learner identities (ibid.).

In Germany, the new approaches have generated a sizeable body of research, although this has so far been largely restricted to evaluations in terms of objective criteria, such as competence development. The findings are ambiguous, with studies related to craft occupations suggesting little or no difference between directive and non-directive approaches, with too great complexity and autonomy negatively impacting on motivation (Nickolaus, Riedl and Schelten, 2005; Nickolaus, Knöll and Gschwendter, 2006). By contrast, studies carried out in relation to business occupations (Sembill et al., 2000) found the effects of self-directed teaching and learning to be wholly favourable, leading to improved student participation and competence development. Schollweck (2007) explored experiences of apprentices of mechanical engineering from their own perspectives. She discovered high levels of satisfaction and motivation. 'Low attainers' in particular, were found to engage with the tasks. Students reported that the approach facilitated their understanding of complex processes and helped to retain knowledge. The study refuted previous findings that students only acquire the knowledge deemed necessary to carry out immediate tasks. Co-operative learning was felt to be particularly motivating, as students felt more readily able to seek or accept advice from students than from teachers.

In England, new approaches to teaching and learning and assessment were introduced from the 1980s onwards with the aim to increase access to qualifications and learner attainment. Thus, vocational education provision has adopted criteria- or competence based assessment methods, based on detailed lists of learning outcomes or competences together with specified assessment criteria. These are typically underpinned by so-called formative assessment, which centres on detailed coaching and extensive feedback to boost individual and institutional achievement. The principles of formative assessment, though more ambiguous than in the German approach, aim to promote motivation and greater learner autonomy. Various studies have sought to gauge the effect of formative assessment, for example on autonomy and motivation (Ecclestone, 2002) and on teachers' and students' attitudes to learning (Torrance et al., 2005). Torrance et al.'s study of various settings of vocational learning (including Motor Vehicle Engineering apprenticeships) found that while competence-based assessment had led to greater numbers of learners it had reinforced the division between academic and vocational learning. Both the tutors' and the learners' focus was on 'criteria compliance' and on achieving qualifications. Success was defined in terms of passing tests and gathering the required paperwork, rather than in terms of, for example, becoming a skilled mechanic. Also, coaching may raise issues of inequity, with learners relying on individual tutor support (see also Colley and Jarvis, 2007).

These findings were confirmed in Ecclestone's study of formative assessment in GNVQ courses. Drawing on James and Biesta (2007), Ecclestone (2004, 2007) argues that the success of formative assessment is strongly dependent on the prevailing expectations and beliefs about student ability and the 'reifying elements' of the learning culture, including assessment regimes and learning materials. Learning cultures were found to be dominated by stereotypical beliefs about how and what students expected to learn or could deal with, which tended to reinforce existing learner identities as 'second chance learners'. Thus, formative assessment encouraged superficial compliance with assessment criteria. Teachers held strongly stereotypical views about learners as fragile and insecure, preferring practical activities in groups within a protected environment. Building up confidence by learning within their 'comfort zones' was widely seen as more important than developing occupational knowledge and skills. The author argues that 'concerns about disengagement from formal education have institutionalised formative assessment practices that raise achievement rather than developing deep engagement with subject knowledge and skills' (Ecclestone, 2007: 331).

The English and German studies suggest that similar approaches have been operationalised in different ways with apparently very different outcomes. These reflect differences in the vocational education systems in the two countries, including their statutes and underlying cultural values.

Conclusions

In conclusion, based on the discussion in this chapter, it seems that the concept of school-to-work transition is still valid if extended to encompass the reality of young people's lives today. This must take account of highly complex transition processes, which are neither linear nor sequential. In the absence of clearly demarcated pathways, young people face difficult choices and often uncertain futures in the face of high unemployment, flexible labour markets and a multitude of (often confusing) educational routes. Most of all, the culture of individual responsibility makes these choices all the more critical. Nevertheless, numerous studies have shown the continued effect of structural factors, notably social class, on young people's decision-making and on transition outcomes.

Studies since the 1960s have developed from simple assumptions of socialisation and smooth transitions to take into account the interplay of structure and young people's agency. Concepts such as structured individualism and bounded agency seek to capture the ways in which actions are circumscribed by socio-economic resources, institutions and cultural values, which can facilitate such actions or pose barriers. A particularly useful concept is that of horizon for action, as it takes account of both, the structural context and young people's perception of it. Much of the research has been highly valuable, highlighting the ways in which learner identities are interlinked with others, such as those rooted in leisure or political participation. Studies have demonstrated that learner identities may change over time, in response to different life events and in different learning environments. The concept of a learning culture underpins the idea that how learning is constructed depends not only on the institutional context and its cultural values, but on the ways in which these are interpreted by the actors within these learning environments, including teachers and learners.

Nonetheless, many of these studies are limited. Some overemphasise social background and leave little scope for agency and for exploring how new experiences may challenge established dispositions. Other research focuses too much on the individualist perspective, whereby young people are seen as reflexively shaping their transitions in a strategic, goal-directed way. Often, young people from more privileged backgrounds are said to be better equipped to become 'individualised'. However, the concept of individualisation is misleading, ignoring young people's quest to forge viable identities in the context of the multiple pressures and discourses that inform youth culture today.

Most importantly, while much research refers to the importance of identity, conceptualisations of identity formation are often inadequate. These are commonly informed by structuralist or individualist perspectives and rely on indicators of outcome and/or selected information from semi-structured interviews, while neglecting the complex processes of identity formation over the young people's lives. In-depth biographical approaches are needed to explore the processes through which learner identities are formed over time, through particular experiences and environments of learning, so that we can explain and understand young people's dispositions to learning and acknowledge that these are neither natural nor unchangeable.

Crucially, as researchers we must not take at face value young people's assertions to the effect that they are not good at academic work or that they had enough of school. Statements such as these have to be interpreted in the context of their biographical experiences. Simplistic conclusions that young people have been 'socialised' to prefer vocational courses, manual work or 'low-skilled' jobs (as opposed to academic pathways and high-status jobs) constructs these young people as non-academic or anti-learning and dismisses vocational education as a positive choice, reflecting the researcher's own prejudice against vocational education and reinforcing the discourse of the academic-vocational divide.

Chapter 4

The study

Introduction

This chapter sets out the conceptual and methodological frameworks. As argued in Chapter 3, previous studies have omitted an adequate conceptualisation of identity, either focusing on structural explanations or individual perspectives. They also neglected young people's biographical experience and hence the complex processes of identity formation. The conceptual and methodological frameworks put forward in this chapter will address both of these issues.

Theorising identity and school-to-work transition

According to Erikson (1968), personal growth and identity formation are linked to developmental stages, driven by the need to construct an 'ego-identity' synthesising fragmented selves into a coherent whole. This process is seen to culminate during adolescence, conceived as a crucial period of 'normative crisis', when young people experience radical changes in body and mind while facing a mass of conflicting possibilities and choices. Erikson refers to youth as a 'moratorium', a period marked by frequent shifts in allegiances and devotions as young people assume a multitude of different identities.

Crucially, Erikson views these processes as being embedded in social relationships. In particular, he stresses the role of parents and teachers in children's development, in terms of, for example, instilling trust and self-worth. Erikson stresses young people's deep seated need to achieve a sense of purpose and 'competence' during school age as they look towards their anticipated futures. This highlights the idea that identity, or identifying with something, is bound up with self-confidence of being good at something and the need for self-expression ('the desire to make something work and make it work well'). He singles out teachers' role in evoking a sense of self-worth: 'a sense of inferiority, the feeling that one will never be "any good", [...] can be minimised by a teacher who knows how to emphasise what a child *can* do' (Erikson, 1968: 125). Where young people are unable to establish confidence and pride at school, they will look for alternative sources of identification.

Erikson provides a detailed insight into the psychological processes of identity formation while stressing its embeddedness in social relationships. However, his theory and particularly the idea of a fixed core-self established early on in life has been criticised by social theorists who emphasise the fluidity and incompleteness of identity formation (Rattansi and Phoenix, 1997). Nevertheless, psycho-social processes, such as the notion that young people have a deep-seated need to achieve a sense of purpose, are highly relevant in the study of transitions.

While psychoanalytic approaches emphasise the individual, writers from the sociological tradition have been concerned with social and political processes of identity formation and the construction of power relations. Bourdieu's (1985) account of power and particularly the notion of *habitus* emphasise the role of structure in reproducing social class. A person's *habitus*—a set of dispositions of how to act in everyday situations—is seen as determined by one's position in the social structure, through the inculcation of norms and values dominant in a social context or 'field'. Thus, position and disposition are closely linked, as the *habitus* mediates between social structures and decision-making.

As discussed in Chapter 3, much of the British literature on youth transition and work-based learning (for example, Bates, 1993; Hodkinson, Sparkes and Hodkinson, 1996; Colley et al., 2003) has drawn on the *habitus* concept to explain working-class young people's transition to particular pathways or occupations. Clearly, *habitus* is a useful concept in that it illuminates the different ways in which structural factors impact on young people's lives. Young people's perceptions of their opportunities and decision-making must be seen as being shaped to a large extent by their social background and the inter-generational transmission of norms and values (Furlong and Cartmel, 2007). However, by focusing on social class reproduction, the concept is of limited value, foreclosing as it does possibilities for change and reflexive agency. For example, it does not explain how young people's new experiences may challenge their established *habitus*. In addition, where agency is informed by *habitus*, many studies, as we have seen, focus on particular indicators and outcomes, while neglecting the processes of identity formation and the ways in which transmitted norms and values inform young people's actions.

Studies on 'occupational' or 'organisational' identity commonly draw on the work of Erving Goffman (1968a, b, 1969, 1971, 1972). Goffman describes the ways in which social interaction is governed by social norms and values that delineate a social identity, for example of an occupation, and its associated attributes, attitudes and behaviours (Goffman, 1972, 1969). However, post-structuralists such as Judith Butler have argued that Goffman's account is ill-suited to our understanding of individuals making sense of the world as it suggests a 'true self' of individuals who put on a particular image in accordance with social expectations of attributes or characteristics associated with a particular role or social identity, which in turn suggests enduring identities and essentialist conceptions of what it means to be male/female or black/white (or a mechanic or retail assistant), with individuals expressing certain truths or core identities through their actions.

If it is assumed that institutions, policies and cultural values do not merely shape individuals' actions in a neutral way, a discussion of identity necessitates an account of power relations, their production, reproduction, regulation and mediation at the level of the individual. Judith Butler (1988, 1990, 1993, 1997), drawing on Foucault's theory of disciplinary power and discursive regimes, has been highly influential in revising existing conceptualisations of gender and gender identity. According to Foucault (1991), rather than being concentrated in the hands of an individual or a government, power is diffuse and exercised through discursive relations and regimes, which regulate social norms and conduct in different societal domains. Drawing on Foucault, Butler argues that identities are discursively produced: rather than reflecting or expressing an enduring identity that exists before the act, it is the actions (discursive practices) of individuals that constitute identity. The conception of identity as performatively constituted focuses attention on the temporal and incomplete nature of identities and, notably, permits individual agency. Regulatory discursive regimes of gender are upheld through the compulsive citation of norms which in turn exert a binding power, a process referred to as sedimentation through the endless reiteration of norms. At the same time, the normative identities are 'phantasmic ideals' and can never be fully achieved. Identity formation is seen as a process of materialisation in which individuals approximate imagined ideals or, occasionally, transfigure them. Herein lies the potential for action.

Butler's notion of performatively constituted identities emphasises that these are inherently unstable and subject to transformation. They appear to be enduring only insofar as they continue to be cited. By the same token, individuals are not fixed or natural but are produced again and again through discursive practices. Their actions are deeply embedded in and only have meaning through the citation of discourses of male/female, black/white and so on as individuals strive to be recognisable in interaction with others. Hence Butler's assertion that 'there is no doer behind the deed' (Butler, 1990). They come into existence and are recognised by others only through discursive practices and the ongoing citation of norms. This conceptualisation also involves a dilemma: While it suggests a potential for individual agency, this is heavily constrained. Borrowing Foucault's (1991) notion of subjectivation, Butler (1990) posits that while individuals are rendered subjects through discourse, they are simultaneously subjected to the disciplinary power of discursive regimes, upholding certain values and norms of conduct.

Butler's theory has not been without its critics. McNay (1999) argues that her concept of performativity constitutes a negative account of agency: rather than changing gender relations, individuals may merely subvert them in a 'process of identity displacement', subverting meanings of male/female or straight/gay. According to her, Butler fails to take account of the multiple values and resources negotiated by young people and the ways in which new value systems are instituted.

In a similar vein, other writers have pointed to the limitations of Butler's theory in explaining contemporary youth cultures. Nayak and Kehily's (2008) approach of 'global ethnography' explores the interplay between institutional discourses, popular consumption, informal cultures, and individual negotiation of gender in the context of transnational flows of people and cultures. Rattansi and Phoenix point to the need for a new conceptualisation of identity that takes account of the multiple social contexts and positionings of young people, drawing on a variety of discourses and giving rise to contradictions as well as the 'profusion of cultural forms' (1997: 124). Most importantly in the context of this study, Butler's highly abstract account neglects the situated subjectivities of people and how they experience and act upon relations of power and negotiate individual identities. This is all the more surprising given Butler's insistence on the 'approximation' of social norms which at the same time she sees as failing to fully determine individuals, presumably giving rise to individually negotiated identities beyond social norms, which she however does not consider. Also, no attempt is made to explore the experiences that encourage individuals to subvert or resist social norms.

Nevertheless, Butler's theory is highly relevant to the study of youth transitions and in particular to examining power relations within specific social settings. Drawing on Butler, Nayak and Kehily (2008) explore the co-construction of gender regimes in English secondary schools, demonstrating for example the powerful and yet unstable nature of heterosexual gender norms and their reproduction as pupils feel the 'extraordinary compulsion to act straight' (2008: 168). Deborah Youdell (2006) in her study of an English and an Australian secondary school adopts Butler's theory of performativity and demonstrates the productive power of institutional discourse, highlighting processes of inclusion and exclusion. She argues that, as schools are governed by discourses of the 'good' and the 'bad' student, these 'are not simply teachers' perceptions or descriptions of students, but are implicated in creating students in these terms' (ibid.: 97). School discourses intercept with social (for example, classed and gendered) identities to create particular discursive frames. These produce certain constellations of identity categories that are more or less commensurate with ideas of the good student, while rendering certain students unacceptable. For example, certain discourses of femininity may be commensurate with the good student, while sub-cultural identities of masculinity are not.

Youdell challenges the idea of students as fixed and abiding subjects and compellingly shows how students and teachers, by deploying discursive performatives in everyday interaction with one another, constitute themselves and others; either explicitly, through language or bodily expressions of gestures and dress, or implicitly, for example by drawing on a particular discourse in speech or text. Many of these practices serve to reinforce hegemonic discourses, such as the girl combing her hair in class, thereby inscribing prevailing meanings of femininity.

A particularly useful Butlerian concept is that of 'discursive agency', which refers to the capacity of individuals (subjects) to 'name' (that is, deploy discursive practices) and thus 'constitute' others. The constraint is posed through the need for intelligibility—practices have to make sense in the context within which they are deployed so as to be recognisable. However, by joining the 'citational chains of discourse', that is, the contextual and historic flows of meaning making, subjects may reinforce as well as resist established meanings and discourses. Hence, the author relates examples of students challenging the teacher-student hierarchy by reinscribing subcultural discourses of femininity/masculinity (and of teachers recuperating the challenge by reinstating their teacher status), or of students subverting derogatory meanings related to disability or 'unfemininity' through 'ironic reinscription' (as in the example of a disabled student subverting the label 'crip' through her joyous and active nature).

While Youdell has successfully related Butler's highly abstract account to the concrete and very real contexts of secondary schools, the focus on power relationships limits our understanding of the students in these terms: the ways in which they reinforce or resist prevailing discourses. Also, Youdell's study, while highly instructive, is bound to a particular period in time and a particular context—it is a case study of two schools. The meanings are those constructed within the particular sites, governed by particular discursive matrices. It neglects the biographical meanings and subjectivities of individual students and how these have evolved over time and in a multiplicity of contexts. Youdell is not interested in *why* certain students deploy certain discursive practices and not others. For the present study, Butler's theory will be useful for exploring the ways in which apprentices are discursively constituted in the different learning sites. However, in order to explore the young people's identity formation over time, we need to draw on other theorists.

Where Butler is concerned with challenging discursive relations, Paul Ricoeur's (1992) theory of identity formation may be better suited to gaining an understanding of how people negotiate manifold and conflicting influences *over time*. His theory encompasses the possibility for change while insisting on the significance of past experience. Ricoeur distinguishes between the 'sameness' of character as a set of lasting dispositions acquired over time ('*idem* identity') and by which we are recognised, and 'self-hood' ('*ipse* identity'), which is concerned with maintaining the self in the context of new experiences. However, this does not happen in an arbitrary way but is always linked to the past and a concern for the future. Thus, identity construction is conceived as evolving over time, and as concerned with establishing continuity as individuals negotiate the present in the light of both past experience and an anticipation of the future, of what they are becoming. By conceiving of it as an ethical project, Ricoeur also highlights the relational aspect of identity construction, which is guided by the moral imperatives of 'being true to oneself' and 'keeping one's word'.

Importantly, it is through the narrative that identity is constructed, weaving together disparate actions and events. The desire for sameness and concordance in the lifecourse is continuously disrupted by new events and circumstances. In the narrative, the individual creates a narrative identity through 'emplotment', linking events and actions which create 'discordant concordance', where contingent events become necessities and chance events are construed as fate (Ricoeur, 1992: 142). The narrative is reminiscent of Butler's performative identity in stressing temporal openness, while leaving greater possibility for the creative actions of individuals.

The weakness of the above accounts lies in the neglect of subjectivity in actual social contexts. The biographical approach recognises the close interrelatedness of individual action and social contexts. It has its origins in the tradition of symbolic interactionism, and is based on the assumption that 'generative structures' (Alheit, 2002: 195) simultaneously shape and are being shaped by individuals, who act upon social structures and in so doing reproduce or modify them. Biography is viewed as a lifelong process of meaning-making and hence identity construction. Indeed, Alheit sees identity as resulting from 'biographical work', driven by the need to continually reconstruct identity in the face of biographical discontinuities (Alheit, 2002).

According to Alheit (2002), it is continually accumulated and renewed knowledge from past experience through which people interpret present situations and which shapes their anticipation of the future. Biography is seen as constituted of meaningfully integrated experiences—people linking new experiences to previous ones, forming particular dispositions over time.

This process does not necessarily happen in a reflected or strategic way, but with an 'inner logic' (or '*Gestalt*'). Thus, biography is conceived as a chain of processed experiences which, to some extent at least, shapes the processing of future experiences. Importantly, biography holds the potential for both continuity and change. Of particular use is Alheit's (2002, 2003) notion of biographical knowledge, which is conceived as the central resource for meaning making as it allows us to integrate new experiences with past ones and thus make sense of our lives. Biographical knowledge includes (often unreflected) knowledge of structures and dispositions acquired through institutions such as the family and the school, shaping our dealing with everyday situations and also encompasses knowledge of alternative, as yet 'unlived', possibilities; an 'intuitive knowledge of potential changes and opportunities' (2003a: 15). New experiences can open up new perspectives. As past experiences are reflected retrospectively, they can lead to new insight. Altheit's notion of 'biographicity' (2003a: 15) describes the capacity of individuals to reflect upon and re-interpret their lives in the light of new experiences and to consciously (re-)negotiate their own biography and particularly the ability to deal with biographical discontinuities by drawing on the as yet unlived potential of past experiences.

In examining identity formation in school-to-work transition, this book draws on social theorists such as Butler and Ricoeur. The analysis of power relations as discursive regimes is an important element in the study of the complex dynamics between agency and structure in youth transition, as is the idea of conflicting pressures of sameness and otherness. The book considers the regulation and performance of gender identities as salient features in vocational education (Fuller, Beck and Unwin, 2005) while also applying Butler's theory to occupational identities, thereby exploring the complex dynamics underlying particular learning cultures in vocational learning environments.

These theories will be combined with biographical approaches (Alheit, 2002; Wengraf, 2001). While identity formation clearly happens at multiple, interwoven levels, it cannot be complete without considering the lived experience (past and present) of the individual. It is imperative from the point of view of understanding young people's perspectives and the ways in which they experience and negotiate structural factors, including and particularly the effects of vocational education and training systems and policy, as well as social disadvantage and biographical discontinuities. The theoretical framework is thus suited to the comparative study of learner biographies, examining the complex interplay between institutional and social factors on the one hand and individual agency on the other.

Constructing a methodological framework

The study was designed as a comparative multi-method ethnography. Adopting a range of data collection methods, it aims to gain an understanding of young people's experiences in a variety of contexts. The focus of analysis is individual learners, that is to say, the study consists of individual case studies (Stake, 1998, 2000; Crompton, 2001). Biographical interviews (Wengraf, 2001) were used to explore young people's learner identities as they are constructed over time and in multiple social contexts. These were complemented by ethnographic studies of the main learning sites, the workplace and the college, using participant observation, interviews with key actors, and documentary evidence. The ethnographies are central to gaining insight into the construction of particular 'learning cultures' in the different sites as important contexts for the young people's construction of identity. Thus, recognising the situated nature of meaning, the study goes beyond a 'place-focused' towards a 'multi-locale' approach (Marcus, 1998). The design therefore aimed to explore the biographical process of identity construction, over time and in multiple social contexts.

Ethnography

The research takes a constructivist-interpretivist approach to ethnography (Denzin and Lincoln, 1998). It is concerned with gaining an in-depth understanding of the lived experience of situated individuals, 'from the point of view of those who live it' (ibid.). Individuals live in social worlds which they construct in interaction with each other, attaching meanings to situations and events. In doing so, they draw on cultural representations of those experiences. Their social reality is thus defined by individuals' interpretations of structural factors, including institutional rules and processes, dominant values and discourses concerning power, class, sexuality as well as organisational roles and occupations. These form a web of interlinked contexts at different levels of society. Denzin and Lincoln (1998) have pointed to the importance of interpreting human action in the light of those contexts and criticised Blumer and Mead's symbolic interactionism, advocating instead what they call 'interpretive interactionism' to highlight the need for sensitivity to the cultural construction of meaning.

Thus, social structures shape and at the same time are being shaped by meaning-making and actions of individuals who simultaneously move within a variety of contexts, each with their own unique social worlds, potentially in conflict with each other. Identities are negotiated within unique social contexts, themselves shaped by societal rules and values governing cultural representations of gender, ethnicity, occupations and learning. It is the inter-relationship of human agency and structure, and identity construction as meaning-making that this book is concerned with.

Participant observation is a critical part of ethnographic research (Atkinson and Hammersley 1998). Individuals construct their social worlds through meaning-making in interaction which each other, uniquely situated in multiple layers of context (Blommaert, 2006). Ethnography therefore holds that we can understand individuals' social realities and meaning systems only through the researcher's full immersion and participation in the community being studied, gradually becoming a 'knowing member of the community' (ibid.: 22). Crucially, this involves building relationships and taking part in interactions with subjects, leading to shared experiences. We are therefore contributing to the meaning-making processes by ourselves interpreting and acting upon situations.

While early ethnographies aimed to produce neutral scientific accounts of the communities studied, it is now commonly acknowledged that representations of the social world are inevitably 'partial truths' (Clifford, 1986: 6). Processes of meaning-making take place in concrete social interactions between members of the community, and within particular social contexts. Under the new epistemological paradigm (often referred to as 'post-structuralist'), the researcher interprets meaning within these contexts, while at the same time recognising his or her own situationality and perspective as well as the power relationship between researcher and informant (Clifford, 1983; Tsolidis,

2008). Central to the new approach is the researcher's active participation in the field, as the 'research instrument par excellence' (Hammersley and Atkinson, 2007: 17). Rather than being fixed, meanings and social worlds are continually constructed and re-constructed in interaction by its members (Blommaert, 2006). Blommaert refers to the 'mutual learning process' which 'enables particular forms of interaction to take place and particular kinds of knowledge to travel between the two parties' (ibid.: 20). Both researcher and participant seek to make sense of social situations governed by rules, values and codes of conduct. My own study has built on this approach.

It was clear that I was not going to be able to conduct a conventional ethnography, spending months in the field. This was partly because of the time constraints of doing a part-time PhD, and partly because of the particular research design. The apprentices in my study were spread across eleven different firms and eight college classes. I had to limit my observations to a maximum of two days in each site.

While some commentators have warned against the diminished rigour of new, compressed forms of ethnography (Walford, 2009), I nevertheless found the participant observations invaluable to my research. Short-term participant observation in the workplaces and college classrooms provided insight into the co-construction of learning cultures in these sites, and of the young people's construction of identity within them. In a variety of 'active' researcher roles (Hammersley and Atkinson, 2007), including those of placement student and auxiliary help, I was able to partake in situations offering opportunities for the co-construction of meaning (for a fuller discussion see Brockmann, 2011).

The biographical method

Whereas participant observation is concerned with communicated interaction and the construction of meaning systems at a particular point in time, the biographical method enables the reconstruction of situated lived experience over time (Rosenthal, 2004). Participant observation may privilege collective, outwardly discernible meanings, shaped by cultural norms and expectations, at a particular point in time, but the insight this provides into individually created meanings and perspectives and the ways in which these change over time may be limited. The study centres on the Biographical Narrative Interpretive Method (BNIM) (Wengraf, 2001) as a powerful tool for exploring the dialectic relationship between agency and structure, the ways in which contexts and situations shape human agency and human beings act upon and shape the world around them.

The biographical method is designed to encourage the telling of life story, generating accounts of events and situations, and bringing the subject closer to the actual experience at the time, rather than giving rise to evaluations or *post hoc* rationalisations, as is often the case with semi-structured interviews (Hollway and Jefferson, 2000). Through eliciting stories of experiences, it goes beyond other qualitative methods and enables the researcher to gain an understanding of situated subjectivity, that is, felt experience, and how this evolves over time, as well as taken-for-granted assumptions, which are indicative of norms and value systems.

Encouraging the subject to tell their story on their own terms, freely and uninterrupted, enables the subject to use their own frame of references and narrate experiences which they regard as important or relevant, without the interviewer imposing their frame of references. Reconstructing the 'Gestalt' of the story (that is, the selection and sequence of events told, the ways in which they are told) gives insight into the subject's current perspective and the ways in which they make sense of their lives, and thus the ways in which s/he constructs their identity from a current perspective and in interaction with the interviewer. Theorists have pointed to the importance of identity construction through the narrative (Ricoeur, 1992).

By distinguishing between 'objective' life events and circumstances (the 'lived life'), and subjective experience (the 'told story'), we can gain insight into the ways in which subjectivities are shaped by and at the same time shape situations, that is, how individual action is guided by societal constraints and enablements and the ways in which individuals experience and act upon these. We can therefore reconstruct people's biographies, how they make sense of their lives, the ways in which they accept, conform with or modify institutional structures, and how their perspectives change over time. Using the biographical method we can construct a sense 'of a historically-evolving situation being subjectively processed and of a historical subjectivity experiencing and acting in their evolving situation' (Wengraf, 2008: 68).

Biographical interviewing usually involves three stages (Wengraf, 1998). It starts with the Single Question aimed at Inducing Narrative(s) or SQUIN, which invites the interviewee to tell his or her story, based on the principle of free association, uninterrupted by the interviewer. Then, when the interviewee has signalled the end of his or her story, the interviewer picks up on issues and events raised in the story (and in the sequence in which they were raised so as to preserve the *Gestalt*), each time seeking to elicit 'more story'. In a final stage, the interviewer may ask questions 'external' to the story, generated by the particular research focus, on aspects not covered in the interviewee's initial narrative. Here it has to be noted that identity construction as a dynamic process of meaning-making is situated within the particular context of the interview encounter and has to be regarded as a result of the unique interaction between the interviewer and the interviewee (Holstein and Gubrium, 1995).

Following Crompton (2001), I have examined learner biographies within the contexts at the macro-, meso- and micro-levels, as young people's biographies need to be interpreted within the contexts of national policies on vocational education as well as the contexts of the college and the workplace, where these policies are played out (Table 4.1). The individual biographies, that is, the contexts of their own life (hi)stories provide a further level.

Table 4.1 Research undertaken at different levels of context

Level of analysis	Information gathered
Macro	National policy on vocational education, including apprenticeship frameworks for the two apprenticeships studied
Meso	Information concerning colleges and workplaces, including their interpretation of the apprenticeship frameworks
Micro	Young people's biographies

Adapted from Crompton (2001)

Sampling

The sample comprised four apprentices on each of the apprenticeship programmes in each country, giving a total of sixteen. Apprentices were selected according to certain criteria to ensure that young people of similar characteristics were being compared. Thus, the age range was specified at sixteen to twenty-four years-old. In addition, the research focused on apprentices in the first year of their apprenticeship who were purposively selected to represent a variety of biographical experiences: men and women, majority and minority ethnic groups, and different educational attainment. The sample reflected to some extent the different gender distribution of the two programmes, while securing an equal number of men and women overall. Thus, the intended sample was, for motor vehicle maintenance:

1 female apprentice

1 male apprentice from an ethnic minority background

2 male apprentices with lower and higher educational attainment

For retailing:

1 male apprentice

1 female apprentice from an ethnic minority background

2 female apprentices with lower and higher educational attainment

The selection of apprentices according to these criteria was facilitated with the help of the college tutors. In Germany, the two-stage design of the apprenticeships served as an indicator of differential school attainment. Motor vehicle maintenance encompasses a three-and-a-half-year programme called 'mechatronic', which is followed more often by young people with at least an intermediate school certificate, and a two-year programme 'car service mechanic' for those with the general secondary school certificate. Similarly, within retail, the programme splits into a three-year apprenticeship 'Retail Salesman/woman' and a two-year apprenticeship 'Retail Assistant'.

Learning sites

Important foci of the research are the different learning sites, that is, the workplace, and the college of further education (in England) and the vocational school (in Germany). The identification of suitable colleges and employers was therefore critical. The identification of sites and the recruitment of apprentices was a lengthy, and in some cases challenging, process. There were a number of practical constraints, such as time and distance, and, notably, people's suspicion of the research and their role within it. The selection of sites was more opportunistic than I would have liked. Given the difficulty of gaining access, this is a common experience, as Troman found in his study of a primary school, where 'the selection of a case to research was more a matter of the school choosing me than me choosing the school' (Troman, 2002: 110). However, as Troman also notes, the research rests on the full co-operation and support of those on the site, so that an opportunistic sample may be the best that can be achieved. The recruitment of apprentices was also somewhat restricted, largely because of the influence of gatekeepers. However, for the most part, the sample accorded with the original sampling criteria.

In England, in the case of motor vehicle maintenance, it was relatively straightforward. After identifying a number of suitable colleges through the internet, one, located in the South-East of England, agreed to support the research and a visit was arranged. Staff were extremely supportive of the study. However, because of the absence of female apprentices in Year 1, it was decided to focus on young people in the second year of their apprenticeship. The tutors' optimism regarding apprentices' willingness to take part proved misplaced. The suspicion of English motor vehicle apprentices was a salient feature in the further process of the research, distinguishing them from their German counterparts. Nonetheless, four young people came forward, and the achieved sample accorded with the specified criteria.

In the case of English retailing, identifying learning sites proved extremely difficult. Few colleges offered retail apprenticeships at the time and the ones I identified were reluctant to take part. This was similar in the case of private providers. It appears that there were concerns with low achievement rates (as this creates problems for the colleges in not fulfilling their contract for government funding) and with comparing unfavourably with German apprenticeships. In contrast, a major food retailer proved much more open and supportive and set up contacts with stores. Two of my apprentices were located in a store in London, the other two in a provincial town in the South-West of England. I was able to sample for sex and ethnicity, but not for educational attainment.

In Germany, the identification of sites and selection of apprentices was difficult because of the geographical distance and because of having to rely on gatekeepers. Initial contact with two colleges (one for motor vehicle maintenance, one for retail, both situated in towns in Western Germany) was facilitated by staff at a German university, which had offered me a base for my research in Germany. These staff had close relationships with the colleges, where they worked as tutors.

The relevant contact persons in the German colleges insisted that I should obtain access to the apprentices *via the employers* (while seeking the colleges' approval for the class observations). This significantly complicated the process of recruitment. For motor vehicle maintenance, I relied on one large car dealership and a smaller garage, again facilitated by the tutors at the university, and the firms put forward apprentices based on my sampling criteria. Unfortunately, there were no white majority ethnic apprentices with the general secondary school certificate in the sample.

In the case of retail, for the identification of suitable employers I had to go through one of the main retail employer associations (*Einzelhandelsverband*). This was a lengthy and largely obscure process which I did not feel I had much control over. Eventually, they established contact with two retail companies (one department store and one supermarket) in an industrial city in Western

Germany. I found that the managers/owners had selected the young people for me based on my description of sampling criteria. Fortunately, I was able to apply the sampling criteria to the retail apprentices.

The individual learning sites and distribution of apprentices will be discussed in detail in the next Chapter. Tables 4.2a and b show the achieved sample of the English and German apprentices.

Table 4.2a The achieved sample of apprentices, England

	Age	Sex	Ethnicity	School attainment
Vehicle maintenance				
Alex[3]	18	Male	White	GCSEs
Ollie	17	Male	White	GCSEs (no English and Maths A-C)
Lisa	17	Female	White	GCSEs
Nathan	20	Male	Chinese	GCSEs
Retail				
Stephanie	21	Female	White	GCSEs (no English and Maths A-C)
Mia	18	Female	White	GCSEs (no English and Maths A-C)
Anita	24	Female	Indian	GCSEs
Robert	19	Male	White	GCSEs

Table 4.2b The achieved sample of apprentices, Germany

	Age	Sex	Ethnicity	School attainment
Vehicle maintenance				
Stefan	18	Male	White	Intermediate (Mechatronic)
Daniel	17	Male	White	Intermediate (Mechatronic)
Erika	18	Female	White	Intermediate (Mechatronic)
Aazim	19	Male	Arab	General secondary (Car Services Mechanic)
Retail				
Claudia	17	Female	White	Intermediate (Retail Saleswoman)
Jeanette	17	Female	White	General secondary (Retail Assistant)
Leena	17	Female	Arab	General secondary (Retail Saleswoman)
Martin	21	Male	White	General secondary (Retail Assistant)

3   All names are pseudonyms.

Data collection

Secondary data

Secondary data collection at the macro-level was conducted prior to the fieldwork. It involved gathering information on the national contexts of vocational education and apprenticeship through a variety of sources, including the existing literature, policy documents, the relevant apprenticeship frameworks, and official databases. At the meso-level, information was collated relevant to the workplaces and colleges, including the adaptation of the apprenticeship frameworks, teaching material, and assessment practices. This material, together with the data obtained through the workplace and classroom observations as well as the interviews with college tutors, enabled me to interpret the learning culture in each setting (introduced in Chapter 5), which provided another layer of context for the interpretation of learner identities.

Primary data

Primary data collection was in two phases:

Phase 1

In each country, the first phase of the research was conducted during a two-week period between February and April 2009 (with the exception of the English retail apprentices who were interviewed in May (1), June (1) and August (2). This phase involved:

+   Biographic-interpretive interviews with apprentices. These started with a 'Single Question aimed at Inducing Narrative(s)' (Wengraf, 2008), inviting the young people to tell their story, giving them the opportunity to develop their own frames of reference. Following this, interviewees were probed concerning particular issues and events they had raised during the interview, each time eliciting 'more story'. This was supplemented by a topic guide comprising further invitations to narrative and open questions concerning the young people's negotiation of identity over time and in specific learning environments. Questions were asked only in so far as the young person had not covered them in the initial story. The interview schedule was developed in English and translated into German by the researcher. The interviews lasted from forty-five minutes to two and a half hours (with initial narratives lasting from five to thirty minutes). They were recorded and subsequently transcribed in their original language.

♦   Observations at each of the colleges. These involved the researcher attending two days at each college, taking field notes using an observation schedule, and, as far as possible, engaging in activities and conversations with tutors and apprentices. Semi-structured interviews were also conducted with the main tutors in each of the colleges, using a topic guide, concerning the tutors' perceptions of their role and of the young people's learning. These lasted around thirty to forty-five minutes and were recorded and transcribed.

Phase 2

The second phase of the study took place during a two-week period five to nine months after the completion of the first phase. This comprised:

♦   Follow-up interviews with the apprentices, focusing on changes in their learning experiences. These took the form of semi-structured interviews and were different in each case, as issues were followed up that were raised during the first interview. As they took place during working hours, they were brief and lasted from fifteen to thirty minutes. They were not recorded. The researcher took *verbatim* notes which were subsequently typed up.

♦   Observations in the workplace. This involved the researcher spending one day at each workplace (two days in the case of the German car dealership), taking field notes using an observation schedule, participating in some of the activities as appropriate (or example, working on tasks with the apprentices, or having lunch), and, as far as possible, engaging in conversations with apprentices and their colleagues.

Unfortunately, two of the retail apprentices in one of the stores in England had left the company by the time I was due to do the workplace observations and follow-up interviews. I was only told this when I arrived there for the workplace observation so that I decided to go ahead and spent a day with the teams as part of which they had worked during their apprenticeships. As the two apprentices chose not to get in touch with me again, I was unable to conduct the follow-up interviews.

Analysis

The secondary data at macro-level were written up to form the wider national contexts within which the primary data were interpreted (Chapter 2). At the meso-level, documentary evidence and primary data obtained in the colleges and workplaces were analysed and written up to provide the context of the case study sites as introduced in Chapter 5. This included the institutional context and, related to this, the learning culture in each setting, which was written up based on the observational fieldnotes, interviews with tutors and documentary evidence (see Chapter 5). The fieldnotes taken during the college and workplace observations as well as the interviews with tutors were analysed according to principles of Grounded Theory (Strauss and Corbin, 1990) in order to identify themes pertaining to the co-construction of learning cultures, such as a hierarchical division of labour, or a participatory approach to learning.

The biographical interviews were analysed according to principles of the Biographical Interpretive Narrative Method (Wengraf, 2001, 2008). The method distinguishes between the 'objective' biographical data (the lived life) and the subjective experience (the told story) which are kept conceptually distinct. The researcher is required to bring to bear relevant knowledge of the particular institutional or social contexts, such as those related to the vocational education systems in England and Germany, which enables us to examine how individuals shape their own lives and how these are shaped by structural factors. By attempting to reconstruct how events have been experienced, the method illuminates changes in perspectives and formation of dispositions and identities.

The biographical interviews were transcribed (in their original language, with transcripts averaging thirty-five pages) and written up according to an analytical framework derived from theoretical and empirical considerations. The process comprised a sequential analysis of the initial narrative, which ranged from one half to four pages in length. This involved the presentation of the self, the identification of major themes, and hypothesising about the meaning of key issues raised (or those that were not raised). Those themes then provided a lens into the remainder of the interviews, and hypotheses were either confirmed or rejected.

Parallel to this, a time line of 'objective' key dates and events (such as birth of siblings, parents' separation, start of primary school) was composed as a structural backdrop in the context of which the young person's narrative was interpreted. Throughout, knowledge of the macro- and meso-level contexts was brought to bear. The interviews were written up (in English, with quotes by German apprentices translated into English by the researcher) as ten-page summaries under key headings (initial narrative; early life; transition to work; transition to college; other life domains). The summaries were up-dated (and revised where necessary) in the light of the follow-up interviews.

Following the completion of the fieldwork, the case studies were written up as short (two to two-and-a-half page) life stories which sought to capture the biographical experience of the young people and the ways in which their learner identities were formed throughout their childhood, adolescence and into adulthood, and in different learning environments. The analysis combined the interview summaries with the findings of the learning cultures, and in particular, the young people's constructions of meaning in these sites, thus enabling me to interpret these in the context of their lives as a whole.

For the comparative analysis, I identified themes across each set of cases (retail and motor vehicle apprentices) according to principles of Grounded Theory (Strauss and Corbin, 1994) and guided by the research questions of the study. I subsequently identified the most meaningful analytical categories for the purpose of comparative discussion and placed the cases onto a matrix. I then selected pairs of individual cases for comparison, in line with the principle of biographical matching (Crompton, 2001), according to which biographies of individuals from different countries are matched on certain biographical criteria, such as age, gender or biographical experience, and compared for explanatory purposes.

My matching criteria were gender and biographical experience, such as a disadvantaged childhood. These proved more fruitful than ethnicity, which I rejected as a matching criterion, because ethnicity either played no role in the relevant young people's stories or proved to be too diverse an experience in order to constitute meaningful comparison. I abandoned educational attainment as a criterion due to limitations in the sample (see section on recruitment of apprentices in this chapter). The pairs were then presented according to the analytical dimensions. By adopting the 'contrast of contexts' approach (Skocpol and Somers, 1980), it became possible to identify the particular structural factors and how these impacted on the young people's transitions and identity formation. The process of analysis is described in more detail at the beginning of Chapter 6. Table 4.3 gives an overview of the analytical steps involved:

Table 4.3 Outputs of analysis

Outputs	Based on:
Macro-level context	Literature, policy documents, official documentation, statistical data sources
Meso-level context, including description of learning cultures	Fieldnotes, interviews with college tutors, documentary evidence
Interview summaries	Biographical interviews and follow-up interviews
Young people's life stories	Interview summaries and learning cultures
Presentation of the case comparisons	Individual life stories, identification of themes and pairs for comparison

Conclusions

This chapter has set out the conceptual and methodological frameworks applied in this book. It introduced theories of identity construction that enable the analysis of both structure and agency, notably Butler's (1990) theory of performativity, and the biographical approach, which draws our attention to the construction of identity as a lifelong process and thus the importance of young people's biographical experience in examining their dispositions to learning. The research design, a comparative multi-method ethnographic approach, was chosen to gather a variety of perspectives and to guard against any simplistic interpretations regarding young people's construction of their learner identities.

While the part-time nature of the thesis posed restrictions, particularly on the length of time I could spend as a participant observer on the different learning sites, these would constituted an invaluable contribution to the overall design. They not only yielded important contextual information at the meso-level for interpreting the biographical interviews. They also provided insight into the meaning-making of individual apprentices within these learning cultures, often in interaction with the researcher, which I was then able to interpret in the context of their biographical experience. The combination of the biographic-interpretive method with participant observation were crucial complimentary elements in a methodological framework designed to understand young people's construction of learner identities over time and within the particular learning environments of motor vehicle maintenance and retail apprentices.

Chapter 5

Introducing the case study sites and learning cultures

Introduction

In this chapter I present my findings in relation to the case study sites. This includes a description of the institutional context of the respective apprenticeships and an introduction to the case study sites. In addition, based on my case study ethnographic work (documentary research, participant observation, interviews with key actors such as college tutors and company managers), I briefly explore the learning culture in each site.

The purpose of the ethnographic work in the learning sites was not solely to set the scene and provide a context for the case study interviews (although this was part of it). Rather, it provided a distinct lens on the ways in which the young people constructed their identities within the different learning sites; the ways in which the institutional structure, notably the structure and content of apprenticeships (Ecclestone's (2007) 'reifying elements') were being interpreted by apprentices and their tutors and co-workers.

The presentation of findings in this chapter reflects to some extent the research design, and in particular, the nature of short-term participant observation. The learning culture in the colleges was much more tangible and can be described more comprehensively (see Brockmann, 2011). By contrast, in the workplaces, particular meanings were more often constructed in direct interaction with the researcher and often pertained directly to the identity of individual apprentices. This material will therefore be presented as part of the individual case studies in Chapters 6 and 7 and will not be repeated here. For these reasons, the description of learning cultures in workplaces in this chapter is at times only sketchy.

Following Butler (1990), Deborah Youdell (2006) showed how subjects are performatively constituted in school environments and how the discursive framework of the school—which constitutes, for example, what it means to be a good student—intercepts with identities of gender, class and ethnicity. Driven by the desire to be an accepted subject, students (and teachers) construct their identities by citing various discourses, rendering students more or less compatible with the school discourse. The performative construction of identities in the college classrooms of my study was highly tangible. Apprentices and tutors co-constructed particular learning cultures in institutionalised and normative environments, in which only certain identities were possible. Nevertheless, while certain identities were dominant, others co-existed, thus refuting the idea that young people in vocational education constitute a homogenous whole. The learning cultures differed between the two countries, as discourses were informed by different values and assumptions of contrasting institutional contexts.

Table 5.1 gives an overview of the different learning sites of the two apprenticeship programmes in England and Germany. For motor vehicle maintenance, the colleges are referred to as 'The German College' and 'The English college' respectively. As the apprentices were spread across different classes, these are referred to as 'Class A', 'Class B' and so on. The workplace sites include 'The German dealership' and 'The German garage', whereas in England they are referred to as four 'English garages'.

In relation to retailing, the workplaces comprise the Emerald Supermarket and the Department Stores A and B in Germany, as well as the Taurus Supermarket and its two stores in London and the South of England. The table also shows the apprentices on the various sites. The young people were referred to as 'students' rather than 'apprentices' in the college environments in England and Germany, highlighting the distinctiveness of the two learning sites of the classroom and the workplace, within which the young people were constituted as 'students' and 'apprentices' respectively. The discussion of the learning cultures in the chapter (and the remainder of the book) reflects this terminology.

Table 5.1 The case study sites

		Germany	England
		Motor vehicle maintenance	
Colleges		'The German College' Class A (Stefan, Daniel, Aazim) Class B (Erika)	'The English College' Class A (Nathan, Ollie) Class B (Alex, Lisa)
Workplaces		'The German Dealership' (Stefan, Daniel, Aazim) 'The German Garage' (Erika)	Four English garages (1 apprentice each)
		Retailing	
Colleges		'The German College' Classes A, B, C, D (1 apprentice each)	No college element
Workplaces		Emerald Supermarket (Jeanette, Martin) Department Store A (Leena) Department Store B (Claudia)	Taurus Supermarket London Store (Robert, Anita) South of England Store (Stephanie, Mia)

Motor vehicle apprenticeships in Germany

The institutional context of the German College

As outlined in Chapter 2, the mechatronics apprenticeship takes three and a half years to complete, while the qualification of motor vehicle service mechanic can be obtained after two years. The apprenticeship combines work-based training with a substantial college element, complemented by a series of external block-release workshops (a total of ten weeks). Apprentices spend up to two six-hour days a week in college (two days a week during the first and third years, one day a week during the second and fourth years).

The scope of activities and associated knowledge and skills as stipulated in the training ordinance are broad and include: labour law; environmental protection; quality management; customer communication; fitting and repairing units; and diagnosing faults and their causes. The college element comprises fourteen learning fields, including: maintenance and care of vehicles; removal, repair and fitting of parts; testing and repair of electric and electronic systems; diagnosis and repair of engine management systems. The theoretical part is complemented by a comprehensive element of general and civic education. Usually integrated into the learning fields are communication (a total of forty hours), English (forty hours) and maths, although in the German College, English was taught as a separate subject. In addition, economic and social sciences, politics, religious education and sport are taught separately. Of these, only economic and social sciences are part of the exam. The pedagogical approach centres on the integration of theory and practice, through situated learning based on authentic situations, and the college workshops, in which apprentices apply the theory.

Assessment is demanding and is carried out through two sets of exams: one after two years and another after the full three and a half years. Both comprise a practical, an oral and a written part. The first exam (lasting a total of seven hours) consists of three practical tasks (diagnosis of one of four systems; servicing and testing a vehicle, including preparing documentation; removal and fitting of parts, including preparing documentation). These tasks constitute a customer order and involve a customer consultation and a written task relating to these activities. The second exam comprises a customer order consisting of four tasks (a total of five hours), and including a 'situated customer consultation' of twenty minutes; a written exam on motor vehicle functions and repair (relating to customer orders); a written exam on diagnostics (relating to customer orders); and a written exam on economic and social sciences. Twenty per cent of the written exam are 'multiple choice' questions, the rest are open questions. In addition, there is continuous assessment at college: oral participation in class and periodic tests each count for fifty per cent towards the college certificate. If apprentices fail the final exam, they can re-sit it once.

The German College

The main branch of the college is situated in a provincial town in Western Germany with another branch in a nearby village. The college services the town and the surrounding rural area. Three of the apprentices (Stefan, Daniel, Aazim) attended classes in the main branch (Class A), a fourth one (Erika) went to the other branch (Class B). In each of the two classes I observed there were about 25 students. Their educational attainment levels were mixed. In Class B, there was a fifty-fifty split of general secondary and intermediate school leavers. Eight students were on the car service mechanics apprenticeships. In Class A, the overall level was higher, with more students having the intermediate school leaving certificate while some had the *Abitur* (the equivalent of A-levels). Class A was all-male and Erika was the only female student in Class B.

The Learning Culture in the German College

The perspective of Mr. Christen, the main tutor
Mr. Christen was the main tutor for occupational theory. He had been a college tutor for many years. His higher education background (a degree in engineering and maths) is typical of college tutors in Germany. He attends regular workshops to keep abreast of the practice field and he explained that with the introduction of learning fields the colleges are much better able to follow technological developments. The learning fields (as broad areas of activity) serve as a guide, and the team of tutors decides the precise content, or learning situations.

Most activities are conceived from a perspective of action-oriented-learning as customer orders. Mr. Christen gave the example of renewing the exhaust system, which involves a whole set of activities and areas of knowledge, including assembling techniques, manufacturer's specifications, and maths, all of which are taught over four or five lessons. He stressed that because of the rapid advance of technology it is impossible to incorporate what is an increasing body of theory. The emphasis is therefore on enabling the students to follow technology. In his view, the advantage of action-oriented learning is that tutors can focus on particular sets of activity on the basis of which they can develop key competences in students, such as learning to learn.

Mr. Christen insisted that the apprenticeship and the exam in particular are very demanding, more so than used to be the case. The students are motivated by what is perceived as a high-status occupation. Thus, they generally do their homework and revise for tests and exams. He insisted that the ability to revise and learn independently from books and other material is an important part of the training, as is the ability to write—eighty per cent of the written exam are 'open questions'.

In addition to the occupational training, Mr. Christen sought to instil certain values in the students, such as respect for each other. He referred to the 'primary virtues'—an old-fashioned term for punctuality and tidiness promulgated by the nineteenth century educational reformer Kerschensteiner (Winch, 2006)—perhaps indicating his own traditional values and belief in discipline, which was reflected in his strict teaching style. Mr. Christen seemed very demanding, believing that the students want tutors to challenge them so as to make sure that they pass the exam. As he put it 'they want tutors to be strict with them (to) get them through the exams'.

Class observation in college: Class A (Stefan, Aazim and Daniel)
I observed Mr. Christen's lesson on occupational theory. The lay-out of the class was traditional. Mr. Christen came across as extremely strict, starting the lesson by rebuking students who had been absent without putting in holiday requests. Throughout, he reprimanded students for what he felt was unacceptable behaviour, such as contributing without raising their hands, or going to the bathroom without asking ('if you need to step out I want to be asked'). On the whole, the class seemed extremely well behaved and attentive throughout. The learning culture had a striking effect on me: I did not dare lean back in my chair, let alone slouch, as everyone else sat upright. I was thirsty, and we were not allowed to drink.

The teaching style was traditional, with Mr. Christen standing in front of the class, explaining the theory related to threads and bolts. Using overheads he asked the students about different types of thread and how to measure the gradient and circumference. He wrote the rules on the blackboard and asked the students to note them down, which they did. They went on to discuss the mechanics of a bolt. It was a question-and-answer style lesson in which all the students seemed attentive and many contributed. Then the students were asked to work on their own on tasks in the workbook, which they subsequently discussed as a class. When the students did not immediately come forward with answers, Mr. Christen again rebuked them. He pointed to the variable level of educational attainment in the class, indicating that students could be divided into three different groups: 'those on the right whom I have to slow down, those in the middle who need encouraging, and those on the left who need a lot of support'. However, all students seemed generally attentive and respectful of Mr. Christen. While they may not have been all equally appreciative of the theory, it seemed that they accepted it as an important part of the apprenticeship. In this sense, following Butler (1990), they can be seen to be performing the social identity of the mechatronic, based on the integration of theoretical and practical knowledge. They were 'conforming' (Bloomer and Hodkinson, 1997) and thus behaved according to the college's discourse of the 'good student' (Youdell, 2006).

It is important to note that this was one particular class, with one particular tutor. There was a different learning culture in other classes with other tutors, and even in the same class with different tutors. This echoes Bloomer's (1997) findings on the co-construction of learning opportunities. The same students, in the politics class with a different tutor, acted altogether differently. The tutor was more relaxed and had a more modern discussion-based approach.

The topic was the recent massacre at a German school. There was a lively debate on the causes and possible prevention of violence which was merely facilitated rather than led by the tutor. The students seemed more mature, like adults, confidently voicing their views. The relationship between the tutor and students was more equal. While much of the discussion was dominated by certain extremely vocal and articulate students, all students seemed engaged and participated to some extent.

Class observation in college: Class B (Erika)
Unfortunately, their theory tutor was ill and there was no substitute. I observed the politics class, held by Mr. Schmidt. Mr. Schmidt had a lot of presence and entertained a fairly casual but authoritative relationship with the students. Just before the class, he explained that the level of educational attainment and motivation of students was 'very mixed'. Half of the students were from general secondary school, the other half from intermediate school.

During the class (on Germany's electoral system) it emerged that the level of engagement was noticeably lower than that of Class A. When students were given a worksheet, many seemed at a loss and a few soon started chatting amongst themselves. One boy expressed his disaffection, indicating his particular learner disposition as a passive recipient of knowledge:

> I have to say I'm not interested in this in the slightest. This is why we are here so that you can teach us these things.

This class illustrates the variable level of students in German colleges. However, disruptive students were rebuked by others so that the class was in effect disciplining itself and it is possible that the learning culture was a different one in the theory classes. Erika informed me that the particular tutor adopted a directive approach and was very strict, similar in style it seemed to Mr. Christen.

The learning culture in German garages

Observation in the German dealership

Stefan, Daniel and Aazim were in a large dealership which was located in a huge compound of adjacent workshops, accommodating thirty seven senior mechanics and twenty one apprentices, as well as a large number of reception and customer services staff. It appeared to be a good place to be an apprentice and was what could be called an 'expansive' learning environment (Fuller and Unwin, 2003b). Apprentices were rotated around several departments at six-monthly intervals, there was a car specifically designated for carrying out training, and there were opportunities for external training organised by the car manufacturer. However, the flipside of a highly elaborate division of labour in this large organisation was that there was also a fair amount of routine work. For example, during the month of November (at the time of the observation) all apprentices had to spend two days a week in the tyre service, changing summer to winter tyres. This involved extremely routinised and hard labour, including loading and unloading tyres onto a truck. Also, apprentices had no customer contact as this was dealt with by customer service staff. Typical for the German system, each apprentice was assigned to a senior mechanic, so as to work alongside them and assist them in their work. As part of this, apprentices were responsible for all the cleaning—they spent the final two hours each day clearing up.

At the same time, it seemed that the firm promoted a culture which fostered participatory learning amongst apprentices—they were encouraged to engage in learning processes with each other. When I arrived, I was told that the morning would be taken up by training, set up to support one of the apprentices (Aazim) in preparing for his exam in the spring.

Aazim was on a two-year programme as 'car service mechanic'. The first training session consisted of Aazim and two of his classmates (both on the full three-and-a-half-year programme as mechatronic) going through exam questions in the breakfast room above the main workshop. The second session involved practical repair work on a car and was led by a fourth year apprentice. The training took place in perfect conditions, with immaculate equipment and tools, more reminiscent of a workshop than a workplace.

The environment was friendly and largely stress-free, as the apprentices were shielded from the pressures of day-to-day work. It was 'okay' to make mistakes. After being gently rebuked by the senior mechanic for a mistake he made, the fourth year apprentice nevertheless carried on in his role of teacher, seemingly unperturbed. While it is of course possible that I picked an exceptionally quiet period I had a strong sense that it was at least not uncommon. Significantly, and in contrast to all other motor vehicle apprentices, the group was shielded from customers and worked away from the immediate pressures common in other garages. By contrast, in the smaller garages in England and Germany, there was little space set aside for learning, which was more *ad hoc* and integrated into the day-to-day work.

Observation in the German garage
Erika worked in a garage which was small by German standards. There were two adjacent workshops with five ramps, a breakfast room, and a separate large reception area and office. There were all in all seven mechanics, including one apprentice (Erika) and one *Meister*. As in the dealership, the division of labour was hierarchical, leaving Erika as the only apprentice with a great deal of menial work, such as clearing up and washing cars. Opportunities for learning appeared fewer than in the dealership.

Motor vehicle apprenticeships in England

Institutional context of the English College
As outlined in Chapter 2, the apprenticeship framework at Level 2 consists of three elements: a work-based element (the NVQ Level 2), a college-based element (the Technical Certificate Level 2), and Key Skills (Communication; Application of Number; ICT) at Level 1. The Level 2 apprenticeship takes two years to complete. The NVQ consists of seven mandatory units and one optional

unit, including: health and safety; maintaining positive working relationships; routine vehicle maintenance; removing and replacing engine units; removing and replacing electrical auxiliary units; and pre- and post-work vehicle inspections. Each of these breaks down into detailed tasks (such as 'remove and replace a camshaft'), which, contrary to the German scheme, are each assessed individually. As will be shown in what follows, a major problem is the lack of integration of theory and practice.

The apprenticeship is structured on the basis of the eight NVQ units. It is strongly led by the various components of assessment, the NVQ being the 'primary learning aim'. Thus, for the work-based element, apprentices have to collect a 'portfolio of evidence'. In the workplace, this involves apprentices carrying out a series of tasks related to the NVQ units, which are assessed through a mixture of observations (by the assessor) and so-called job cards. The latter require apprentices to carry out a task and to subsequently write down the work in a step-by-step manner. The job card evidence is witnessed and signed off by the employer. The apprentices are guided through the work-based element by an assessor, who draws up an assessment plan, makes sure apprentices are ready to be assessed in relation to each task, and monitors the apprentices' progress. The NVQ element is strongly formative and relies on the assessor coaching the apprentices and providing feedback. If an apprentice does not fulfil the criteria, he or she will repeat the task at a later stage.

The college curriculum is guided by the teaching programme which is provided by the awarding body and maps on to the NVQ units. Teaching at college is based on the Technical Certificate, which mirrors (and overlaps with) the NVQ units. The Technical Certificate consists of practical tasks, which the students carry out in the college workshop and which form part of the assessment. Again, students have to write down 'the procedure they used' as well as demonstrate some of the knowledge underpinning the tasks. As with the NVQ, each task needs to be signed off, in this case by the college tutors. The theoretical knowledge is assessed through formative 'phase tests' and on-line multiple choice tests at the end of each unit. The college also has its own internal Technical Certificate which breaks down tasks into further detail and which they use for training purposes.

In order to get admitted to the apprenticeship, students need a minimum of four Ds at GCSE level. During the first year, they do their key skills and the Technical Certificate Level 1 (they do not do the NVQ Level 1). In the second year, they do their Technical Certificate Level 2 and the NVQ Level 2. The students attend the college one day a week, and for a total of two hundred and ten hours per year. The six teaching hours break down into four and a half hours of classroom teaching, and one and a half hours of workshop practice.

The English College

The college is situated in a small industrial town in South-East England and serves the surrounding towns and villages. The students were spread over two different classes: The Monday class, Class A (Nathan and Ollie), and the Wednesday class, Class B (Alex and Lisa). There were about fifteen to twenty students in each of the classes. The Monday class was entirely male, while there were two female students in the Wednesday class. By far the vast majority of students were from comprehensive schools and had left school at sixteen. The main tutors were Steve and Alan. Graham was the NVQ assessor.

The Learning Culture in the English College

The perspective of the tutors

In contrast to the German tutors, those in the English college did not have a university background. Indeed, Steve, the main tutor, who used to run his own garage, stressed the importance of 'coming from the trade', explaining that this was important in building relationships with the students:

> If you're on the same level as them normally you can get a lot more out of them, you can get a lot more respect from them ... you know a bit of banter doesn't matter in the classroom, if you're just talking at them all the time, you've got to break that off from time to time, perhaps come outside the box of the education ... and I think that comes from my background of doing exactly what they're doing, and that makes it a lot harder for people that have only done education work. I haven't, I went to a normal school and came out of it and learnt a trade, a proper one, I feel, and that's what the students are actually doing.

I also overheard a conversation between several tutors about a recent job advertisement for a new tutor, which specified a diploma or university degree as a requirement. They all agreed that this would over-qualify the tutor. It may also have undermined their authority and construction of motor vehicle maintenance as a trade.

Steve suggested that the links with the industry should be improved to foster a better understanding of what apprenticeship should be about. Some employers expected too much of the apprentices too early on. He also bemoaned the current dominance of awarding and audit bodies and felt they were out of step with developments in the workplace. While the teaching time was limited even considering the required workload, it was a struggle to equip the students for what is a rapidly developing field. He pointed to the limited resources and stressed that students would benefit from technological equipment or being sent on courses (for example, air conditioning or diagnostics). He had been trying his best to address this shortfall by teaching them material from his own courses that he attended as a tutor ('they'd be given that extra lesson'). But he pointed to the potential of tension that this created with the audit body, as the tutors were 'judged on achievement'.

Tutors suggested that by far the bulk of the students would not tend to revise for exams. They did not think that this was much different from other colleges. Students were not perceived to be 'particularly academic' and they suggested that a few would read up their notes but not many. Tutors would not give them homework and most would not do it anyway. Steve's teaching style was informed by his belief that the students were not academic and learned through practice:

> A lot of these students that we deal with are visual students that learn from visually looking at things, doing things, monkey see monkey do, ya know what I mean yeah, and they will get a lot more out of that.

Both Alan and Steve complained that the time in the workshop was not well used. They would prefer to use the workshop to follow up the theory taught in the classroom. Students resented the workshop class as was evident in their behaviour—on each occasion many had not brought their shoes or overalls and were not permitted to be in the main part of the workshop. They stayed in the classroom-end of the workshop, working on their folders. Others worked in groups of two or three on different cars. It appeared that they disliked having to do the same (mostly routine) tasks they already did for the NVQ (for the same reason one tutor described the Technical Certificate activities as nonsense). In this sense, the assessment-led structure of the apprenticeship impeded more imaginative learning.

There was also some evidence that the tutors' primary concern was to 'get the students through', partly through building up their confidence. Ecclestone (2007) suggested in a previous study that tutors aimed to build protective environments (comfort zones) to improve students' achievement, at the expense of more quality teaching. For example, Graham the assessor insisted that during assessments he would 'try to be as unobtrusive as possible to try and make them feel confident' and 'make it as plain and simple as possible so they're really relaxed, and I just casually watch them'.

Classroom observation in the English College

Throughout my observation at the English college, I had a strong sense that the structure and content, the tutor discourse and student interaction all combined to construct motor vehicle maintenance as a *practical craft*, with little value afforded to theoretical knowledge, in stark contrast to Mr. Christen's class in the German college. The general atmosphere in the classroom was casual, the students were very boisterous and there was a lot of banter, contrasting sharply with Mr. Christen's class in the German college. There was a strong sense that students were not taking the classes seriously, as they opted to pay attention for a while before talking amongst themselves again. The casual attitude was also evident in their postures, as they slouched or rocked on their chairs or lay across the table. Failing to engage and motivate students more substantially and over longer periods of time, the focus was often on behaviour management and the use of disciplinary measures, with tutors taking students outside the classroom and rebuking them for turning up late.

There was a sense that while the rejection of theory was compatible with the discourse of the good student, turning up late was not. It is important to note, however, that, while a particular identity dominated, others co-existed, with some students attentive throughout, raising the possibility of reinscribing the identity of vehicle maintenance. Nathan, for example, was one of a few students taking notes.

The construction of vehicle maintenance as a practice was confirmed by the main tutors. Steve felt it important to develop a matey relationship with the students which suggested that he was one of them. Their respect for him appeared to be founded on his practical expertise as a craftsman and his experience of working as a mechanic. His main teaching approach was a question-and-answer style, focusing largely on procedural knowledge related to authentic situations they were likely to encounter, and, crucially, involving the students by drawing on their experiences in the workplace. In one class, Steve started by asking the students to write down the components of an air conditioning system and their functions. Then he asked them to name them while he wrote them down on the whiteboard.

In this and other sessions, it was noticeable that very few students took notes (though some did). The second part of the class was practice-oriented. Steve asked questions related to possible defects in air conditioning systems, how to diagnose them, and how to repair them. It was a very interactive, fast moving session. Steve asked many leading questions (often getting very short answers), in the following style:

> Customer comes in, has a problem with the air conditioning, what's the first thing we're going to do, evacuate the air conditioner ... how do you check the air conditioner, what's your first port of call ... . How much vacuum did I say you'd be pulling on a normal air conditioning system?

Students told of their experiences and most of them seemed to enjoy the class. They tried to guess answers and it was very playful. Later Steve told me that he felt it important to make it interesting so as to retain their attention. At the end of one class he had a quiz (but most of the questions were completely unrelated to motor vehicle maintenance).

By contrast, Alan, the new tutor, who had worked as a technician with a major car manufacturer for thirty years, was rejected by the students for his perceived lack of practical craftsmanship. He was teaching systematic theoretical knowledge. Not only were the students less engaged, they were noticeably hostile towards him. On one occasion, he was challenged by a student who asked what his role was as a technician and whether he could actually do manual work. This challenge had performative force (Youdell, 2006) and was one of many practices that reaffirmed vehicle maintenance as practical craft, successfully it seemed, as one morning he introduced the lesson with the words: "We're doing electrical theory unfortunately ... unfortunately you've got to learn it and I've got to teach it". Seeking to gain the respect of the students or at least pre-empt their disapproval by empathising with them, Alan had started citing and reinforcing the dominant discourse. The effect of his statement was for the students to disengage even further.

In his class, students paid attention for a while but did not seem to take it seriously. They made fun of him. When he asked for definitions, they had a laugh guessing the answers before engaging in conversation with their neighbours. Alex, Lisa and another female student, Katie, were chatting most of the time. Katie told Alan that she had already passed the unit, while the student next to her joked that she guessed the answers. This again suggests just how little they were taking it seriously, indicating that college is about passing tests, and that 'guessing' was entirely possible (as they can re-sit tests as often as they like) and thus inside the discursive framework of the college.

Previous studies have highlighted the way in which assessment has come to dominate learning in 'competence-based' approaches, exemplified by the NVQ ('assessment as learning'), fostering an instrumentalist attitude to teaching and learning (Torrance et al., 2005). Portfolio-building is certainly a very time-consuming task and students spent up to half the time at college doing 'folder work': one and a half hours of classroom 'learning' and much of the workshop sessions were dedicated to writing up 'evidence' in one of three folders: the NVQ folder, the Technical Certificate folder, and the college's internal Technical Certificate folder. In the classroom, students used the time to fill in their 'job cards'. Katie asked how to write up the task of removing a switch—the tutor's answer was to write up literally what she did (lifting it up with a screwdriver). It seems that writing up 'what you did' can be a very tedious task, albeit one which students took seriously, as this counts towards the assessment—these classes were the only ones where they worked away quietly, mostly in groups.

The Learning Culture in English Garages

Observation in English garages

Two of the English apprentices worked in very small garages. In Alex's case, this was a tiny ramshackle workshop which was part of a yard with other workshops. It was an extremely crammed space with two ramps, and a separate office. It was run by the owner, a senior mechanic and the apprentice. There was no modern diagnostic equipment and they offered no M.O.T. service. Ollie's garage was only marginally larger but did have a separate reception area. There was the owner, two older mechanics and Ollie.

Whereas apprentices in Germany always worked alongside a senior mechanic, these two apprentices routinely carried out jobs on their own. Also, there was no clear division of labour. Alex and Ollie were expected to 'work out' more complex jobs by themselves. Cleaning was not left to the apprentices, but each mechanic would look after their own work area, and once a week someone would come in to do more general cleaning.

Lisa's garage was only slightly larger. There was one workshop, with three mechanics and two apprentices. It had a more formal set-up than the two small garages, with a separate reception area and a workshop manager allocating the work. The owner revealed that he always had apprentices and that he valued developing his own staff. The division of labour was reminiscent of the German garage. Apprentices were not expected to carry out more complex work on their own, but largely assisted senior mechanics and were responsible for clearing up. The relaxed and light-hearted atmosphere in the garage—everyone seemed to be singing along to the radio—seemed in no small part due to Lisa's outgoing and chatty nature, a good example of the co-construction of learning cultures. However, in interaction with me she also voiced unhappiness about being restricted to fairly menial tasks, something which I will discuss in Chapter 7.

Nathan's was another independent garage, slightly larger than Lisa's, consisting of one large and airy workshop with six ramps and one pit, a separate reception area, and a waiting room for customers. There were four mechanics and two apprentices, with reception and administration staff. The learning environment struck me as very supportive. Nathan carried out routine maintenance work on his own and, in common with other English apprentices, was given time to work out non-routine work by himself. However, senior mechanics were always available to help and give advice. It was a kind of supervision at arm's length. Nathan was not worried about asking for help, which he frequently did, and it appeared that asking for help (and making mistakes) was an accepted part of apprentices' learning.

Conclusions

In some contrast to Germany and certainly to Mr. Christen's class, the learning culture in the English classes was dominated by the social identity of the mechanic as craftsman/woman with little value attached to theory and it seems that the young people were performing this identity, drawing on the discourse of the academic-vocational divide as an alternative to identities based on academic learning, which they appeared to reject outright. However, it is important to note that there may be a range of identities in classrooms and not to treat young people as homogeneous wholes.

The identity of vehicle maintenance as practice was certainly reinforced by tutor discourse and by the structural elements of an apprenticeship framework that is heavily biased towards workplace practice and procedural knowledge and is reflected in the assessment process, which is primarily concerned with the practical knowledge necessary to carry out tasks rather than a deeper theoretical understanding of how cars function. The teaching itself was dominated by procedural knowledge referring to diagnosis, maintenance and repair. 'Theory' for the most part was about naming components or listing advantages or disadvantages of particular systems (for example of suspension) and of 'knowing how' to do something.

The teaching guidance provided by the IMI is extremely detailed, specifying particular systems (for example, brakes, or transmission), naming every possible component and listing a vast range of possible faults. Similarly, the NVQ and the practical part of the Technical Certificate relate to very specific tasks (for example, 'remove and replace fuel filter'; 'remove and replace alternator').

It seems that this detailed approach, seeking to cover an exhaustive list of tasks, imposes a considerable workload on the tutors and leaves little room for flexibility (and indeed, for covering new technological developments). It also promotes an instrumental approach whereby the focus is on passing the prescribed tasks. In addition, the tasks are dealt with in isolation and impede an 'action-oriented' approach, focused on the wider work process.

Steve's more flexible teaching style based on authentic work situations sought to encompass new developments in technology, but is partly at odds with the approach of detailed learning aims (he was rebuked by a reviewer for teaching over the students' heads and for not regularly checking their learning—apparently an OFSTED requirement). Rather than enabling students to learn and develop with the technology, the learning is focused on detailed and specific task lists that seek to be exhaustive, something the German tutor described as an impossibility given the rapid development, and thus bound to always lag behind the latest technology.

In terms of the learning culture in the workplace, what was most notable was the strict hierarchy of mechanics and apprentices in the German garages which contrasted sharply with the learning cultures in the two small English garages of Alex and Ollie. Lisa's and Nathan's workplaces were more reminiscent of the German ones in terms of the division of labour. In the German dealership, high importance was afforded to learning, with time and space dedicated specifically for these training purposes.

Retail apprenticeships in Germany

Institutional context of the German college

As shown in Chapter 2, the dual system training occupation Retail Salesman/woman takes three years to complete, while the qualification of Retail Assistant can be obtained after two years of the same programme. Apprentices spend one and a half days (ten and a half hours) per week in college and the rest of the time in the workplace.

The German Retail apprenticeship programme is comprehensive in terms of content and like all dual system occupations is guided by the principle of *Handlungskompetenz*. The work-based content, as stipulated in the training ordinance, covers knowledge and skills in relation to: the training firm; information and communication; product range; basics of customer advice and sales; checkout; basics of marketing; merchandising; and accounting. There is one optional unit out of four (goods reception and storage; customer advice and sales; checkout; marketing). The three-year programme lists three additional units: One mandatory (retail processes) and three optional out of seven, including Information Technology (IT) and Human Resources Management (HRM).

The fourteen learning fields of the college element cover a broad range of workplace activities, including: presenting the retail company within the industry; buying and storing stock; administration, including accounting and merchandising; and customer interaction. The sequencing of learning fields reflects the division into the two training occupations. During the first year, they cover the sale of goods and customer orientation; in the second year, they concern stock control, replenishment and accounting; and in the third year learning fields cover specific areas of activity pertaining to the profile of the salesman/woman, including HRM and leadership. The comprehensive element of general and civic education covers maths, IT, English, economic and social sciences, politics, religious education and sport. Of these, only economic and social sciences form part of the exam.

The assessment is through two sets of exams. The first exam (identical for both programmes) takes place at the beginning of the second year and is in written form (two hours). The final exam for Retail Assistants takes place after the full two years and comprises three written exams on the different areas of activity (sales and marketing; stock control; economic and social sciences) and an oral part in the form of a customer consultation (whereby apprentices are given fifteen minutes for preparation and twenty minutes for the consultation). For apprentices on the Retail Salesman/woman programme, the final exam takes place after three years and comprises three written elements (Retail Sales-related activities; retail processes; economic and social sciences) and an oral exam in the form of a customer consultation.

The German College

The college is located in an industrial city in Western Germany. It specialises in vocational education courses in business and administration. The four apprentices were each in different classes (see Table 5.2). In all classes, there was an even split between male and female students. Three of the classes (B, C and D) contained a high proportion (up to fifty per cent) of students from migrant families. Class sizes were around twenty.

Table 5.2 Retail apprentices in the German college

Clothing retail	Food retail
Class A (Claudia) (Retail Saleswoman)	Class B (Jeanette) (Retail assistant)
Class C (Leena) (Retail Saleswoman)	Class D (Martin) (Retail assistant)

The learning fields were structured in terms of clusters of subjects, such as 'customer communication and service', and 'goods-related processes'. During their first year, students were also taught the following subjects: 'economic and social processes'; 'data communication and accounting'; IT; politics; German; and English.

The college participated in a pilot study on self-regulated learning in vocational schools (hereafter referred to as SEGEL) from 2005 to 2008, financed by the federal and *Länder* governments. The initiative arose from increasing recognition among policy-makers and practitioners of the importance of the ability for self-directed learning in the context of lifelong learning (Krakau and Rickes, 2007).

The SEGEL project had been introduced into nine classes of the Retail assistant/Retail salesperson programme. It focused on developing students' competence for self-learning through the imparting of particular learning strategies in especially developed learning situations. Upon being given a relatively broadly defined task, students decide how to organise the solving of the task, including how to organise the groups, the time scale required, what resources are needed, and how the tasks are to be approached. The classes were particularly well resourced, with a classroom layout facilitating group work and with access to a range of multi-media resources. Of the four apprentices, only Claudia was part of a SEGEL class.

While there were marked differences between the classes, the learning culture also varied between different lessons and tutors. The level of student engagement varied among and within classes and the young people's dispositions to learning or 'studentships' ranged from 'conforming' to 'strategic compliance' to 'retreatism' (Bloomer and Hodkinson, 1997). The different ways in which learning opportunities (Bloomer, 1997; Bloomer and Hodkinson, 1997) were interpreted by tutors and learners in different classes and lessons were striking.

The learning culture at the German college

The main tutors
Table 5.3 gives an overview of the lessons and tutors observed.

Table 5.3 Tutors and lessons observed

Class	Tutor
A (Claudia)	Mr. Karstens
B (Jeanette)	Ms Bielenberg, Mr. Drechsel
C (Leena)	Ms Meier
D (Martin)	Ms Junge

There are many aspects which affect the construction of learning opportunities, including the particular teaching and learning style, and the tutor's interpretation of the students' needs. The narrative of the exploitative nature of many retail employers was prevalent and shaped teaching and learning arrangements. Some tutors (Ms. Bielenberg, Ms. Junge, Mr. Drechsel) remarked on the long, irregular working hours of apprentices, and the exploitative nature of the work in certain retail firms. This perception induced a high level of empathy in tutors, with some of them asserting that they would never give the students any homework. Mr. Drechsel expressed his outrage to me at the exploitation of apprentices as cheap labour. He bemoaned what he perceived as the decline in the quality of retail apprenticeships in response to pressure from employers who do not see the value of classroom learning. His empathy led him to tolerate students leaving the classroom to smoke, and to finish the class early.

This empathetic approach contrasted sharply with that of Mr. Karstens in the SEGEL class, who came across as very strict. The tutor, who was one of the most ardent promoters of self-directed learning at the college, suggested that the main difference between SEGEL and conventional classes was the level of student engagement, which he regarded as resulting from the self-directed approach (although this was questioned by other tutors who pointed to the generally higher level of attainment of students in the SEGEL classes). Mr. Karstens also made a point about not tolerating disruption and during the class repeatedly rebuked students for minor disruptions or lapses of concentration. During my observation, I found a more variable level of motivation and engagement in the non-SEGEL classes. The tutors of conventional classes pointed out that this was due to the differential educational attainment levels in these classes, with generally higher levels in the SEGEL classes.

Many tutors stressed the importance of educating young people to become rounded human beings. When I told Ms. Bielenberg that there is no college element in the English apprenticeship of my study, she seemed bewildered and referred to the 'education mandate' of the college, the importance of developing the young people, including their ability to develop careers and move across firms. As she put it, 'it's not just a case of making sure they can work at [major German cut-price retail chain]'.

Class observation in college: Class A (SEGEL) (Claudia)
In the lesson I observed (economic and political sciences), students worked in groups to answer questions in relation to labour law and collective agreements. The groups followed a division of labour, whereby one student would look up the information on the internet and another would type it into the PC, using Word or Powerpoint. The idea was that knowledge of a particular topic was obtained and developed by a group and then shared with the wider class. Claudia in particular seemed to enjoy creating the layout of slides, using photos, graphs and other illustrations.

I felt that the level of the class was high, and students seemed engaged throughout. There was little disruption. A group of students presented their findings on the role of collective agreements. All students participated, asking questions, generating a discussion, facilitated by the tutor, on the impact of strike action on employees. The tutor, Mr. Karstens, came across as very strict, repeatedly rebuking students for appearing tired, even though this was the final lesson of a long day, and for failing to take notes as the groups presented. However, there was no rebellion (nor deference) but some discussion with students seeking to justify not taking notes. Their studentship can be described as 'conforming' in Bloomer and Hodkinson's terms (1997). Be it through inadvertent selection or because of the particular teaching and learning approach. The young people for the most part constructed themselves as well-behaved, disciplined and highly motivated learners.

Class observation in college: Class B (Jeanette)
In conventional classes there was much greater variation in the level of student engagement. In Jeanette's class, Ms. Bielenberg, teaching 'goods-related processes', explained the principles of window displays. In one group activity, the students were requested to develop ideas for a display, considering particular aspects they had just been discussing, such as the effect the display has on shoppers and the target group it is aimed at. The students seemed to enjoy the creative nature of the task, although after a while the noise level increased and students talked about private matters. Ms. Bielenberg explained the task was too long and the students were losing interest.

Some students could be said to be 'conforming' while others adopted a more instrumental approach, similar to what Bloomer and Hodkinson (1997) referred to as 'strategic compliance'. This latter, instrumental approach was apparent in the final lesson of the day, 'economic and social processes', taught by Mr. Drechsel. He asked students to read a chapter on 'skill requirements of retail employees' and write down the most important points. He then asked for one student to come forward and write down the competences on the blackboard as the remaining students were encouraged to name them. No doubt aware that she was being observed but also reflecting her general enthusiasm and motivation, Jeanette volunteered. While there was some level of participation, most students phased in and out of paying attention. Some listened to music on their MP3 players. After a while, most students switched off, talked about private things or played games, which they interrupted only to copy what was written on the blackboard ('let's just copy this and then we'll carry on'). As the level of disruption rose, the tutor's lack of intervention was noticeable. Even when groups of students left the class for ten minutes at a time (to have a cigarette as I realised later) the tutor did not object. Rather, and remarkably, other students in the class rebuked the disruptive ones, for example by asking them to turn the music down.

Class observation in college: Class C (Leena)
Almost half of the students were from migrant families. The tutor, Ms. Meier returned a test which had turned out badly, and went through the questions. She had a remarkable presence and her teaching style reminded me of Steve's in the motor vehicle class in England. Like Steve, she was 'from the trade' and adopted

a leading question style (going through methods of payment), always referring to authentic workplace situations, while frequently making jokes and engaging in banter with the students. Notably, she always drew on the experiences of students, who participated throughout the class, and there was no disruption.

> What do you say when it turns out that the customer's EC card is barred?...
> What do I do when I'm on checkout and someone pays with a counterfeit note? Who's experienced this?... What do I do if it is fake?

It is possible of course that the same students were less engaged in other lessons.

Class observation in college: Class D (Martin)

Ms. Junge was teaching 'economic and social processes'. The mood amongst students was very boisterous. The proportion of students from migrant families was nearly fifty per cent (mainly Turkish). There was a high level of disruption, with students playing with their mobile phones, listening to their MP3 players, and shouting across the class. Ms. Junge struggled to assert herself as students ignored her warnings, for example not to go to the toilet in pairs. The subject of the lesson was to revise for a test on labour law and employee rights by going through some of the slides the students had previously prepared in group work. Many students' disposition to learning seemed to lie somewhere between 'strategic compliance' and outright 'retreatism' (Bloomer and Hodkinson, 1997). They continued to talk amongst themselves about private matters, and only temporarily disrupted their chats to take photos of the slides with their mobile phones—which the tutor seemed to tolerate without question. One boy repeatedly tried to get my attention, keen to express his lack of interest in the lesson and possibly his 'disidentification' (Skeggs, 1997) with the retail occupation, shouting across the classroom:

> I swear to you, if I'd won the lottery I wouldn't be sitting here.

By contrast, Martin, while also at times listening to music and chatting to his neighbour, was one of a handful of students participating in the lesson, taking notes and asking questions, again highlighting the idea that classrooms encompass a range of identities. After the class, Ms. Junge asked me how

I selected the apprentices for my study, pointing out that Martin was not 'representative'.

In these classes, many students may not have viewed retailing as desirable and invested instead in their sub-cultural status. Their chatting and listening to music rendered them unacceptable students, although empathetic tutors did little to challenge their behaviour. Nevertheless, as in the vehicle maintenance classes, other identities co-existed and many students (including the four of my study) seemed motivated and engaged.

The learning culture in German retailing outlets

Observation in the Emerald Supermarket

Jeanette and Martin both worked at the meat and cheese counter at a franchise of Emerald, a reputable supermarket chain located in the same city as the college. I joined them at the counter on a busy Saturday. This was not constitutive of their learning culture, which was in fact 'expansive' and involved a thorough in-house training programme on top of the college element, including product knowledge and maths. Jeanette and Martin were working together with three senior assistants and two other apprentices. All retail assistants were busy serving customers. It seemed a highly stressful environment with a constant queue of customers, although I was assured that it was much quieter on other days of the week.

It appeared that staff performed the identity of retail assistant according to an 'interaction ritual' (Goffman, 1972), a formalised routine behaviour which guides the exchange between staff and customers. As soon as they faced a customer, the assistants assumed a different posture and tone of voice, adopting a recognisable pattern of behaviour and phrases ('anything else madam?'). It is what Hochschild (1983) refers to as 'emotional labour'—the ability to regulate one's own feelings in an effort to present a particular image. As demonstrated elsewhere (Brockmann, 2012), interaction with customers is an important part of the social identity of the retail occupation and one which is actively negotiated and interpreted by apprentices as an integral part of the retail assistant's competence.

It seemed to me that by adopting these normative phrases and behaviours the retail assistants became professionals, a status which afforded them a degree of detachment, while allowing them to appear polite and friendly. However, at the same time this also left them vulnerable. While Martin appeared to relish the performance, enthusiastically serving customers and engaging in friendly small-talk, he seemed to lack the detachment of his colleagues. Similarly, Jeanette told me that she finds it difficult when her efforts of being friendly are not being acknowledged by customers. Again it is important to note that the unique meanings the young people attach to the apprenticeship are not apparent from the observations alone, but need to be explored through their biographies, as will be shown in Chapters 6 and 7.

Observation in Department Store A
Leena and Claudia both worked in outlets of two of the largest department store chains in Germany, located in the same city as the college. Like the supermarket above, both stores run extensive off-the-job training programmes for apprentices. Leena worked in the children's clothes department with two senior retail assistants, the head assistant, a woman in her fifties, and one or more placement students.

Leena worked largely independently and autonomously and had her own area of responsibility—the section for girls' clothing. She seemed to know what needed doing, for example when to get new stock or to mark goods as reduced items. The head assistant instructed her from time to time, setting priorities after consulting with the departmental manager. Advising customers was a key activity, and one that Leena thrived on. It was clear that she enjoyed this activity, in which she could use her knowledge creatively. It was a good example of co-constructing the learning culture, which allowed her to develop her own creative style (and which may have gone beyond how her colleagues interpreted their roles).

Observation in Department store B
Claudia worked in the ladies' knitwear section of another department store. The set-up was similar. She worked with an older head assistant and one or two senior assistants. All around her were various other sections selling particular brands, each staffed with young retail assistants, whom she interacted with in a friendly manner and who seemed an important source of social support.

The day of my observation was very busy, as they were having a promotion which involved getting stock from the storeroom and displaying it on the shop floor. It seemed hard work and involved not only standing up all day but moving around long rails, large boxes, and hundreds of items of heavy winter clothing.

Leena and Claudia, while both performing the identity of retailer, interpreted their roles very differently. Where Leena was working largely independently, Claudia always awaited the head assistant's instructions or advice on how to display items and what to do next, although she insisted that she could bring in her own ideas regarding, for example, the order of colours of sweaters on a rail. This suggests that, while young people do conform to the norms and values associated with the retail occupation, they nevertheless interpret these in unique ways. As will be discussed in Chapter 6 and 7, the reasons for the differing interpretations are to be sought in the young people's biographical pasts.

Retail apprenticeships in an English supermarket

Institutional context of Taurus's apprenticeship programme
As we have seen in Chapter 2, the Retail Apprenticeship framework consists of the NVQ Retail Skills at Level 2, the Technical Certificate in Retailing at Level 2 (including the unit 'Employment Rights and Responsibilities'), and Key Skills at Level 1 (Application of Number and Communication).

The NVQ element comprised one mandatory ('Work effectively in your retail team') and five optional units (out of forty-eight). The optional units are grouped under areas of activity: Sales, Stock Management, Product Expertise, Merchandising, Visual Merchandising, Management and Leadership, Finance and Administration, Customer Service, and Organisational Effectiveness. The units comprised narrow tasks. For example, 'select, weigh and measure dough ingredients', 'hand divide, mould and shape fermented doughs' and 'maintain food safety while working with food in a retail environment' are all individual units. Anyone of these could be combined with, for example, 'help customers to buy National Lottery products' or 'promote loyalty schemes to customers' to make up a highly fragmented and company specific programme. As NVQ units are developed based on a detailed and exhaustive analysis of tasks in the workplace, any retail firm's internal training is likely to comply with the framework.

The NVQ element is assessed through observations of skills by an assessor, who may be a member of staff trained by the awarding body. The Technical Certificate involves an assessment through a multiple choice test at the end of the apprenticeship, requiring no teaching and learning element. This test and the Key Skills assessments have to be marked by the relevant Awarding Bodies. The apprenticeship at Level 2 is equivalent to 5 GCSEs grades A* to C.

Taurus's Apprenticeship Programme
Taurus started their apprenticeship programme in 2004, and the number of apprentices has been steadily increasing since then (to 800 in England in 2009). The programme is open to people of all ages from sixteen to sixty-five. The

apprenticeship co-ordinator for Taurus assured me that the apprenticeship entailed 'massive benefits' for Taurus and for the staff. Taurus introduced the scheme out of a concern with high staff turnover and resulting skill shortages, particularly for management positions. The apprenticeship co-ordinator explained that the scheme had considerably improved retention rates (particularly among the sixteen to twenty-four age group) and that around fifty per cent of apprentices progress to the first management level. She and the personnel manager at one of the stores insisted that the scheme serves to overturn the poor image of the sector and to create worthwhile careers within the company. They explained that it is highly motivating to staff who value gaining a recognised qualification by having their skills validated and having a clear progression route. Neither of the informants denied that the apprenticeship is closely aligned with the internal staff training and that the NVQ units consist of knowledge and skills that staff would have acquired anyway. In the words of the apprenticeship co-ordinator, the scheme is 'a way of saying thank you by validating the work they do already'.

Taurus has a comprehensive in-house training framework, with a clear and well-publicised progression route. The general staff training distinguishes between three progressive levels, and the policy is to train everyone up to the second level (and up to first level within twelve weeks' of joining). The training is entirely on-the-job and consists of informal demonstrations and talking people through. Staff may progress to semi-skilled and skilled status within their specialist area, by acquiring relevant units up to third level (for example, in the bakery the progression is from packer to semi-skilled baker to skilled baker). In addition, there is a management programme.

In contrast to other apprenticeship frameworks, prospective apprentices are required to have worked for Taurus for at least six months, reflecting the work-based nature of the programme and the extent to which it is part of their regular staff training. As a result, by the time they start the apprenticeship, individuals will have already covered all or much of the training. The apprenticeship takes ten months to complete (which is well below the average of fourteen months specified in the SSC guidance) and runs from October to July.

The two available programmes are Service (Customer Service or Checkout) and Replenishment, which have four units in common: Team Work (the compulsory unit), Customer Perception, Security, and Health and Safety. The Service programme further includes Operating Check-outs and Refund Policy, while the Replenishment programme comprises Filling Stock and Promotion.

In order to provide the required NVQ units, Taurus have put together relevant units of their internal training (largely at Level 1, some at Level 2). As NVQs and Taurus' own units are both developed based on a detailed task analysis in the workplace, one can presume that they are easily mapped against each other.

For the NVQ, apprentices have to work through a folder containing the six units. Each unit is divided into several sections, including the aims of the unit, a list of 'what you need to know/do' which refers to the relevant internal training units and corresponding training handbooks should apprentices need to consult these, a section 'your chance to practise' in which apprentices are asked to carry out certain activities and describe their experiences, and a series of 'validation questions', probing the knowledge deemed necessary to underpin the tasks. The assessment is based on the folder work (the activity and the validation questions), Witness Statements collected from other members of staff about their ability to carry out tasks related to the units, and Skills Observations carried out by the Taurus-internal assessor.

The NVQ units are extremely narrow and relate to specific and detailed tasks, tightly controlled by the store's standardised procedures. Thus, for example, the unit 'promotion change' involves obtaining relevant information on which products are to go on promotion, preparing labels and placing these appropriately, clearing old stock from shelves and replacing it with new stock, and communicating with the team leader. Many of the procedures are specific to Taurus (such as those related to retrieving stock from the warehouse, or to waste disposal). The training reflects the hierarchical and Taylorised division of labour in the store and the routinised and fragmented work processes this involves.

The Personnel Manager of the London store insisted that the apprenticeship, while based on in-house training, nevertheless goes beyond what other staff would learn. She explained that the apprenticeship is broader, giving trainees a better understanding of the whole work process. She felt they were also highly motivated by the particular way of learning, and get a real sense of achievement:

> I think it just gives them a more global understanding of the business and retail as a whole, so it's not so much specific to their particular department … and what we do with the apprenticeship programme is to get them to kind of dissect the store almost on different levels and understand how everybody else works … people are really rounded, knowledgeable

and deliver a great service ... you get a sense of achievement from these individuals, from the detail they put in and the effort they put into these workbooks, it's really important to them; it's something that they hold really high in their esteem.

It thus appears that Taurus' apprenticeships may be somewhat broader than their regular staff training, particularly as managers are encouraged to rotate apprentices around the store and units may relate to areas outside the apprentice's immediate department. This seems to reflect Taurus's concern with developing their own staff and managers. The fact that different units are combined to reflect the NVQ units may demonstrate a more systematic approach to training than other staff may experience. I was also informed by a retail assistant in one of the stores that training for general staff was 'sometimes forgotten about'. In addition, the workbook is designed to facilitate learning through reflection. Apprentices are required to apply the knowledge and information provided in the workbook to a specified set of workplace situations and to subsequently write up their experiences. However, while this process may encourage young people to externalise and articulate knowledge, the extremely restricted scope of activity and knowledge mean that the scheme is a far cry from the development of competence so central to the dual system in Germany.

In terms of support, Taurus's scheme foresees that apprentices have monthly review meetings with their assessor to discuss their progress and identify any additional support, as well as 'sign-off meetings' at the end of each unit. Nevertheless, apprentices in the study complained about the lack of support with the apprenticeship overall, and with the folder work in particular. All described the unavailability of assessors and the difficulty of having units signed off, as well as constantly changing assessors, leading to significant disruption in progress. This was commonly due to a lack of trained assessors, or existing assessors moving to a different store or leaving the company altogether. The lack of support was a major concern for Mia who ended up having all her units signed off in the last week of the programme. In addition, while apprentices are to be given one hour per week off the job in order to complete the activities in the NVQ folder, Robert and Mia complained about a conflict between the demands of their job and the activities involved in the apprenticeship. It seems that this lack of support served to undermine the rhetoric of the apprenticeship as a valued programme.

Key Skills and Technical Certificate

The Key Skills and Technical Certificate elements are delivered by an external training provider. A trainer runs monthly four-hour sessions in the in-store staff training room (a total of eight to ten sessions). For Key Skills, apprentices are required to put together a portfolio of work which relates to actual workplace situations. There are two assessments, one at the beginning and one at the end. The level of key skills depends on the apprentice's GCSE grades. Those who did not obtain GCSEs grade A-C in English and Maths are put on level 1.

The Technical Certificate is based on assessment only (a multiple choice test). According to the Apprenticeship Co-ordinator, apprentices gain all the necessary knowledge through completing the NVQ. She explained that 'that's probably the easiest part of the programme ... they don't have to follow a separate course for that'. It appears therefore that the Taurus retail apprenticeship lacks a meaningful theoretical underpinning beyond the procedural knowledge deemed necessary to carry out a narrow task range.

The learning culture in the Taurus Supermarket

Observations were carried out on two sites, both large stores or 'hypermarkets'. Robert and Anita were employed in a large store on the outskirts of London, while Stephanie and Mia worked in a store in a provincial town in the South of England.

Observation in the London store (Robert and Anita)

Robert worked in the bakery. The team consisted of a team leader and four staff, including Robert, on shift work (Robert worked from four a.m. to twelve p.m.). In the morning, they worked as a team of four, each being responsible for one of the four tasks of what was a highly routinised process: making bread, baking bread, packing bread and packing cakes. Robert was making bread on the day of the observation. There was a set amount of loafs, rolls and French sticks to be prepared each day. There was a noticeable absence of customer interaction. The bakery area was more or less shielded from customers and was separated from the shop floor through walls of shelves. If a customer requested a service (normally having their bread sliced) they had to come through a relatively narrow gap between the shelves. Robert said he preferred making or baking bread which are tasks carried out at the very back of the bakery, as he did not enjoy contact with customers.

Robert and two of his colleagues engaged in a narrative about the importance of being 'skilled'. One stressed that they were all multi-skilled—they were all able to work on each of the four tasks. This is a narrative based on the supermarket's 'story' of recognising and valuing their staff's skills, partly through the internal training structure, which involved a validation of skills. Chatting to the young people it was apparent that this was something which gave meaning to their work. Part of their narrative was to differentiate themselves from other, unskilled staff, such as the fourth member of the team who, according to his colleagues, only ever did packing.

Anita worked part-time (twenty-five hours a week). I observed her on a late shift (five to nine p.m.) on a busy Friday night at the Customer Service Desk. Her responsibilities included dealing with refunds and exchanges, selling cigarettes, lottery tickets and working on the photo lab. There were two other retail assistants behind the desk—one senior assistant and one A-level student—and a manager.

Anita seemed very experienced—she dealt with the various tasks confidently, and the calm and gentle way in which she interacted with customers was striking. She managed to diffuse tension of which there was a lot. At times there was only one person serving, while the queue was getting longer and people impatient. There were a number of people returning perished food, or complaining about having been overcharged. These complaints require a standard procedure which Anita followed confidently. But it was her skill in dealing with angry customers which was most impressive. As shown in Chapter 6, her confidence stems partly from her quite varied experience of different educational pathways and work environments on the basis of which she developed a secure identity.

Observation in the South of England Store (Stephanie and Mia)
As explained in Chapter 4, I was told that both apprentices had left only when I arrived at the store for the workplace observation. I therefore spent the day observing Stephanie's and Mia's former teams, without the young women being present.

Stephanie worked at the Electrical Desk, which was in the far corner of the shop floor and seemed isolated from other parts of the store. She was responsible for the sale of electrical goods (from vacuum cleaners to multi-media goods, such as laptops, TVs and mobile telephones) and for the return and exchange of such products. Processing the return and exchange of goods required following a detailed and largely computerised procedure, stating the conditions upon which products may or may not be returned and how to input it into the system. Items are re-ordered automatically, as the computer records each sale and an order is generated as the stock is depleting to a certain minimum.

Mia worked at the delicatessen counter. The set-up was not dissimilar to the one in Germany, and the counter included cooked meats, cheese and fish. There were two assistants at the cooked meat counter and one at the cheese counter. It was a quiet Tuesday morning and there were few customers. The staff were polite, using similar phrases as in Germany ('What would you like madam?', 'Anything else madam?'). There was some banter between the three assistants. I asked one of the assistants whether one of them would have gone through the different types of meats and cheeses with Mia when she started. The answer was no, she would have just picked it up. In contrast to Germany, product knowledge is not taught formally as part of the apprenticeship.

Conclusions

It seems that both German retail programmes (retail salesman/woman and retail assistant) are comprehensive, providing for competence development and identification with the occupations, while the English scheme is restrictive, consists of a fragmented set of skills, and is almost deplete of noteworthy theoretical content other than procedural knowledge. While the learning culture in two of the German classrooms was characterised by varying levels of engagement, this may reflect the high proportion of apprentices for whom this was not the occupation of their choice (see Chapter 2). The German workplaces of the young people in the study constituted expansive learning environments (although this is no longer the norm in German retail) with larger areas of responsibility and greater autonomy for apprentices. By contrast, English workplaces were characterised by routine and highly prescribed tasks.

As indicated in relation to some of the apprentices, the observations tell us little about the meaning of apprenticeship to individual young people. They do not tell us, for example, why they draw on certain discourses and not on others. In the next two chapters, I will explore these issues by examining the young people's construction of identity in the context of their biographical experience. In order to explore young people's interpretations of different learning opportunities and the meaning they attach to apprenticeship, we have to reconstruct their biographies.

Chapter 6

The learner biographies of retail assistants in England and Germany

Introduction

The purpose of this and the following chapter is to present the comparative analysis of the individual cases. In biographical data analysis, it is important to compare cases without losing the sense of the whole (Wengraf, 1998). This involves presenting each case as a life story, rather, than simply comparing cases thematically so as to understand the meaning young people afford to apprenticeship in the context of their lives as a whole.

Given that much of the interview data was unstructured, the challenge was to identify meaningful themes and concepts that cut across cases and that allow for comparative discussion. Following Wengraf (1998), I started by looking for themes across each set of cases (retail and motor mechanics). This process was guided by a) the focus of the study and b) principles of Grounded Theory, whereby the researcher allows for themes to emerge from the data, informed by his or her theoretical and contextual knowledge (known as 'theoretical sensitivity') (Strauss and Corbin, 1990). I then went on to identify the most meaningful concepts to serve as analytical dimensions for comparative discussion and subsequently placed the cases onto a matrix. For selecting the pairs for comparison, I followed the principle of biographical matching according to which biographies of similar (or different) individuals from different countries are compared for explanatory purposes (Crompton, 2001: 186).

The pairs were selected according to gender and biographical experience, such as a disadvantaged childhood or a negative school experience. These proved to be more fruitful than ethnicity which I rejected as a matching criterion. I then presented the pairs according to the analytical dimensions. In doing so, I tried to maintain the full integrity of each of the individual life stories.

The process of reconstructing biographies throws light upon the ways in which structural dimensions and macro-processes are played out in individual lives. It is in comparing the life stories that the divergent contexts come to the fore (Chamberlayne and Spanò, 2000).

In this chapter, I will present the retail apprentices, while the motor vehicle maintenance apprentices are discussed in Chapter 7. In the following section,

I will discuss the main findings of the analysis. The paired cases are presented thereafter.

The retail apprentices in England and Germany: secure and fragile identities

Table 6.1 lists the apprentices in the two countries.

Table 6.1 The retail apprentices

Germany	England
Claudia (17)	Anita (24)
Leena (17)	Mia (18)
Jeanette (17)	Stephanie (21)
Martin (21)	Robert (19)

In Table 6.2, I provide an overview of the themes that I identified across the cases. For each of them, the table shows: whether or not a theme applied to the individual case (for example, whether or not they had family support); the extent to which a theme applied (for example, whether the identification with the apprenticeship, either over time, guiding the transition, or in the course of the apprenticeship, was low, limited or high); or the nature of a particular theme (for example, whether their school experience was positive or negative).

What stands out the most is the problematic nature of many of these young people's biographies. For example, for five of the eight young people, personal or family problems dominated during the transition, five had experienced their general schooling as negative and five had experienced a particularly difficult rather than a smooth transition. However, all of these apprentices were nevertheless able to renegotiate their learner identities as a result of the apprenticeship. These themes will be addressed in the discussion of the young people's narratives in this chapter.

Table 6.2 Analysis of Retail Apprentices: Common Themes (German and English apprentices)

	Leena	Claudia	Jeanette	Martin	Robert	Stephanie	Mia	Anita
Secure/fragile identity	Secure	Secure	Fragile	Secure	Fragile	Fragile	Fragile	Secure
Means for identification over time (social identity of occupation)	High	Low	Low	High	Low	Low	Low	Low
Means for identification during apprenticeship (content, learning sites)	High	Limited	High	High	Limited	Limited	Limited	High
Dominance of family/personal problems	No	No	Yes	Yes	Yes	Yes	Yes	No
Family support	Low	High	Low	Low	Low	High	High	High
Sees apprenticeship as personal development	Yes	Yes	Yes	Yes	No	Yes	Yes	Yes
School experience (perception of own learning)	Negative	Positive	Positive	Negative	Negative	Positive/ then negative	Negative	Positive

	Leena	Claudia	Jeanette	Martin	Robert	Stephanie	Mia	Anita
Identity formation through informal learning	Yes	Yes, not retail	Yes, not retail	Yes	Yes, not retail	No	No	Yes
Apprenticeship as positive choice	Yes	Yes	No	Yes	No	No	No	Yes
Transition	Smooth	Smooth	Difficult	Difficult	Difficult	Difficult	Difficult	Smooth
Learning sites confirm identity	Yes	Yes	Yes	Yes	Limited	Limited	Limited	Yes
Apprenticeship viewed as in line with own abilities/ personality	Yes	No	Yes	Yes	No	Yes	No	Yes
Renegotiates learner identity due to apprenticeship (more confident)	Yes	Yes	Yes	Yes	Yes	Yes	Yes	No
Meaning of apprenticeship	Valued in its own right	Instrumental	Valued in its own right	Valued in its own right	Instrumental	Instrumental	Instrumental	Instrumental
Actively negotiates identity	Yes	Yes	Yes	Yes	Yes	Yes	Yes	Yes
Preference for practical learning	Yes	Yes	Yes	Yes	Yes	Yes	Yes	Yes

The most powerful categories that emerged were whether apprentices had developed secure or fragile identities (Ball, Maguire and Macrae, 2000a), and the extent to which they were able to construct an identity through the apprenticeship (Table 6.3).

Table 6.3 Secure and fragile identities by strong and limited identification with the apprenticeship

Identification with apprenticeship	Secure identity	Fragile identity
Strong identification	Leena Martin	Jeanette
Limited identification	Claudia Anita	Mia Robert Stephanie

Thus, the extent to which the apprenticeship provided a means of identification emerged as a crucial factor in young people's ability to construct secure identities. Following Ball and colleagues (2000a), secure identities are constructed in the context of stable transitions and often linked to long-term perspectives, whereas young people with fragile identities are confronted with disruption and difficult circumstances and struggle to make sense of themselves, who they are and what they want to become.

As outlined in Chapter 2, based on the *Beruf*, the retail apprenticeship in Germany enables the transition to a recognised social and occupational position. The particular notion of competence with its broad knowledge and skills base and its emphasis on autonomous and reflective action-taking allows for identification, while offering a clear pathway and future perspective (Harney, 1998).

For Leena and Martin, the apprenticeship played a major role in their formation of identity. It guided their decision-making throughout the transition and enabled them to confirm and strengthen their identities within the different learning sites. This was much less the case for three of the apprentices on the English programme, Robert, Stephanie and Mia. The narrow and fragmented skills base and the routinised nature of the work meant that opportunities for identification were limited. Nevertheless, with all three apprentices having experienced highly discontinuous biographies, the apprenticeship fulfilled an important function in restoring their confidence in their own learning, but there was disillusionment with the apprenticeship and their identities remained fragile as the future was still uncertain.

Anita was the exception here. Being slightly older and from a family of small business owners, she already had a range of work experiences and the retail apprenticeship was just one option of many made available to her. Similarly, for Claudia on the German scheme, the apprenticeship was a stepping stone and part of a broader career perspective. In a way, both Anita and Claudia could be said to have 'choice' biographies (Wyn and Dwyer, 1999). By contrast, Jeanette, another German apprentice, was unable to develop a secure identity because of her experience of a highly disruptive family background and because the retail apprenticeship was a second choice.

Another critical factor in the analysis below is the learner identity as it develops on the basis of learning experiences throughout the young people's biographies, notably at school, and the way it is transformed and (re-)negotiated during the transition from school to work. It becomes clear that, rather than being passively socialised, the young people actively negotiate their identities on the basis of their experiences. Here, Butler's notion of performativity (1990) provides a more useful theoretical framework than the concept of *habitus*. The analysis demonstrates the power of social norms as young people actively perform the social identities of occupations to achieve socially recognised positions (Butler, 1990). However, they do not just blindly conform to social expectations. Rather, their particular interpretations of occupations and the ways in which they make sense of learning opportunities reflect their unique biographical experiences and backgrounds. Learning opportunities may be appropriated and made sense of in ways that serve to strengthen emergent identities. In many ways, the apprenticeships are central to the young people's overall formation of identity and their transition to adulthood. Many commented on how the apprenticeship had contributed to their development as persons, for example, in overcoming shyness. Importantly, young people on retail apprenticeships do not reject learning. Many prefer experiential learning and practical skills, so often dismissed in academic discourse. For others, their 'rejection' of academic learning is a reflection of a struggle with difficult circumstances and disadvantaged backgrounds rather than of academic ability.

Presentation of the cases

Pair One:
Martin and Robert: A retail apprenticeship to overcome battered self-esteem?

Martin

Martin had a difficult childhood in the industrial city in Western Germany, where he still lives today. When he was six years old his mother died. His father was frequently absent from the home, at times for long periods, so that Martin and his brother had to look after themselves. Lacking parental support and with hunger preventing him from concentrating, Martin struggled at school ('nobody took an interest and revised with me'). In the end he failed his grade.

Indicative of the structured and comprehensive nature of German vocational education, he was absorbed by the 'transition system' (see Chapter 2), which enabled him to retake his school qualification. In a supportive environment, he was able to regain confidence in his learning. However, his story also illustrates the ineffectiveness of the system as he was forced against his will to train as a bricklayer. It is testimony to his growing confidence at the time that he decided to drop the course in favour of pursuing his dream job of retail assistant, enlisting the support of his tutors in writing applications. As was indicated in Chapter 2, parts of the retail sector can be ruthless, and Martin tells of several employers who exploited him, in jobs with little pay, and who reneged on their erstwhile promise of an apprenticeship place. Eventually, he was able to obtain a training place with current employer Emerald, a traditional and reputable food retailer.

Martin has a sense of himself as an 'intelligent human being' who was let down as a child. In the narrative he presents himself as the 'self-made man', who struggled in adverse circumstances and succeeded against the odds. Always concerned with seeking the approval of others, it is the story of a boy striving to overcome rejection. At the same time, Martin's story illustrates the power of the social identity of the retail occupation in Germany. The *Beruf* of retail assistant has been critical in the formation of his identity, providing a clear long-term perspective (Harney, 1998). It is what guided and motivated him throughout his transition. Performing this identity (Butler, 1990), conforming to the norms and expectations associated with the occupation, critically serves to build his self-esteem and thus takes on a unique meaning in the context of his biography.

Ever since he was a small child, Martin had wanted to become a retail assistant. His particular image of the occupation centred on the customer consultation, as he may have experienced it in shops or on television. He would make up fantasy games, whereby he would 'sell' items, such as his bicycle, to imaginary customers. Referring to his otherwise poor performance at school, Martin sees himself as a smooth communicator ('what I'm good at is talking'), and it is likely that the retail occupation appealed to him as something through which he could confirm his own identity (Ulrich, 2006). Asked about his expectations regarding the apprenticeship, he replied,

> Well, I only had one expectation, that of becoming a fully skilled worker. German workers have a reputation as quality workers, which means that I want to be trained in a way so that when I later go abroad that people will say 'this is a top notch guy, that fellow really knows his job'. This is what I expect from my apprenticeship, to be trained to a very high standard.

However, it is on the shop floor, behind the meat and cheese counter, where Martin really comes into his own. During the interview, he talked with great enthusiasm about the customer consultation, which he presented as a highly professional activity. It became clear that it was important to him to draw on theories of customer communication in order to facilitate 'a positive buying experience'.

> I start welcoming the customers in a very friendly way, you see, and build up a small conversation so that they feel comfortable in front of the counter and with me as assistant ... .and smiling throughout, being friendly. Yeah, and that, most people really like that ... and there are people who will only be served by me ... mostly older people ... I can sell them products they don't know, you see. I offer them a slice of sausage as a taster, they taste it and before they say anything I will say 'tastes delicious doesn't it?', with a broad grin on my face, and then they're happy, having a positive experience while tasting. And then they want to buy the product. This also creates a social bond you see. This is something I'm proud of and that I enjoy.

In many ways, Martin's emerging learner identity is confirmed in the different learning sites. The apprenticeship has been critical in developing his confidence and his identity as a communicator and a sales person. Central to this have been the notion of competence, allowing identification through a sense of purpose, and an expansive learning environment in the workplace (Fuller and Unwin, 2003b). Emerald's reputation is built on a knowledgeable workforce and the apprenticeship includes a comprehensive internal training course consisting of monthly seminars (including assignments and tests) on theoretical knowledge. While he finds these hard, the importance attached to competence is central to his identity.

Martin shines at college in a class with, as described in Chapter 5, an otherwise low educational level and a high level of disruption. It is interesting that the relaxed atmosphere in class means that the identities of 'the good student' and 'the good classmate' are not incompatible. It allows him to engage in learning activities while taking part in banter, listening to his classmates' iPods, and being popular with both tutors and students. The teaching and learning arrangement also enables him to take the initiative in group work, where he prefers being the one 'doing all the work' to make sure it corresponds with his own high standards.

> When the others do it I always fear it won't be right, you see ... because I always try to do it really well, it has to look really good by my own standards ... and then I get a lot of praise from my tutors and my classmates. Some say I'm top of the class ... and when I think that I was bottom of the class during fifth, sixth and seventh grade it means a lot to me.

At college, his experience has connected with previous positive learning experiences, and he has a strong sense that he can achieve (he passed the interim exam with a grade 2[4]). Wanting to prove to himself and others that he can succeed is what motivates him. Importantly, the structure of the retail apprenticeship and the learning culture in college and the shop are supportive of this endeavour.

In terms of the future, Martin is remarkably clear about what he wants to achieve. His goal is to climb up the career ladder and earn a 'decent salary' by the time he is 30. It is because of his positive experience during the apprenticeship and the progression structure at Emerald that his career plans have become a realistic option.

4   The German equivalent for the English grades A to F is 1 to 6.

Robert

Similar to Martin, initially Robert told a story of success, of how the apprenticeship had given him the opportunity to turn his life around and to prove himself.

> Ever since I've worked here [at Taurus] ... I've just progressed up and up ... I think I took the apprenticeship ... to show people and myself that I can achieve things and to, er, to all those people that doubted me, sort of, chuck it back at them in a way.

Robert grew up in a socially deprived area in East London. His parents split up when he was six months old and he was raised by his mother to whom he developed a close relationship. When Robert was ten, his mother met a new partner with whom she had another child and the family moved to a different area. Being no longer able to rely on his mother's undivided attention, away from his friends and having to start a new school were major uprooting events that the shy young boy perceived as overwhelming.

> That was really hard and I think that's why I had- just weren't bothered about school so much because I didn't really- I weren't friends with no-one.

What was now at the forefront of his mind was how to deal with the discontinuity. It appears that his teachers did not recognise his circumstances and failed to engage him, as Robert withdrew and resisted the school culture. He was excluded on four occasions, for truancy and disruptive behaviour. With poor marks in most subjects, he decided that school was not for him. This was despite the fact that he enjoyed English and maths—in his GCSEs he got Bs in both subjects. He explained that he 'naturally adapted' to English and enjoyed interpreting literary works such as Lord of the Flies, where he valued the autonomy involved in creative writing.

> We could write our own opinion, it wouldn't be, like, a question and that that everyone is going to have the same answer to, you could write what you thought and express it why and, like, defend your argument and that, so it was quite fun having your own opinion, er, as opposed to getting told what to write.

As a young teenager, through informal learning experiences outside the school context, Robert developed an emerging identity as a 'practical person'. He started accompanying his mother's partner (who had a carpentry business) at weekends, helping him install kitchens. While he enjoyed the work as something he was good at, he was also attracted to the male image of the carpenter and the 'white van' as something that would reinforce his gender identity. However, by the time he left school, his disaffection was such that carpentry was no longer within his 'horizon for action' as he could not envisage classroom education beyond the age of sixteen.

> … 'cos it's like the whole white van thing … it's quite a man- manly job and that, but … I would have had to go college, most likely, and I really didn't want to do that so I didn't pursue that.

In the final year at school, he was so concerned with getting to the end of it that he had no perspectives beyond that. On leaving school he was faced with a new reality as his mother expected him to contribute to the household, and his friends all started work or college. It was through his grandmother who worked at Taurus that he applied for and was offered a job in the supermarket's bakery. This marked a critical turning point in his life, which eventually led him to renegotiate his learner identity.

Robert was emboldened by his initial work experience, and for the first time started taking the initiative in shaping his learning career when he applied to go on the apprenticeship scheme after a year in the shop. He saw the apprenticeship primarily as a means to progress (to team leader and manager), reflecting the ways in which he had made sense of a company narrative that strongly advertises its progression structure. Several events served to boost his confidence: He was among four employees selected for the apprenticeship scheme out of fifteen candidates. Importantly, of the four apprentices he was the only one put at Key Skills Level 2 rather than Level 1, due to his GCSE grades. The experience of being an 'achieving' student was clearly transformative as he rose to the challenge of a key skills assignment which involved giving a talk on the history of the company based on his own research.

> I found it interesting … to see how such a big company come about, so I thought that would be something good and it's a good thing to discuss

in front of the other ... people doing the apprenticeship 'cos they might want to know ... so yeah, I chose to do that.

Initially at least, he also derived a sense of achievement from being a baker and the idea that people would buy and take home and eat something he had made. Importantly, the apprenticeship enabled him to consolidate his latent identity as a practical person. He insisted that it suited his disposition for learning by doing, in seeming contradiction to his experience in Key Skills.

I like it here because it's a lot of physical work ... I can't sit and write, I just- I can't- ... I'm more of a practical person, I like to physically have to do stuff like lifting thirty-two kilograms of dough [laughs] ... it's something that I enjoy doing.

Seven months later Robert's perspective on the scheme and on Taurus more generally had changed radically. While he completed the apprenticeship, it had become very stressful towards the end and he had thought of dropping it. He had completely abandoned the idea of progressing, stating that managers 'aren't respected in the store', a statement which perhaps reflects his own disillusionment with the work.

A major factor in this disillusionment became apparent during the observation. Robert was 'making bread', one of his four tasks as a baker, which also included 'baking bread', 'packing bread' and 'packing cakes'. He followed a prescribed routine of what was a highly automated process. There was a set amount of loafs, rolls and French sticks to be made each day, involving preparing the dough according to a standard recipe, and cutting and weighing pieces of dough which were then further processed by a machine. He perceived his work as boring and menial and repeatedly stated almost apologetically that 'there isn't much to learn, you picked it up already'.

Robert struggled with the monotony of the work, stating that he 'can't stand the sight' of dough. Also, the lack of support for the off-the-job aspects of the apprenticeship led to conflict between his work and the apprenticeship activities, and he kept 'being pulled away from work to meetings'. When I mentioned to him that apprentices in Germany attend college, he indicated that he would find that much preferable ('here you were given the book and told to get on with it'). Thus, whereas Martin thrived in an expansive work environment, for Robert, his employer's lack of support may have signalled to him the low importance attached to the learning activities of the apprenticeship and was highly demotivating.

One of the most interesting facets of Robert's story is his change in perspective over the course of the research. In a further chat with him two months later, while I was in the store to observe Anita, he revealed that he was toying with the idea of doing engineering with London Underground, something suggested to him by a family friend. Remarkably, he indicated that he would now consider going to college. It means that while his work at Taurus initially enabled him to renegotiate his learner identity, in the end it did not fulfil him because of the menial and highly routinised nature of the work and the lack of challenge it presented to a bright and creative young man. It would seem that, based on his experiences at Taurus, his horizon for action broadened as he finally considered going back to college.

Finally, it is highly significant that Robert continued to stress his practical identity, insisting that he cannot 'sit and write', despite his success in English and maths at school and during the apprenticeship that suggest the opposite. It appears that he drew on the discourse of practical or vocational learning which in England is constructed in direct opposition to academic learning and thus excludes any form of creative writing. The discourse of a practical person provided a legitimate alternative identity and investing in it allowed Robert to distance himself from a school experience dominated by fear and rejection. His story flies in the face of the idea that young people on vocational courses are not academic learners. Not achieving at school may be bound up with the children's or young people's personal situations. However, practical learners are also 'constituted' as non-academic through discourses upon which the young people themselves draw.

Summary of Pair One

Like Martin, Robert had a difficult upbringing which disrupted his learning career at school. For both young men, the apprenticeship was important as a means to 'prove' themselves and to build their self-esteem. Both stories illustrate the ways in which learning careers are deeply interwoven with other life domains, and school pupils may be more concerned with dealing with discontinuities than with learning (Rosenthal et al., 2006). The difference between the biographies is the extent to which the apprenticeship provides a long-term identification. For Martin, the comprehensive nature of the occupation and high quality of the scheme enabled him to construct a secure identity and provided him clear future perspectives. In contrast, while the apprenticeship served to restore his confidence as a learner, Robert was ultimately unable to identify with a narrow and undemanding occupational profile.

Pair Two: Leena and Mia: Renegotiating negative learner identities

Leena

Leena was born in Germany of Moroccan parents and was raised in an inner-city migrant community. As a migrant, she occupied a fragile position in German society, as evident in her school experience. The family spoke Arabic at home, which is likely to have impeded her educational attainment.

Leena did not enjoy school. After primary school, she went to intermediate school but did not feel comfortable in a learning culture which she found academically challenging, so she was transferred to general secondary school. This would have been a critical blow to her confidence at the time.

Her experience of general secondary school was equally difficult. Reflecting a dominant trend in the German school system, there was a high concentration of pupils from poorer social backgrounds and migrant families. Leena felt there was no individual support. Her experience at the time must have been daunting, always at risk of being left behind and confirming her perception of not being good at school. In the end she lost her motivation and withdrew. She no longer revised, reasoning that learning was not important as she planned to enter the labour market on leaving school. In this she would have followed a common pattern within the migrant community.

However, during Year 9, a critical turning point occurred. Over the past year, Leena had developed an interest in fashion and beauty. This was no doubt part of her adolescence and the need to experiment with different identities, drawing on images of popular consumption (Rattansi and Phoenix, 1997). Thus, she explained how, aged fifteen, she became more adventurous in terms of choosing outfits, and more confident in trusting her own judgment. This was to a large extent fuelled by outside influences, including fashion magazines, glamour models and a styling show on TV.

> It was at the beginning of ninth grade, that's when I became interested in make-up, how to dress, because previously I wasn't bothered by that. Then I started going into the shops, and for instance, say pink wasn't trendy, it will be in the summer, I still bought it and wore it, because

fashion just interested me … I always found it fascinating how fashion how clothes can transform a person into someone else [referring to TV show].

Leena recalled how her best friend started to consult her on fashion matters, thereby further consolidating her new identity.

In Germany, during the final two years at school, the transition to work constitutes an important element of the curriculum and includes placements at local firms. Thus faced with the reality of having to choose an occupation, the idea of becoming a retail assistant crystallised in Leena's mind. The school environment was highly supportive, providing help with the process of finding placements and, later, apprenticeships. She respected the new teacher, who convinced her of the importance of a good school leaving qualification. Determined to get an apprenticeship place, the real prospect of achieving prompted her to revise her disposition to learning and her grades improved dramatically. Driven by her own enthusiasm, her experiences during two placements at the women's fashion sections of large department stores (three weeks in Year 9, and one day a week throughout Year 10), confirmed her emerging identity, as she was popular with customers and colleagues, who, in the latter store, encouraged her to apply for an apprenticeship place, which she did and was successful in getting.

Based on her experiences of success, Leena developed a confidence that enabled her to practise biographicity (Alheit, 2003): reflecting on and taking control of her learning career and negotiating the vocational education system. Interestingly, and reflecting the status of vocational education in Germany, she was able to participate in the vocational education discourse despite her parents not being familiar with it. She was determined to obtain a quality apprenticeship in a large department store. She even hedged an alternative plan should she not get it, of obtaining her intermediate school certificate and applying for an apprenticeship further afield.

The most interesting facet of Leena's biography is how she expressed and negotiated her self-identity through the social identity of retail. She drew on cultural representations of fashion, but equally on the social identity of the role of retail assistant and associated competences, such as approaching customers. In other ways, too, the apprenticeship went far beyond providing an occupational identity. From a present perspective, Leena saw the retail apprenticeship as important for her personal development, helping her to overcome her shyness.

Based on situations with customers, she had discovered a new facet to her character, one which is outgoing and communicative even with strangers, facilitated by her identification with the retail occupation. She illustrated this describing a situation during her first placement.

> We were a bit afraid of customers, I didn't like to talk, ... and then after three or four customers I somehow forgot that I was a placement student ... she [a customer] told me she wanted to buy a new pair of trousers, I saw that she was wearing jeans, but I gave her something completely different so that I could see how she is transformed and starts wearing other things, and then the customers kept coming back, they became regular customers.

Participant observation on the shop floor further revealed her agency in co-constructing the learning culture. She had her own area of responsibility, from time-to-time receiving instructions from the head assistant. Advising customers was a key activity, and one that Leena thrived on. She enjoyed using her knowledge creatively. She took the initiative to approach customers and came across as extremely competent and knowledgeable about the product range, sizes and materials, suggesting alternatives when they did not have what the customer asked for. However, while the learning culture allowed her to develop her own ideas of customer interaction and lay-out of the department, this also put her on a collision course with colleagues, notably the older head assistant whose judgment she mistrusted.

Leena preferred the work environment to vocational school. Nevertheless, she passed her interim exam with top marks. She benefited from the interactive teaching and learning arrangement which contrasted with her experience of school. In terms of future expectations, Leena anticipated completing her apprenticeship, being taken on by the firm and progressing to management level. Thus, despite coming from a disadvantaged background and her rejection of learning during much of her time at school, Leena was able to construct a secure identity through the retail apprenticeship. The identification must be seen as being facilitated through the comprehensive nature of the occupation and the social recognition it confers (Harney, 1998).

Crucially, the apprenticeship was about much more than becoming competent in an occupational field. It coincided with and facilitated Leena's transition to adulthood and becoming a person. The learning site of the workplace in particular enabled Leena to negotiate her identity as somebody who expresses herself through fashion, both in the way she dresses and in terms of how she is able to give competent and trusted advice in her retail role. While she drew heavily on readily available images of retail and fashion which guided her formation of identity, how she combined these and the ways in which she interpreted learning opportunities reflect her particular biography, and notably the desire to construct a viable alternative identity to academic learning through fashion. It illustrates the ways in which young people perform identities in more creative ways than is perhaps foreseen by Butler's (1990) notion of the compulsive citation of norms. As we will see, her interpretation of the retail apprenticeship contrasts sharply with that of another retail assistant in a German department store, Claudia.

Mia
Like Leena, Mia had a negative school experience. Mia grew up in a provincial town in the South-West of England. She had dyslexia but was diagnosed very late (aged fourteen), which meant she had to endure year after year with a sense of not achieving and being left behind. The sense of helplessness and 'otherness' was expressed in her account of school.

> I used to hate ... having books to take home and read ... cos I didn't know there was something wrong with me.

Her story of destroying an essay indicates the shame she felt about her poor spelling, preferring the punishment of detention for not doing the essay over humiliation.

> I had to write an essay ... and I struggled quite bad with that, and I was reading mine and then you had to read ... someone else's, and I thought, nah I screwed mine up and I threw mine in the bin and said that I didn't do it, cos their's was so much better and the spellings were spot-on but what I could read of it.

The diagnosis constituted a critical turning point in her life. Whereas before, she had resigned herself to the idea that she was unable to perform at school, leading her to withdraw, she was now able to name her disability. At school, she was given a permanent support teacher who would sit with her in lessons.

However, she still failed her mock GCSEs, which led her to abandon her dream of becoming a police officer. Instead, based on a recent experience of caring for relatives, Mia decided to go to sixth form college where she completed a one-year vocational course in Health and Social Care. She enjoyed the more practical activities involved, finally giving her a sense of being good at something. The learning culture contrasted with that of school, and the idea formed in her that she was better at practical than at written work. She was no longer 'different' but a confident student. However, the prospect of entering work filled her with anxiety, as she thought she might be unable to cope without the support with dyslexia. Although she did not say so, it may have been a major reason why she dismissed the idea of working in care.

Still at sixth form college, and with the help of her father who worked at Taurus, Mia took up a part-time job in the store. Here, she found an opportunity to confirm her emerging identity (being good at practical work), proving herself to be hard-working and keen to learn. This was acknowledged by her managers, who, after a few months, put her forward for the apprenticeship scheme. Gaining reassurance that she would receive support with her dyslexia, Mia accepted and started working full-time.

It appears that Taurus provided an environment in which she felt comfortable and in which she could thrive. This is confirmed by her narrative, which was dominated by accounts of coping with dyslexia, accepting it rather than hiding it, and asking colleagues for support as of right.

> I've built up the confidence in myself to start letting people know, see [the apprenticeship co-ordinator] knows, there is some managers that know already ... so I've got that extra help ... spelling can be quite difficult, but where people here know that I'm dyslexic, I just need to go and ask someone and they'll tell me, so it's not too bad.

Working at Taurus helped her to build up her confidence as the environment was conducive to strengthening her emerging identity as a practical learner. She keenly took up new learning opportunities and, following Youdell (2006), became recognised by her managers as a 'good retail assistant' ('everyone wants me in their department cos I'm trained on every department within the store').

Mia's story illustrates the role of Taurus's apprenticeship scheme in building the confidence of young people who may have underperformed at school by recognising their skills and offering them prospects for progression. For Mia, being an apprentice gave her a recognised status within the company, making her more visible, with managers taking time to provide training.

Crucially, the apprenticeship enabled her to renegotiate her learner identity by learning to cope with dyslexia. Her determination to succeed was based on the support she received from people within Taurus, but also her parents, who would correct her work in the NVQ folder. Whereas previously at school she would have given up, she now persisted, knowing that she was able to succeed.

> I failed one of my exams ... it was the math one I failed ... [the key skills tutor] gave me the practice paper to take home ... and I was writing the answers down, I was doing it three times a week, and when he come in then I passed it again, and he was quite impressed ... errmm really actually got more experience in maths now then when I did when I was at school, cos I never used to concentrate ... so I just used to click off.

Thus, like Leena, after a difficult time at school, Mia was able to renegotiate her learner identity through the apprenticeship, which enabled her to find a way to live with dyslexia. In the narrative, she constructed an identity of someone who had struggled with a learning disability but who was learning to cope with it through persistence ('it's four years of picking up slowly but surely the spellings and what I need on a day-to-day basis'). It is in this sense that the apprenticeship was meaningful to her. Beyond this, and in contrast to Leena, her identification with the occupation of retail assistant was limited. Indeed, the apprenticeship opened up a further perspective—at the time of the interview she was planning to apply for a job as security guard within the store. This plan connected with long-held ambitions.

> It was either health and social care or a police woman, cos I knew I wouldn't be a very good police officer cos I didn't get the grade in my mocks ... and then I went on to health and social care, but since then this apprenticeship I've it's opened my eyes again to looking how you can do things, what to spot in like a shoplifter, and all that.

It is unclear what happened to Mia. Six months after completing the apprenticeship she had left the firm. She may have been unable to get a job as security guard and was looking further afield. Thus, while she could not construct a secure identity as a retail assistant it might have given her the confidence to pursue other options and thus widened her horizon for action.

Summary of Pair Two

Both Leena and Mia had negative experiences at school and perceived themselves as failing or non-academic. Both were able to renegotiate their learning careers through the retail apprenticeships. For Leena, the social identity of the occupation guided her transition and provided an important means for consolidating her learner and gender identities. She was able to construct a secure identity on the basis of the comprehensive vocational education system and a multi-dimensional conception of competence. In contrast, for Mia, similar to Robert in the other store, the apprenticeship was primarily a means to gain confidence in her own learning.

Pair Three:
Jeanette and Stephanie: Retail apprenticeships as second choice

Jeanette

Jeanette experienced a highly disruptive childhood. Like Leena and Martin, she grew up in an inner-city area of an industrial town in Western Germany. Her parents separated when she was young. As her mother struggled to earn an income, Jeanette was effectively raised by her grandparents, to whom she developed a close relationship. Four years ago, her mother entered a new relationship and the family moved into their current flat. Jeanette has a very acrimonious relationship with her stepfather and a complex relationship with her mother, whom she might view as unreliable. It is against the background of highly volatile family relationships that we have to understand Jeanette's narrative which is about having learnt through the apprenticeship to be 'independent', despite it not being her 'dream occupation'.

Her first choice was to become an old people's carer, a desire that first developed when Jeanette was fourteen, when the family took in her grandparents who needed full-time care. Because of their close relationship, she took an active part in looking after them. Based on this experience, when required to do a work placement during her final year at school, she chose the local home for the elderly, an experience which she found highly rewarding. Jeanette spoke about a Christmas party when a resident told her she should never leave. It confirmed her sense of purpose and her desire to work in elder care. When it turned out that she would not be able to secure a training place at the home, Jeanette was devastated. Tensions mounted between her and her family as her parents put pressure on her to find a training place in a different occupation, a prospect that horrified her as it meant having to give up her dream. She eventually followed her parents' advice to look into food retailing (both her parents work in retailing).

After several rejections, she was accepted at the Emerald store. She described how shocked she was, trying to regain some control by convincing herself that it may not be the be all and end all, as she could leave after the probation period.

> And then my parents said "this is your last chance", errrm yeah and then I thought about it, and I was shocked that I should be trained in something that I didn't want to be trained in, errm and I thought about how this apprenticeship would pan out and what kinds of problems I might come across.

Nevertheless, Jeanette presented her transition as a success story. In important ways, the apprenticeship became crucial to her personal development as she sought to build her fragile self-esteem. It appears that the particular learning sites enabled her to develop an identity through the occupation and increase her self-confidence, and to become, in her words, 'independent'. She interpreted the learning environments not merely as opportunities for learning an occupation but a chance to take control of her life, to develop as a person and to prove to herself and her parents that she could achieve. Thus, in her narrative, Jeanette is exuberant about the apprenticeship, displaying her eagerness for learning.

It was important to her to become 'competent' and she talked at length about the many learning opportunities in an expansive learning environment, insisting that being a retail assistant required specialist knowledge and involved much more than just cleaning (a reference to the often menial tasks delegated to apprentices). It was critical to build her own expertise in order to gain the trust of customers.

> You always have customer contact … and you always have to look neat, always be polite with the customers that's important, and errrm of course the customers place trust in you and you have to return the trust, you have to be able to advise them, you have to have the confidence … so for example errrm these differences in filet, maybe it is well hung and it is more tender, and they'll say "it's so dark and it looks dodgy, no, I won't buy

it", but in principle it's better meat ... but if you don't believe it yourself it's difficult to convey it to the customer.

Jeanette was thus able to construct her identity through the occupation. She clearly cites the normative expectations in terms of demeanour and appearance, as she wanted to be recognised as the good retail assistant. However, the broad knowledge base was critical. It was what made the customer interaction meaningful and enabled Jeanette to develop a professional competence of which being friendly was a part.

Also, being a retail assistant suited her extrovert nature, and she could rationalise her 'choice' as in line with her personality. Interaction with people was important to her, and something she found she was good at, as for example in the home for the elderly.

Just working with people is so fascinating, like customers, older people, just contact with human beings really, that was important to me, for my future.

The college was important to her as part of the qualification, and she easily adapted to the demands of college. She was familiar with the student-centred style as she thrived in group work and relished presenting in front of the class.

It is interesting how she made sense of an environment with mixed ability students as her attitude veered between conforming and strategic compliance (Bloomer, 1997). She was able to take advantage of learning opportunities while at other times taking a more instrumental approach (explaining that she only needs to participate three times in class to get her oral mark for the day).

While the apprenticeship had offered her an opportunity for identification, it appears instrumental to the much bigger task of being able to stand on her own two feet, as she returned to the theme of 'being independent' and looked beyond the current apprenticeship when asked what it meant for her future.

I have acquired specialist knowledge ... I am able to progress ... and the apprenticeship means errm that I am able to do something by myself, without support ... without being dependent on someone ... it means to have learnt for the future.

Once more, while occupations play a powerful role in the young people's identity construction as they strive for social recognition, the meaning of apprenticeship for individual apprentices seems to be strongly rooted in their biographical experiences.

Eight months on it was clear that Jeanette's personal life had continued to interfere with her work life. Still only seventeen, it seems that she gained some control over her family difficulties by moving into her own flat. However, another event, the death of her grandfather, had a devastating impact on her performance at college and at work. In the interim exam she finished bottom of the class.

Nearing the end of the apprenticeship, she was determined to complete it. Jeanette's story demonstrates the close intertwining of apprenticeship and family lives, the impossibility of escaping her troubled past, and the fragility of her identity as she still struggled to become someone. Nevertheless, the apprenticeship had afforded her a sense of purpose and some latent future perspectives, which may include fulfilling her dream at last. She explained that if she was not taken on, she wanted to do an apprenticeship in elderly care.

Stephanie

Stephanie was brought up in a rural area on the outskirts of a provincial town in the South-West of England. It appears she was a bright and lively pupil who enjoyed school. However, her life changed dramatically when, aged fourteen, she started to suffer from headaches and extreme tiredness caused by a severe disorder of the adrenal glands. She was no longer able to attend school on a regular basis and was eventually prevented from going altogether. Although passing her GCSEs with the help of a home tutor, she was deeply unhappy about the poor grades she received, what she refers to as 'proper pants results'. It prevented her from fulfilling her long-standing dream of becoming a police officer, an occupation which would have chimed with her outgoing and communicative nature.

> Ever since I can remember I've always been a real people person, that's why I've always had jobs where I've been dealing with people ... I think I'm one of very few people like that in my age that can talk to younger children, middle-aged people, older people or teenagers, I can talk to anyone.

Deemed unsuitable for work with the police force on account of her illness, she started looking into related fields, such as forensics, but soon realised she lacked the grades these jobs required. In the end, she felt her only option was to join the labour market. Five years on, her remark that 'there's a lot of things that I could have done but I can't' is indicative of the continued resentment she felt about the disruption the illness had brought to her life.

For the next three years after leaving school, she worked in a number of jobs in the local area, but none of them worked out. At the age of twenty, she got a job at the electrical appliances counter at the local supermarket.

Taurus is one of the largest local employers, but for Stephanie and her family it was 'where you go to work if you can't do anything else'. It is unlikely that she would have considered it, had it not been for her disrupted career. She had joked with her parents that she would end up at Taurus. The fact that she did may indicate how restricted she perceived her options to be. However, in the interview it soon became clear that she now saw Taurus as offering an opportunity to reconstruct her learning career through an alternative pathway.

> It just goes to show that if you haven't really got sort of very good GCSEs it doesn't mean you can't progress.

It appears that the work enabled her to relate to and reinforce her existing identities as a 'people person' and a practical person. The latter had formed at school ('I was much better doing the hands-on stuff than I was at writing') and she proudly related that she had been trained in several departments and that she was now 'multi-skilled', thus interpreting the company narrative of staff progression. Keen to develop a sense of purpose, Stephanie started seizing learning opportunities far beyond of what was expected of her. Reflecting her eagerness to learn and her ability to reach out to other people, she offered colleagues to 'help out' wherever she could. As staff and customers acknowledged her growing expertise and friendly nature, this reinforced her emerging confidence. When, a year later, the store started advertising the apprenticeships, she immediately enquired about the scheme. However, what attracted her was the prospect of making up for her poor GCSE grades.

> ... because I didn't have the best sort of end in my school, I thought it would help me get a little bit further if I do something like that, just to get the grades more than anything else.

The apprenticeship greatly enhanced Stephanie's confidence in her own learning. She enjoyed Key Skills, involving a work-based project (requiring apprentices to obtain and analyse sales figures for a product, and creating an advertising poster). Her remark, 'you're actually learning it at the same time but it doesn't feel like that, it doesn't feel like you've been sat down and getting told this, this blabblablablabla', reflects her association of learning with conventional directive teaching arrangements which seem to have dominated her school experience. In the end, she got 84% in maths, leading her to revise her original perception of being 'rubbish at maths'.

Stephanie explained that learning new skills and knowledge (for example, in relation to customer communication and the company's returns policy) has increased her confidence in dealing with customers and has made it a much more rewarding experience.

> So before I'd just sort of say 'oh no, you can't return it' and not really give them an explanation why whereas now I'll be like 'well the problem that we have unfortunately is because it's branded, as far as we're concerned if you have not got your receipt you could have bought that in (shop x) or in (shop y) and you try and make them see it, you try and explain it so that you can- they sort of see it from your point of view, so then by the end of the conversation they sort of think 'hmm, yeah, fair one' so you'll find that you're talking to the customers differently and [yeah] things like that, you'll find that you're like that your body language is different when you talk to the customers as well, it's not as sort of defensive.

At the same time, and in contrast to Jeanette's experience, Stephanie's occupational knowledge, such as in relation to the products sold in her department, was restricted and there was no off-the-job learning element. All she knew about the products she had learnt, rather haphazardly, from reading information on the packaging, and from talking to colleagues or, at times, customers. In addition, although working largely unsupervised, her autonomy was highly constrained, with key activities, such as dealing with a customer returning a product, tightly prescribed by the step-by-step approach laid down in standardised procedures. Stephanie left the company shortly after completing the apprenticeship. As she did not get back in touch with me, I cannot be certain as to why she left.

Summary of Pair Three

The cases of Jeanette and Stephanie illustrate the close intertwining of learning careers with other life domains. Like Jeanette, Stephanie had not envisaged a career in retail and was devastated not being able to embark on a training course in the occupation of her choice. Again like Jeanette, she discovered that the apprenticeship was achievable and it enabled her to construct a learner identity that related to previous experiences. Crucially, while for both women the apprenticeship fulfilled an important function in rebuilding their confidence, neither of them were able to construct secure identities. For Jeanette, the comprehensive nature and relatively high status of the retail apprenticeship provided a stronger means of identification and offered a long-term perspective. Experiencing continuing difficulties in her family life and unable to give up her dream of working in elder care, her identity remained fragile. As for Stephanie, it seems plausible that, in the end, the narrow and routinised nature of retail work at Taurus did not fulfil her, and that, with her confidence in her own learning restored, she was looking for new challenges that before would have seemed unrealistic.

Pair Four:
Claudia and Anita: Retail apprenticeships as part of 'choice' biographies?

Claudia

In contrast to some of the other retail apprentices, Claudia's biography was marked by stability and continuity. She was brought up in a medium-sized town in Western Germany, in a Catholic lower middle-class family, and had lived all her life in the close-knit white Catholic neighbourhood where 'everyone knows everyone else'. She went to the local Catholic intermediate school.

The most salient aspect in Claudia's story is the nonchalant way in which she describes her learning career, including her experience of school and the apprenticeship. Another striking theme is the active support and encouragement she received from her parents. There never seems to have been any doubt that she would achieve and 'become somebody' (Ball, Maguire and Macrae, 2000a). While she said she did not enjoy school, she left aged sixteen with an average grade of 2.4 (between B and C), indicating the relative ease with which she succeeded. She was bored with the particular teaching and learning approach: rigid by-the-book and rote learning of factual information, leaving no room for interpretation. She preferred subjects that stimulated her practical creativity, such as arts, or sports.

Affording relatively low importance to school, her focus throughout her school years seemed to have been instead on her extensive out-of-school activities. This included participating in events organised by the Church and membership of the local scout group, both activities she was still pursuing at the time of the research. She also did jazz dance from the age of seven and played tennis from age nine. Tennis in particular required a considerable level of commitment on her part, involving daily training sessions and playing at competitions.

Her horizon for action always included both, a dual system apprenticeship and higher education. In her perception, the dual system and higher education were both part of an education system that she could negotiate on her terms. Echoing Evans and Heinz (1994b), the vocational education system enabled an extended transition that allowed her to 'experiment' and find out what she wanted to do. Thus, the decision-making process was facilitated by the knowledge that doing an apprenticeship was a good and highly reputed basis for a career but that there was the prospect of doing something else afterwards, including continuing school, doing Abitur (the German equivalent of A-levels) and going on to university, a path her best friend had chosen. Her parents persuaded her to do the apprenticeship.

> At the beginning of tenth grade ... my parents said, what would you like to do ... which direction would you like to take, and then I was always so undecided, and then they said just try it [an apprenticeship], it is only three years and then you'll be nineteen, and then you'll still be able to do something else, or continue with school.

She was still undecided about which occupation to choose, despite the extensive guidance she received at school (including visiting advisors from the employment office). She had done two placements neither of which she particularly enjoyed: a two-week placement as a nursery nurse in her local kindergarten in Year 8, and a three-week placement at the local publishing house, where her parents knew the owner, in Year 9. In the end, her parents helped her decide to do retailing ('you like clothes [...], wouldn't that be something?').

When she applied for a training place with the major department store in the nearby city and did not hear for a long time, she believed she had been unsuccessful and started pursuing an alternative pathway: vocational A-levels

(*Fachabitur*) in business studies. She had already been offered a place at a full-time school. However, when she received the acceptance for the training place she went for it, but for her, the apprenticeship was a stepping stone, and she was clear from the beginning that she wanted to do something else afterwards. The options Claudia was considering included progression within the company to managerial level, or taking her Abitur and studying for an MBA.

Of particular interest was the way in which she co-constructed the workplace environment and the role of retail assistant, which she interpreted very differently to Leena. Claudia worked in the ladies' knitwear department, together with an older head assistant and two senior assistants. The day of the observation was busy, and we were restocking the display area with the winter collection. It was heavy and rather menial work. However, she insisted she liked it, particularly the varied nature of the work, comparing it with the much greater division of labour in another large store.

Her instrumental approach to the apprenticeship was evident in her interpretation of the role of retail assistant. Where Leena was working on her own initiative, Claudia always awaited the head assistant's instructions, although she insisted she could bring in her own ideas. Moreover she also did not relish the customer consultation in terms of advising them what to wear. The information she related to customers was always brief and pragmatic, concerning, for example, where to find certain products. While she performed basic aspects of the role (and did well at college), which made her a docile and well regarded apprentice in the eyes of her employer, the act of retailing played only a partial role in her formation of identity.

In contrast to school, Claudia enjoyed college where she was part of the pilot project of self-directed learning. She felt she benefited from this approach as she had to work out the knowledge for herself, within the context of authentic situations.

> At intermediate school we covered everything that was in the book ... and now in the [self-directed] class we [the students] make the lesson.

The apprenticeship was an important part of her transition to adulthood, introducing her to the world of work and contributing to the development of her personality. Like Leena, she explained that through the requirement of doing frequent presentations in front of the class, she had become much more confident with people.

Anita

Anita is of Indian origin and was brought up in an East London borough with a large ethnic minority population from the Indian subcontinent. While her immediate family live on modest means by UK standards (her mother is a retail assistant at another supermarket, her father was a construction worker), they have a large property in India and Anita had been spending time there every year since she was little. They are part of a large and tightly-knit family network, locally. Several of Anita's aunts and uncles live close by, while others live in their home community in India and in the US.

Anita went to an all-girls' comprehensive school. Here, she was for the most part unhappy, because her own emerging learner identity was at odds with that of her classmates. She felt that most of her peers were interested in things outside school, notably boys, and were disruptive during class. She did not seem to have sought the other girls' recognition, indicating that she felt secure in her learner identity, which was shaped by being brought up in a family of small business owners. Her exposure to this (by visiting and watching her relatives) offered her a variety of role models and perspectives, which were major motivating factors in her learning career. Similar to Claudia, as an only child, she received a lot of support from her family. They would arrange for her to travel, and facilitate and encourage experiences in different business environments.

While still at school, there were several experiences of informal learning which provided Anita with positive experiences and future perspectives. From a young age she was encouraged to experiment with make-up and from the age of seventeen she started helping out in her aunt's beauty salon, where she was given her own stand to practise and experiment with different designs. She developed considerable expertise which was drawn upon by her family as she started doing family members' make-up. Since working in her aunt's salon, becoming a make-up artist had always been an option.

At fifteen, she started helping out in the office of her uncle's local building firm. A year later, just before her GCSEs, she worked in another uncle's travel agency in San Francisco, an experience which motivated her to do Business Studies in a Sixth Form College, and she embarked on a three-year course, where she thrived. She was highly motivated through her recent experience. Her knowledge and motivation was recognised by the teachers and she was able to build on and confirm her learner identity.

My teachers, er, they used to, erm, ask me if I could help them and people used to come up to me and ask me for help, and ... and teachers always used to say to my mum, oh she's really good, she's like- she's like a teacher herself teaching them and helping students.

On completion of the course, despite having considered going to university, Anita decided against it, as she wanted a 'break' from studying, despite her parents' reassurances that she did not have to work and could go to university. Instead, she worked for almost two years as a membership advisor at a leisure centre. In the end, the routine nature of the work and lack of progression opportunities caused her to leave. With the money she had been able to save she went on to spend the summer travelling to India and America.

It is striking that Anita, like Claudia, at no point seemed worried about her learning career. This meant that she was able to take risks and experiment with different options as she perceived them, reminiscent of 'choice biographies' as described by Wyn and Dwyer (1999).

On her return from travelling, aged twenty-one, she decided, apparently on the 'spur of the minute', to enrol on a beauty therapy course at her local college. She enjoyed the course content, if not the learning culture, which she perceived as too lax, and again she was unable to identify with her classmates who to her did not seem to be interested in learning. She had completed the Level 2 course and was starting Level 3, when, tragically, her father died of Legionnaire's disease. For Anita's learning career it meant that she had to give up her course—and her dream of becoming a make-up artist—as she had to get a job to support her mother.

She started working at the checkout at the local Taurus store. With her background in business studies, her managers were quick to spot her potential and after six months, she was employed in administrative positions, including HR and the cash office. Her experience at Taurus served to consolidate her 'business' learning career as she received confirmation from managers, whom she perceived as 'fighting over' her. When she was approached by the manager regarding doing an apprenticeship she accepted as she saw it as a 'stepping stone' on the managerial ladder.

During the interview, Anita was very positive about Taurus, as an opportunity to learn new things. The apprenticeship had a particular meaning in the context of her previous experience. She enjoyed being able to put into practice what she had learnt at the sixth form college.

Her responsibilities and abilities far exceeded the requirements of the apprenticeship. She was highly motivated as she could relate the knowledge directly to her work and to her existing knowledge of business studies. She was able to pursue learning opportunities to a greater extent, confident that she would use the knowledge, if not in her current job, then in the future.

> I'm learning some things which I didn't know before, while I was, you know, actually doing my course … being outside it and writing about it and researching on the internet is completely different than actually being in there and watching the procedures and how they do it.

Looking to the future, Anita was planning to get on to Taurus' internal training programme and become a manager. However, she insisted she still had two options.

> I do enjoy make-up more than this but … I've left myself two options, business and beauty. But … I think I'll be going towards the business side of things.

Summary of Pair Four

Like Claudia, past experiences of being able to succeed with relative ease in learning activities and being able to count on her parents' support were important biographical resources for Anita. In addition, the experiences in her family's various businesses provided a wealth of opportunities and what Alheit (2002) refers to as 'unlived potential', which she would be able to draw on at later stages in her life. Both young women seem to have always been certain of 'becoming somebody' (Ball, Maguire and Macrae, 2000a). Importantly, in Anita's case, her experiences in a family of business owners who valued highly the different trades may explain why she, in contrast to other English apprentices, always saw vocational education and apprenticeship, including in retail, as positive options, not drawing a sharp distinction between vocational and higher education. Thus, for both Claudia and Anita, the horizon for action always included both. On the other hand, neither of the girls depended on the apprenticeship to develop a sense of purpose. This was part of a broader learning career and an already secure learner identity.

Chapter 7

The learner biographies of motor vehicle maintenance apprentices in England and Germany

Introduction

In this chapter I will present the motor vehicle maintenance apprentices. The comparative analysis and pairing of cases was conducted as described at the beginning of Chapter 6. In what follows, I will discuss the main findings, while the paired cases will be presented in a further section.

The motor vehicle maintenance apprentices in England and Germany: secure identities through practical know-how

Table 7.1 lists the apprentices in the two countries.

Table 7.1 The motor vehicle maintenance apprentices

Germany	England
Erika (18)	Lisa (17)
Daniel (17)	Ollie (17)
Aazim (19)	Nathan (20)
Stefan (18)	Alex (18)

As with the retail apprentices, I have mapped the dominant themes identified across the cases, as shown in Table 7.2. What is most striking is the homogeneity across the German and English apprentices. Not only was the social identity of motor vehicle maintenance critical in the young people's construction of identity and school-to-work transition, for all of them this identity centred first and foremost on the practical know-how associated with car mechanics. Both the English and the German apprentices said they preferred experiential and workplace learning.

All eight apprentices had developed an informal learning career based on an interest in cars in the context of problematic school careers during which they had come to reject a particular style of directive, academic learning. The analysis of the young people's biographies also shows that they were not passively socialised into taking up the occupation. They acted upon and developed learning dispositions based on their experiences of formal and informal learning. They gained self-confidence through their informal careers and their emerging identities enabled them to actively and reflexively shape and negotiate their learning careers. In all

Table 7.2: Analysis of Motor Vehicle Maintenance Apprentices: Common Themes (German and English apprentices)

	Erika	Stefan	Daniel	Aazim	Lisa	Ollie	Alex	Nathan
Means of identification through practical know-how	High	High	High	High	High	High	High	High
MV as practical trade or training occupation	Training occupation	Training occupation	Training occupation	Training occupation	Practical trade	Practical trade	Practical trade	Training occupation
Learner or worker	Learner	Learner	Learner	Learner	Learner	Worker	Worker	Learner
Secure identity	Secure	Secure	Secure	Fragile	Secure	Secure	Secure	Secure
Institutional guidance during transition	Good	Good	Good	Good	Poor	Poor	Poor	Poor
Transition	Smooth	Smooth	Smooth	Relatively smooth	Relatively smooth	Relatively smooth	Difficult	Difficult
Family support	v. high	High	High	Low	High	Low	High	v. high
School experience	Positive	Neg. then pos	Negative	Negative	Negative	Negative	Mixed	Pos. then neg.
Preference for practical learning	Yes	Yes	Yes	Yes	Yes	Yes	Yes	Yes
Long-standing passion for cars	Yes	Yes	Yes	Yes	No	Yes	Yes	Yes
Strong identity through informal learning	Yes	Yes	Yes	Yes	Yes	Yes	Yes	Yes
Apprenticeship as positive choice	Yes	Yes	Yes	Yes	Yes	Yes	Yes	Yes

	Erika	Stefan	Daniel	Aazim	Lisa	Ollie	Alex	Nathan
Meaning of apprenticeship	Valued in its own right	Valued in its own right	Valued in its own right	Valued in its own right	Instrumental	Instrumental	Instrumental	Valued in its own right
Learning sites confirm pos. identity	Yes	Yes	Yes	Yes	Yes	Yes	Yes	Yes
Value attached to college	High	High	High	High	Low	Low	Low	Moderate
Actively negotiates identity	Yes	Yes	Yes	Yes	Yes	Yes	Yes	Yes

cases therefore, motor vehicle maintenance was a positive choice, based on the young people's passion for cars and a preference for experiential learning.

A key difference between the two groups is that, although both apprenticeships constitute vocational education programmes, the German apprentices valued the practical know-how as embedded in a comprehensive and highly reputable training occupation, based on the integration of theory and practice, while in England, the young people saw the apprenticeship primarily as a way into the trade of motor vehicle maintenance, where the college was perceived as adding little to their (practical) knowledge. Thus, the German apprentices valued the apprenticeship in its own right, whereas their English counterparts focused largely on the occupation as a practical trade. The contrasting contexts within which transitions took place were powerfully illustrated by the nature of the school-to-work transitions. Whereas in Germany, the young people's choice of doing an apprenticeship was facilitated by the vocational education system as a regulated and well-established institution, in England, the low status of vocational education and the lack of guidance resulted in more problematic transitions. From the perspective of the young people, they differed in terms of the meanings they afforded the apprenticeships. Broadly following previous commentators (Evans and Heinz, 1991; Ryan, 1999), we can distinguish between 'apprentice as learner' and 'apprentice as worker'. The German apprentices valued the institution of apprenticeship which posits them as learners, whereas in England, three of the young people constructed themselves as workers, keen to work in the trade as equals to the other mechanics in the workplace. Whether the apprentices see motor vehicle maintenance apprenticeships as a valued training occupation or a way into a trade and whether they are constructed as learners or workers emerged as the most useful analytical categories. I have mapped the apprentices according to these categories, as shown in Table 7.3.

Table 7.3 Value of motor vehicle maintenance as a practical trade/ a training occupation by apprentice 'as worker' or 'as learner'

Identification as apprentice	Value of Motor Vehicle Maintenance as a practical trade	Value of Motor Vehicle Maintenance as a training occupation
Apprentice as worker	Alex Ollie	
Apprentice as learner	Lisa (reluctant)	Nathan Erika Stefan Daniel Aazim

While this to some extent confirms previous studies (for example, Evans and Heinz, 1994a), I want to focus on the ways in which these identities are discursively constructed and thereby challenge common stereotypes, particularly of English vocational education students. Thus, for example, the English apprentices are not naturally 'anti-theory', but are constituted as such through the prevailing social discourses. Young people perform social identities as they strive to be socially recognised. In important ways, the different identities reflect the contrasting vocational education contexts, within which they are constructed.

While Butler's theory of performativity (1990) will become useful in this regard, my emphasis will be not so much on young people performing identities but on exploring why they draw on certain discourses and not on others, and on how they integrate different past experiences to make sense of the present.

In Chapter 5, we saw the power of social norms, which was demonstrated most clearly in the English college classroom, which served as a vehicle for the young people to confirm their practical learner identities through an open rejection of learning, similar to Willis' (1977) 'lads' or Bates and Riseborough's (1993a, b) FE students. In doing so, they drew on the English vocational education discourse which is based on a dichotomous relationship between academic and vocational learning, between theory and practice. This identity (and the rejection of theory) is reinforced by the structure and content of the apprenticeship which emphasises procedural knowledge. It is telling that all English apprentices perceived theory as knowledge 'how to', which, perhaps unsurprisingly, they felt they could learn more adequately in the workplace.

Many of the young people in England perform identities which centre on practical work, eschewing theoretical knowledge. However, the observations and interviews revealed a highly differentiated picture, calling into question the findings of previous studies which so often present vocational education students as a homogenous group with a collective identity. Clearly, a multiplicity of identities co-existed as young people interpreted learning opportunities according to their particular biographical experiences and social backgrounds. The interviews in particular enabled me to explore the meaning of apprenticeship to individual apprentices. Even where young people outwardly displayed an identity in conformance with the dominant classroom culture, their learner identities were much more complex, based, for example, not on a rejection of classroom learning *per se*, but of a particular style of academic learning. Like their German counterparts, they disliked conventional directive approaches based on a passive intake of knowledge and preferred interactive and experiential learning.

The biographical interviews allowed me to explore the ways in which certain learning dispositions were formed over time, in specific experiences of learning, how they were interpreted and actively negotiated by young people as they moved through different life stages and social contexts, and how they interacted with identities of class, gender, and ethnicity. The question is therefore not so much that they are performing identities, but which ones, how and why.

Three of the English apprentices identified through the social identity of the practical trade, perceiving themselves as workers. This was the case for Alex and Ollie, who both worked in small garages with a high degree of autonomy. For Lisa, who aspired to the identity of worker, her positioning within the garage as learner produced conflict. All three dismissed the learning of theory and took an instrumental approach to the apprenticeship—a qualification they needed to work in the sector. Nathan, on the other hand, is the exception amongst the English apprentices. Coming from a different cultural background to his peers and with a more varied range of experiences, including that of a successful academic learner, he did not perform the identity of worker in a trade by drawing on the dominant social identity, but combined his interest in science with his preference for experiential learning and constructed himself as a learner. However, all of the apprentices had complex identities, which did not rest on a rejection of all learning. Indeed, they valued elements of college learning.

All German apprentices constructed themselves as learners. While they identified through the practical know-how, this was based on the integration of theory and practice. Thus, they accepted and valued college which facilitated this integration (most notably through the alternance of classroom and workshop learning). For Stefan and Daniel, the apprenticeship also opened up perspectives which included study in higher education.

All but one of the young people developed secure identities through the apprenticeship and in particular, the practical know-how of motor mechanics, something which, particularly in English academic discourse, is so often regarded as inferior to academic ability and on the basis of which apprentices are described as 'second-chance' learners. It is clear that all apprentices in this study made a positive choice to become motor mechanics, based on a practical expertise as an invaluable skill in its own right.

Presentation of the cases

Pair One:
Stefan and Alex: 'apprentice as worker' and 'apprentice as learner'

Stefan

Stefan grew up in a small provincial town in Western Germany. His parents split up when he was two years old. His mother worked as a retail assistant. At primary school, Stefan was a quiet and shy pupil who was bullied because of his tall height. He was a good student and was transferred to grammar school (he passionately told of his fascination with the natural sciences from a young age). However, he disliked the teaching and learning approach and his performance started to dip. His 'hate subject' was Latin, which for him epitomised the way he did not want to learn: rote learning of knowledge which he saw as irrelevant.

While Stefan seemed unable to develop a sense of purpose at grammar school, an alternative learning career gradually developed outside school based on his interest in cars. He was already passionate about motorsport, an interest which had been nurtured first by his grandfather, who took him on rides on his quadbike and later his stepfather with whom he had been to watch Formula One races at the Nurburgring. At age eleven, he was given a cross-country motorbike. At fourteen, he started socialising with a group of boys, who were into tuning scooters and later cars and who initiated him into the practice. This youth culture of young guys tuning engines and the thrill of doing something illegal made a big impression on him. In the context of his declining school performance, it provided an alternative means for identity construction.

> I got into fixing cars ... a good friend of mine took me with him ... we went there on our bikes ... I was sitting there by the scooter watching and I went 'great!', he got on the scooter and I saw that it was faster than before, wow! the fascination of it.

Based on his developing sense of purpose and attracted by the occupation, during eighth grade he vowed to leave school to do an apprenticeship in car mechatronics. This decision was aided by a serendipitous event, when, during Year 9, the family moved to another town which required him to change schools, and he insisted on transferring to intermediate school. Crucially, this change enabled him to practise biographicity and shape his own learning career, and to actively consolidate his formal and informal careers, as he found the curriculum and the teaching and learning approach more suited to his interests and learning preferences. He chose more vocational subjects, such as technical science, which included learning about automotive technology. He enjoyed the project-based teaching and learning such as constructing a hot air balloon. From a current perspective he describes the move to intermediate school as 'the best thing that could have happened to me' as he was able to take control of his own learning ('now I was able to finally make a difference').

The favourable learning environment enabled him to make a reality of his plans and enabled a smooth transition. From ninth grade, the need to choose an occupation and to do a placement further focused his interest. After a three-week placement with his current employer, he applied for an apprenticeship (one of only two applications!) and after a three-day trial was offered the place. His initial experience in the workplace and the expansive learning environment chimed with his natural curiosity and his interest in sciences and encouraged him to seek out opportunities for progression even during the placement.

> The placement was great … I was completely fascinated because basically that was completely new to me, and I've got this curiosity always wanting to discover something new and all that … and the many doors this apprenticeship will open, how many routes one can take … I talked to the *Meister* about the opportunities available.

The recognition he received in the garage further strengthened his confidence and learner identity. Because of his good school leaving certificate, he was one of three apprentices who was sponsored by a major car manufacturer to go on regular training courses. Similarly, a learning culture in which apprentices are encouraged to learn from each other positioned him in an authoritative position, assisting other apprentices. Nevertheless, Stefan performs the recognised identity of apprentice as learner in a strictly hierarchical organisation, where apprentices are allocated to senior mechanics, assisting them and involving a great deal of menial tasks on a daily basis, including cleaning and making coffee for 'his' senior mechanic. However, Stefan perceives that compared to other apprentices he enjoys an unusual degree of autonomy, as he is occasionally entrusted with more challenging tasks, further endorsing his skills.

Some aren't allowed to do it even in their second or third year … but that's what I liked that basically right from the start that they saw that I can do it … and that I was allowed to work on my own right from the start.

Reflecting his preference for experiential learning, Stefan is in no doubt that he prefers learning in the workplace to that in college.

Because it is more about practical work … it's also good to do the theory and all that but I've always preferred the practical work … and it's really through practice basically that I learn … the theory basically underpins it … in the workplace I learn more than in college but here [in college] it basically becomes clearer.

However, as evident from this quote, it also clear that he values the learning of theory and is keen to get a thorough understanding of the technology ('getting to the bottom of things'). Unlike the English apprentices, his understanding of learning is not based on a theory-practice dichotomy, but on their integration. What he values most at college is the alternation of classroom and workshop. The occupation of mechatronic represents an exciting challenge to him and asked what he expected from the apprenticeship he replied.

That I will be able to expand my knowledge and practical know-how further. With cars you basically never finish learning, and that's what I found so fascinating, because … some occupations, for example tiler or or err painter, they deal the whole day with paint or with tiles but in the motor vehicle sector, cars change all the time … it evolves all the time, you never finish learning.

Theoretical knowledge is important to him as an accepted and recognised part of the apprenticeship but also in view of his long-term perspective: becoming an engineer with a major German car manufacturer. At college, Stefan is a model student who Mr. Christen, the main tutor, finds he has to slow down to let other pupils have a chance to participate. Mr. Christen is also somewhat of a role model to Stefan in view of his long-term perspective and he respects his expertise.

Yes, he is a very strict tutor, but he can explain things very well, and he draws perfectly I find, he really can draw. The stuff that he draws, I never cease to be surprised, and that I think is really good, cos later engineering also goes in that direction of drawing and all that, and that I find really fascinating. That's superb in his class.

The detail with which Stefan has planned his professional future is striking. On completing the apprenticeship he will join the professional army for eight years to train as a sniper—he already had the contract at the time of the follow-up interview! While in the army, he will obtain his *Fachabitur* (A-level qualification that gives access to certain professional courses in higher education) to study automotive engineering.

Alex

Alex's story is similar to Stefan's. It illustrates the centrality of the social identity of the trade to his transition to adulthood. While he tells of a difficult transition with false starts and setbacks, he has been able to consolidate his identity as a practical learner and to overcome his shyness.

> Me personally it's been quite good where I work now because I deal with a lot more customers and eh … I was quite shy, didn't really like to talk to new people, but I suppose when you get chucked in the deep end you gotta learn how to do it and it's been good, so, it's one thing that I take out of it it's been good for me, yeah, yeah, just carry on doing it.

Alex was brought up in a working class family in rural areas in the South-West and South-East of England. Similarly to Stefan, at comprehensive school, he resisted what he described as the passive intake of knowledge. He described himself as not good at written work and 'a lot better with my hands'. But contrary to common assumptions about English vocational education students, this did not reflect a rejection of learning *per se*, and he enjoyed the interactive teaching and learning arrangement of one his teachers.

> There is Mr. Green who would take his own knowledge of history and tell us, whereas the other one would read it out of a book, it is just boring. I don't want to learn like that, [with Mr. Green] no-one was stupid in that class, it was like everyone had their own kind of view on things … you learnt more from talking about something instead of just reading something in a book and copying it out.

Like Stefan, his experience outside school gave him an alternative to classroom learning. His grandfather was a mechanic and his passion for cars has been a key influence in Alex's life. From the age of five, Alex helped him working on cars. Based on this interest, at the age of fourteen he took a job as a Saturday boy at a local garage. Here he was put off by the menial work he was asked to do, an experience which might have caused him initially not to pursue car mechanics as a future career. By the final year at school he did not consider it an option. He had developed an alternative learning career playing guitar in a band and he and his friend enrolled on a music course at the local college, which, however, he found too demanding, and he dropped out after one year.

Here lies one of the key differences between Stefan and Alex. While for Stefan the choice of occupation was encouraged and facilitated through the institutional system, this was not the case for Alex who experienced a difficult transition. Staying on after GCSEs had not been an issue because, based on his learning experience, Alex had decided that 'that wasn't for me'. Regardless of his negative experience in the garage, there was no guidance for students who wanted to leave school at sixteen, such as information on apprenticeships. This lack of guidance was reflected in his repeated assertion that 'it's hard when you leave school, you don't really know what to do'.

It was his stepfather, also a mechanic, who persuaded him to do an apprenticeship at a garage. Again, this was far from a smooth process. Before finding his current workplace he worked in two garages with bosses unsympathetic to apprentices' learning and who instead expected them to be fully-fledged workers, reflecting the English 'apprentice as worker' discourse. Alex felt that whatever confidence he had was eroded by bosses who put him down in front of other people for making mistakes.

The learning environment in his current garage caused his confidence to increase significantly. As described in Chapter 5, it is a tiny ramshackle place, run by the owner, another mechanic and Alex as apprentice. His boss invests a great deal of trust in him and he enjoys a high level of responsibility and autonomy. He often stands in for the owner, dealing with the whole process from taking on work, carrying it out and handing it over, including the administration of bookings and billings. There is no clear division of labour. Menial tasks such as clearing up are done by a boy on work experience. Thus, in contrast to Stefan, Alex sees himself as a 'worker', stressing equality in status with the other mechanics. This experience of success has led him to grow in confidence.

I suppose it gives you a bit of a boost, gives you a bit of a high when you work something out yourself ... like when you put a car back together, and you turn the key and it starts up, it's a good feeling.

Like Stefan, for Alex, the apprenticeship is about learning by doing and about knowing how to do something. This is what he perceives himself as being good at ('I remember stuff cos I've done it instead of writing it down'). However, in contrast to Stefan, he attaches little value to college, which he describes as more of a break from work and an opportunity to meet with his mates. Indeed, as we saw in Chapter 5, college may serve as confirmation of identity as a practical learner, which is constructed by the group in direct opposition to theory. Thus, he values Steve's practical experience over Alan's theoretical expertise.

I think he owned his own garage at one point, yeah he is good, it's all about past experiences ... I much rather go on someone's past experiences than reading the book.

However, it appears that his distrust of books is because of his understanding of 'theory' as procedural knowledge rather than underlying theory (such as physics) and he insists that he learns this knowledge better in the workplace.

... and like a lot of these books as well, these manuals that I got, like they've got they say 'twenty minutes doing this' and that's with a brand-new car, but nothing is like that. You haven't got this brand-new car coming to you, you got a car that's got all sorts of things wrong with it, like you got to, like get round that problem just to solve that problem ... that's why I don't like reading the manuals, and I like to work it out and get moving myself.

It is perhaps not surprising that for Alex the value of his apprenticeship seems to be largely instrumental. Asked what he hoped to get out of the apprenticeship, he replied.

A bit more experience, and my certificates I guess. You need them these days, whereas in the olden days you didn't really need them, if you can show someone that you do it, but now nobody gives you the chance to show that anymore without the certificates.

It is interesting to which extent Alex draws on the dominant discourse of vocational education learners as rejecting classroom learning. He has negotiated a learner identity as a practical learner who is not good at written work and who distrusts books. However, Alex does not reject learning or reading books *per se*. He has a wide range of interests and apart from his passions for cars and music he has a keen interest in Latin America, stemming from a family holiday in Mexico. He has accumulated a large collection of travel books and spends a great deal of his spare time reading, illustrating once again that learner identities may be constituted in different or even contrasting ways in the context of different life domains and discourses.

Summary of Pair One:
Based on their experience of school, both young men felt that academic learning was not for them as they were able to construct alternative identities through informal learning. Through this experience, they developed biographicity and directed their learning careers reflexively. For both, the apprenticeship was central to their construction of identity and to transition to adulthood more broadly as it served to guide their decision-making and build up their confidence. However, within the context of German vocational education, for Stefan this meant combining his interest in science with his preference for experiential learning and the integration of theory and practice. By contrast, Alex, drawing on the discourse of the academic-vocational dichotomy, constructs his identity through motor vehicle maintenance as a predominantly practical trade.

Pair Two:
Aazim and Ollie: Disadvantaged childhoods

Aazim
Aazim was born in Germany to Lebanese parents. He is the youngest of nine siblings. When he was two years old, his parents divorced and he had no contact with his mother until he was sixteen. His father remarried and Aazim has had a difficult relationship with his stepmother, whom he experienced as uncaring. He explained that he was raised largely by his seven-year older sister.

Aazim experienced difficulties at school which was in large part due to his poor German language skills (the family speak Arabic at home). However, he was also lagging behind in his mental and intellectual development, possibly because of the emotional upheaval experienced during his early life. He did not start primary school until he was seven. This 'lagging behind' and difficulties learning have shaped his learning career and is deeply ingrained in his learner identity. He did not pass second grade and had to repeat the year, which he put down to having nobody at home to revise with him. He started receiving extra tuition at school and his grades improved somewhat, at least temporarily. From a current perspective he recalled how for once he was not the 'dumbomb' of the class.

An informal learning career developed from the age of fifteen. His father had long owned car workshops in Lebanon, but it was only when Aazim's brother-in-law opened a garage in Germany that he developed an interest in becoming a mechanic. He started helping him out during holidays and at weekends and indicated that his brother-in-law was very supportive. Aazim was encouraged and the idea of becoming a mechanic formed. When having to do a placement in ninth grade, he took the initiative and arranged to work in a local garage.

At the same time, his performance at school deteriorated and in Year 9, his grades were so poor that his teachers recommended him for a one-year BUS (*Beruf und Schule*) class, a scheme specifically designed for disadvantaged youth to facilitate their school-to-work transition. It involves the close integration of school and work. The tutor arranged a work placement in a car dealership. Aazim certainly preferred the year to the conventional school.

> It was rather better because you're interested in the placement, and then you think well, less school and all that. You looked forward to having to go to school only three days a week and the other two days you learnt something perhaps for the future.

At the end of the placement, he was offered an apprenticeship as car services mechanic. Thus, with considerable institutional support Aazim was able to enter the dual system. However, labelled 'disadvantaged' and in need of support, his learner identity remains fragile. This is most clearly manifested in him being on the two-year car services mechanic programme rather than the full three and a half year mechatronic apprenticeship. It positions him as lower in status *vis-à-vis* his fellow apprentices.

This positioning is reinforced both at work and at college. In the workplace Aazim is closely supervised, working to detailed instructions. In the period running up to his final exam, the *Meister* had arranged weekly sessions, in which his classmates Stefan and Daniel revised the theory with him, followed by a practical session led by a fourth year apprentice. At college, Mr. Christen was concerned about Aazim's performance and he received extra tuition twice a week. Unlike Stefan and Daniel, he struggles with Mr. Christen's directive approach.

> ... he talks and talks and sometimes I look at him and think we're at grammar school or something. It's too fast for me, I can't follow.

As his learner identity as a car mechanic remains fragile, he defines himself first and foremost through his football playing, which is the dominant theme in his initial narrative. Football has provided Aazim with a positive identity since childhood, contrasting with his experiences of formal learning. He started playing from a young age and at thirteen joined the local football club. It always took up a considerable part of his spare time, and he currently trains three times a week. At work, he joined the firm's football team, enjoying a high status amongst his colleagues as a good player. Perhaps most tellingly, during the workplace observation he approached me to make sure that I also noted down his football activity, which for him is a far more important aspect of his identity.

> Do you only write down what the apprentices do here ... or also what the apprentices do with the other mechanics, because I also play football.

At the time of the workplace observation, just before his final exams, it was clear that he would not be taken on by his employer and his future is uncertain. He would prefer to find employment in Germany. Failing this, he is considering going to Lebanon where he feels he would enjoy a high social status as someone who has trained in Germany. However, he is deeply ambiguous about his feelings of belonging, and moving there would present different challenges, not least the unstable political situation.

Ollie

Ollie similarly had a troublesome childhood growing up in a rural area in South-East England. He was shy, lacking in self esteem and had few friends. He explained that he was left alone a lot by his parents who were both working. His father, a policeman, did shift work.

There is a strong sense that Ollie felt rejected by his father, who he said he does not get on with, possibly because he was unable to meet his expectations, and his story is infused with wanting to gain the recognition of others. However, unlike Aazim, he has been able to develop a secure identity as an 'apprentice as worker' based on his practical know-how. He presented himself as an 'old hand' having worked as a mechanic for nearly five years and someone who is highly appreciated by his boss.

He was unhappy at the all-boys' secondary school, explaining that he 'just wanted to go home every day because I didn't really want to be here'. He felt unable to integrate socially in a school which he described as rough. Worst of all, a learning disability which was not diagnosed until he started college, meant he had poor reading and writing ability and was soon left behind, as teachers appeared to have made no effort to engage him ('I just sat in the back of the room just doing my own thing'). At the same time, he enjoyed art and craft subjects, such as metal and wood work, which gave him a sense of being good at something. He developed an alternative identity as a practical learner early on. Aged ten he started building walls in the garden with bricks left over from some earlier DIY work. The experience initially left him wanting to become a builder.

As he grew older, Ollie became very close to his brother who started an apprenticeship as a car mechanic when Ollie was thirteen. Ollie's interest in cars was soon kindled when his brother invited him to work with him, initially on their father's car. A year later, when Ollie had to organise a week's work experience as part of school, it was his brother who encouraged him to come to his garage.

This was a critical experience and a turning point in Ollie's life. It provided an alternative identity in sharp contrast to that offered by school, and Ollie started working there all the hours he could spare. The quote below reflects the pride that he felt about having a paid job.

> All my mates was like, oh why don't you come down the beach with us, so … we are all going to go down there … and I was just like, nah, I got work, mate … I got a job, ain't I … and he was like, but … you're- you can't have, and I was like, yeah I work with my brother.

Based on his practical expertise (and despite poor grades in English and maths) Ollie's school-to-work transition was relatively smooth. During his last year at school, after he had worked at the garage for two years, the owner offered him a place as an apprentice. However, he was expected to work with an undue level of autonomy, which led to mistakes and tension between him and the owner. When the working relationship became increasingly strained, his college found him his current workplace. Here the learning culture is highly supportive, confirming Ollie's practical ability. Ollie highlighted the fact that the owner was not interested in his GCSEs but 'in what I can actually do'.

Ollie still works with a high level of autonomy as the only apprentice in a small garage with two other mechanics, but he is always able to ask the senior mechanics for advice. There is no hierarchical division of labour, and, for example, everybody is expected to clear up after himself. During the observation, I found it a very friendly place, and people treated each other with a lot of respect. It seemed a relationship of equals. Thus supported, Ollie considerably gained in confidence (the owner told me that 'he has really been coming on' over the past six months). Ollie is highly motivated to prove himself. He talked a lot about the importance of gaining his employer's trust and respect, showing that he wants to be treated like a full member of the team.

> I was always there at half-seven on the dot ... and he was like, what are you doing here so early and I was like, well, that's what time you open, 'en't you? And he's like, yeah, but you only- you don't have to get here till like nine ... and I was like, no, I'd rather get here early than late ... and then like from then there's ... realised that I was actually interested in doing the trade and not just tagging along for it ... and like, so ... they trusted me more with like more jobs and that.

In the light of his school experience, it is unsurprising that he found the college environment daunting. His learning disability was picked up following the initial key skills test and he receives support during classes. However, he still finds the theory element challenging and is deeply suspicious of it. Like Alex, he understands theory as procedural knowledge and insists that one cannot learn to be a mechanic from a book.

> The practice, you can't beat it because, like, if you practice something already then you can know how to do it already instead of like the theory. It just, like, shows you a couple of pictures and, like, if someone gives it to you you're like, okay, I don't have a clue what to do, and it might be that if you do it yourself you're just like, why, you've got to figure it out instead of just, like, looking in the book.

Nevertheless, Ollie is by no means 'anti-learning'. He is one of few people regularly participating in class and he explained that he values the opportunity to exchange ideas with classmates about how to approach problems in the workplace. His story compellingly illustrates the way in which motor vehicle maintenance as a trade has served to build his confidence and self-esteem, particularly with members in his own social network of family and friends. Through his private work, he very visibly is recognised as someone 'who is good at something'.

> I fix my mates' cars at weekends and do a lot of private work … which is good money (laughs) … yeah … and, like, it's always good to have someone in the family that's a mechanic because you can get a lot of work out of it.

Summary of Pair Two

Both Aazim and Ollie were constructed as 'failing' in school, but were able to negotiate alternative identities through informal learning. However, Aazim's identity remains fragile as it was not confirmed in the learning sites of Germany's high-status but stratifying dual system of apprenticeship which still constitutes him as disadvantaged. This contrasts with Ollie's experience, who, despite, his learning disability, has been able to negotiate his learner identity as 'apprentice as worker' in the context of English vocational education, where the occupation of motor vehicle maintenance is constructed as predominantly practical.

Pair Three:
Daniel and Nathan: Apprentices as learners

Daniel

Daniel grew up in a working class family in a provincial town in Western Germany. He did not like school. Significantly, at primary school he felt that he was unfairly treated by his main teacher, who always gave him poor marks. With his confidence dashed and believing that he was unable to make a difference he withdrew and stopped trying altogether.

> I was always so bad, at primary school … and errm then we always sat these tests and yeah and then she always assessed them and she always

gave me a six, time and again always a six, I don't know why … and in fourth grade I no longer even tried, I really could not be bothered any more.

It seems that Daniel's primary school experience had a lasting impact on much of his remaining school career. He continued to lack motivation and from a current perspective evaluated that 'school isn't for him'. While his performance improved intermittently, in seventh grade, when he was thirteen, it dropped again when his parents broke up and his father left the family home. This was a traumatic experience and he still remembers worrying he would never see him again. He recalled how he managed to 'get by' with mainly fours, narrowly avoiding having to repeat a year.

Daniel countered his largely negative school experience with a long and continuous informal learning career fuelled by his interest in cars. This started with his collection of toy cars, something perhaps not unusual for a young boy. He developed a keen interest in automotive technology. At the age of twelve he started reading up on the latest technology in car magazines and on the internet. He shared and cultivated this interest with his friend whose mechanic father encouraged the boys to watch him repair cars. His interest was supported by his parents, who suggested to him to become a car mechanic.

In grade nine, faced with the need to find a work placement and to choose an occupation, he was able to draw on his earlier experience and interest in cars to help him in his decision. Thus, as with Stefan, his transition was facilitated by the standardised vocational education system.

Aided by his parents, he organised a placement with his current employer. It was a positive experience and the garage accepted him for another placement later that year. This was the decisive turning point in his learning career and he started practising biographicity: taking control of his own learning. Motivated by his goal of becoming a car mechatronic, he made an effort during the final year at school to get a good leaving certificate, which he succeeded in doing. This is part of his success story in the initial narrative. The fact that he was able to improve his grades in the final year indicates that underlying his previous poor performance was a lack of motivation rather than lack of ability. It also points to the power of the occupation as a motivating force.

During the final year Daniel applied to firms in the area and was successful getting a place with his current employer. He flourished during the apprenticeship. He said he was excited to see in practice what he had read about in magazines. For the first time in his life he was able to do hands-on work and the learning culture confirmed his emerging identity as a practical learner. He explained that he was entrusted with working on cars by himself, although during the observation it appeared that these are relatively minor tasks, common for first year apprentices in Germany, such as servicing cars and changing tyres. His responsibilities also include clearing up and assisting senior mechanics. He clearly sees himself as a learner, valuing the time allocated to learning in the workplace, for example by using the specially designated car. His aim eventually to be able to work 'independently' must be seen as his quest for a sense of purpose, of being good at something, which was denied him in academic study. His own perception of having difficulty learning means that he still is apprehensive. Asked about his expectations regarding the apprenticeship he said,

> ... that everything will be explained that I have read, that it will be explained to me more thoroughly, that I will be able to work independently ... yeah and that I will find it easy to learn. Do you know what I mean, that I won't have the same problems learning cos then I would quit if I found it hard.

Not surprisingly, Daniel prefers learning in the workplace.

> I prefer being here [at work] cos at college everything is so dry ... that's not for me. I learn better when I can see it and do it, then I learn much better than when I get told everything theoretically, cos then I cannot imagine it, cos when I do it in practice then I can see it much better and I can understand it much better.

Nevertheless, linking in with his interest in science and technology, he is keen to learn the theory which he feels is important to underpin the practice and to understand why things are done in a certain way. Like Stefan, his favourite tutor is Mr. Christen because he is 'good at explaining things'. Daniel is highly motivated which is reflected in his grades: he has mostly ones.

As with Alex and Stefan, the occupation and particularly the practical know-how of motor vehicle maintenance, have been central to Daniel's construction of identity and have served to guide his decision-making in the school-to-work transition and to consolidate his identity as a practical learner. As for Stefan, for Daniel, this centres on mechatronics as a comprehensive training occupation which he envisages will lead to higher education study. Encouraged by his positive experience, he has a clear idea of what he wants to do after the apprenticeship, which is to obtain his *Fachabitur* (vocational A-levels) in order to study mechanical engineering and become an engineer with a major German car manufacturer.

Nathan

While Nathan's identity also centres on practical know-how, he came to the apprenticeship with a perspective which distinguished him from his fellow English apprentices. Being slightly older than his fellow apprentices and with positive experiences as an academic learner at grammar school, for him the apprenticeship is a route that enables him to pursue his interest in science and his preference for practical activity. In this sense he values practical work without rejecting theory.

In the workplace, Nathan expresses that he sees himself as a 'learner' who is keen to learn from his senior colleagues, rather than a 'worker'. Also, having been brought up in a multi-cultural environment, he does not identify with British male working-class culture. Notably, in the classroom, he does not strive for acceptance by his classmates and hence does not have to renegotiate his identity, which is based on a broader experience, his relationship with his girlfriend of many years (a university student) and his former schoolmates. In many respects therefore, he subverts the identity of the English motor vehicle maintenance apprentice.

Nathan is of Chinese origin and was adopted by his English parents when he was six months old. With his father in the army and on frequent deployments around the world, Nathan had an unsettled upbringing. He went to primary school at a British army base in Belgium. When he was ten years old, the family returned to Britain, where, a year later, his parents divorced. Nathan went to live with his mother in the south of England. He did well at grammar school, where he took his GCSEs aged sixteen. Learning came easily to him. His fascination with science and technology extended to life outside school and was actively encouraged by his parents, whose presents to him included science books and an interactive encyclopaedia. His interest in cars was fuelled from an early age by his father who routinely worked on cars at home.

Nevertheless, the transition to sixth form constituted a highly disruptive phase. Nathan increasingly clashed with his mother, and after his GCSEs, decided to move in with his father who lived in another county. Here he joined the sixth form at the local comprehensive but, after less than two months, had to move to yet another school when his father changed jobs. He had difficulty adapting to the new learning environment and an unfamiliar teaching style. In the end, he failed his AS levels.

Nathan insisted that, up until sixth form, he had never thought about what he wanted to do after school. Based on his school record, he and his parents had always assumed he would go to university. Suddenly, he found himself confronted with the need to make a decision regarding his future. Supported by his father, he explored the possibility of doing an apprenticeship as a car mechanic. However, his applications to private training providers were unsuccessful and left him disheartened. Within a year he had gone from successful GCSE student to being unemployed and he took up casual employment for the next few months.

Nathan's problematic transition again illustrates the paucity of information available on vocational pathways and apprenticeships, with young people having to rely instead on parental support. When his father went on another overseas deployment, Nathan moved back to his mother, who helped him enrol on a one-year full-time course in motorsport engineering (Level-2) at his current college and on completion he started an apprenticeship.

It is interesting how, in doing the apprenticeship, Nathan was able to draw on his informal learning career (his 'unlived potential') to present a continuous learner identity.

> Luckily I did- I have always had this interest, erm, in vehicles ... cars, aeroplanes, et cetera, et cetera. I- I'd always had a fascination for them because ... I've just always been quite a curious person ... I used to ask my dad about how things work and pull things apart when I was younger and put them back together again.

Failing his AS levels presented a turning point in Nathan's life, which for the first time in his life caused him to reflect on and actively shape his learning career and to question the value of university. The following passage illustrates the weight of normative expectations on young people. Faced with a major discontinuity, he was forced to renegotiate this pathway because of serendipitous life circumstances. However, crucially, he was able to present it as a positive choice, subverting normative expectations of going to university by calling himself 'fortunate' not to have done so. Tellingly, he refers to the apprenticeship as 'a way out of academia'.

> I didn't have a clue what I wanted to do as far as courses go but I knew that I wanted to get to university because I thought that's what I needed to do to get on in life. But as it turns out you don't have to obviously … and especially now this- er, as it turns out this country is now in recession, so, basically, going to university isn't really going to help that much because everyone is going to university … so in a way I'm quite fortunate I didn't go.

Nathan works for an independent garage, with four mechanics and two apprentices. The learning environment is highly supportive. While he carries out routine maintenance work on his own, senior mechanics are always available to help and give advice. Nathan is not worried about asking for help, which he frequently does, and it appears that, as with the German dealership, asking for help (and making mistakes) is an accepted part of apprentices' learning. Again as in the German dealership, the apprentices are encouraged to learn from and support each other and Nathan is not expected to carry out the more complex work of the senior mechanics. He appreciates the supportive learning environment which posits him as a learner rather than a worker.

> The work itself is very, sort of, involved and based around what I am able to do and what I am not able to do and if I ever get stuck I don't really feel … like it would be a problem to ask for help or anything because the people that I do work with are very friendly.

Nathan perceives college as 'quite boring', both because he knows much of the theory already and because it is largely procedural, which he finds he learns a lot better at work. However, he does not question the value of theory, which has always been of interest to him and he passed all his exams 'first time, in one go, in an hour' without revising. During the classroom observation he was the only student to take notes throughout and was regarded by the tutors as a model student. During the interview, he stressed the importance of taking notes so that he can refer back to them later.

I do take notes on things that I possibly don't understand very well
... what you learn at college ... is purely, er, theory based and the
understanding of how different components work, so I find it quite
helpful to make notes. I mean I notice quite a lot of people in my class
don't ... it's up to them ... it doesn't bother me.

It seems therefore that by subverting the identity based on a rejection of
theory (for example, by asserting the value of taking notes) Nathan is also able
to get more out of the theoretical element. In terms of his future career, he has
no definite long-term plans beyond completing the apprenticeship, although he
assumes he will progress in some way.

Thus, while his identity is based on technical know-how, his more varied
experience, including as a successful student at grammar school, means that
he does not have to 'compulsively cite' the normative identity of the apprentice
as worker, or indeed, that of the working class lad, an image from which he
distances himself. During his cosmopolitan upbringing he was exposed to
different cultures from an early age (he remembers that in Belgium he preferred
playing basketball with the American children rather than football with his
English classmates), and does not identify with English working class culture
and distances himself from his fellow students. He explained that he always
shunned the boisterousness of working class youth. Living further away has
enabled him to avoid socialising with his classmates.

I live further away so ... in that sense I, I quite like that because it means
I'm not forced to ... form friendships that ... perhaps ... would put me
off doing something or whatever ... because I'm not a very going out sort
of person ... I'm twenty years old and I don't even drink.

Summary of Pair Three

While both young men developed a keen interest in science and technology early
on, they rejected certain forms of conventional academic learning. Both value
the apprenticeship as a way of integrating their interest in science with practical
know-how. For Daniel, his learner identity based on the integration of theory
and practice was facilitated through the standardised German dual system and
he experienced a smooth transition. In contrast, for Nathan, because of the low
status of vocational education and the lack of guidance in England, this was a

much more difficult process. However, now in the apprenticeship, he is able to draw on his positive experience at grammar school and his interest in science, thus going beyond the 'common' social identity of motor vehicle maintenance in English vocational education.

Pair Four:
Erika and Lisa: Motor vehicle maintenance apprenticeships and tomboy identities

Erika
Erika grew up in a rural area in a working class family in Western Germany. Her father is a road builder and her mother works part-time in a supermarket. The most dominant theme in the narrative is Erika's construction of her tomboy identity, which she negotiated and confirmed through the social identity of the car mechatronics occupation. Typical for tomboy identities, it is constructed in relation to the polar opposites of hyper- (or girlie-girl) femininity and heterosexual masculinity (Renold, 2005; Paechter, 2010). In the initial narrative she explained that she does not conform to common gender stereotypes.

> I'm different I know (laughs). You know, I'm not your typical girl, you know, I don't need three hours to get ready.

It is striking that she describes her experience of intermediate school largely in terms of her social relationships with fellow classmates. It appears that, as she resisted the identity of 'girlie-girl' femininity in the classroom, she struggled to get accepted by her female peers. Her anxiety of being marginalised (Renold, 2005) still preoccupies her and was a major theme in the interview. She referred to what she perceived as the girls' obsession with fashion and staying slim.

> They start talking about 'Germany's Next Top Model', and 'oh my god' … 'how do I look, I'm too fat', you know … That's not my thing … I don't have a problem wearing men's trousers occasionally, you know, so, I'm more like … I don't care what they think of me, you know, and pink and that is not my colour, and I have absolutely no problem with … belching in class in front of everyone, you know …

Erika defines herself in direct opposition to the hyper-femininity, drawing on signifiers of masculinity. She referred to her close friendships with several of her male classmates and her affiliation with 'rockers' and their outfits and out-of-school activities as she became an 'honorary boy' (Renold, 2005: 48).

Her tomboy identity was encouraged in the parental home from a young age. Her relationship with her father is pivotal and it seems that in many ways she was raised as a boy. Practical skills were encouraged and rewarded in a household where DIY and self-help were central activities. When she was eight, her father showed her in great detail how to fix her bike until she 'got the hang of it'. At twelve, she helped him build a shed and soon afterwards she started to help him fix the many cars they always had in their courtyard.

Overall, Erika did well at intermediate school, but preferred more practical subjects, such as chemistry and IT. Remarkably, and unusually even in the German context, from the age of thirteen, she spent almost all of her holidays doing one- or two-week work placements, a total of ten! Her parents and particularly her father were instrumental in organising them, frequently drawing on local or family contacts.

Her father was adamant that his daughter should learn a manual craft. After her first placement as a hairdresser, he persuaded her to do something 'genuinely manual' and facilitated a placement as a tiler, which she found physically too demanding. The following year, after a placement at the local chemist, her father suggested she try working in a garage. Thus, aged fourteen, she undertook two two-week placements at a local garage, again arranged by her father. She enjoyed it, partly because she was able to bring in her experience of working on cars and proudly related that she was given a high level of responsibility early on.

It seems that this experience linked in with an emerging identity, which eventually led her to decide in favour of car mechatronics. In Years 9 and 10, she did further placements in garages, the final two with her current employer, in a small independent garage, who offered her work on Saturdays. She felt that she was given the opportunity to demonstrate her growing competence, and when she applied for a training place she was accepted.

The constant need to overcome gender stereotypes is another salient part of Erika's narrative. She had preferred to work in a larger dealership, but her many applications were turned down, which she attributes to employers preferring male apprentices. This is strongly reinforced by her father who puts a great of deal pressure on her, pointing out to her that as a girl she would have to do better than boys and reprimanding her for failing to get top marks. In the workplace, she finds some of the tasks physically challenging and frustrating. However, she is determined to work out techniques that allow her to accomplish the tasks, rather than applying physical force, and she resists calling for help straightaway (which she may perceive as a threat to her tomboy identity).

> Very quickly I tried to manage on my own, without needing help, you know, yes even now from time to time I go 'can you come and help?' ... But ... on the whole, you don't need much force I'd say, it really depends on the technique, you know, so for a big bolt I won't use a half inch or quarter inch spanner but the big torque wrench, you know, main thing is that it works.

In a garage with a hierarchical division of labour and where Erika is the only apprentice, much if not all of the menial work is left to her, something which she seems to fully accept. In this sense she is the typical (German) learner apprentice whose main tasks include assisting senior mechanics and menial work. On the day of the observation (a quiet day), she spent most of the time clearing out rubbish, washing cars and changing tyres. Under pressure to keep herself occupied, this is the work she resorts to. Nevertheless, the younger mechanics in particular are also a source of social support, and Erika socialises with them outside work.

Like all apprentices, Erika feels that she learns more in the workplace than at college. While college was about theory, this did not reflect reality in the workplace, which was mainly about practical tasks. However, while she does not value theory to the same extent as workplace learning, she accepts it as a vital part of the apprenticeship. Compared with school, she finds college much more demanding, insisting that it is vital to revise and do the homework as otherwise one would get a poor mark. It is not helped by the directive approach of the tutor and a climate where she does not feel she can ask questions. However, she is determined to get on top of the material. She has no concrete future plans apart from staying on at her current garage. Progressing to *Meister* or technician and even owning a garage all seem achievable options.

Lisa

Similar to Erika, Lisa's tomboydom seems based on her close relationship with her father. At the age of six her mother left the family to live with her new partner. Lisa lived with her father for a few months, before moving in with her mother and three-year older sister. She may have felt abandoned by her mother and came to identify with her father instead. Lisa and her father developed a close relationship and to this day regularly spend time together.

While Lisa has had no long-standing interest in cars, she presented herself as someone who always enjoyed practical activities, referring to creative and outdoor games as a child. This must be seen as an attempt to construct a continuous alternative learner identity against a negative school career. Her experience of secondary school in an all-girl comprehensive invoked in her a strong sense of failure, as someone who 'struggles' with academic learning. She constructs her identity in opposition to her older sister, who 'is the clever one of the family and I'm the one that goes out and gets dirty'. This sense was reinforced through her sister going to the grammar school next-door, making Lisa one of the 'rejects'.

> I went to … next to a grammar school … and we was like the rejects school … They was all like pushed, like, to get the best grades and that, but we- 'cos, like, everyone just got sent to my school if they didn't get into the grammar school, but we was all just like- I don't know, no-one bothered with us.

Lisa found it hard to learn at school. She hated 'being made to sit down all the time' and frequently came into conflict with teachers who she felt would 'give up' on her. While she resisted classroom learning, she identified with physical and practical activities and with signifiers of masculinity, notably football, which she has been playing regularly from the age of twelve. Her father accompanied her to matches, thereby endorsing his daughter's ability, and in this way may have reinforced this identification.

In terms of deciding what to do on finishing school, there were no obvious choices. Her one reference point was the garage next door, where in passing by she would have experienced some of the daily routine of working on cars. The image of car mechanics as a male-dominated trade may have appealed to her as it held the prospect of an alternative learner identity, one associated with practical activity and masculinity.

It is this prospect which motivated Lisa to take charge of her learning career in the absence of any institutional support. In the final year at school, while teachers stressed the importance of getting good grades to get into college, there was little or no support with the process. With the help of her mother, Lisa managed to get a Saturday job in a garage. This was crucial in confirming her identification, enabling her to delineate her identity from the other girls in the class, many of whom chose Hair and Beauty, which she dismissed as boring.

Lisa enjoyed working in the garage. Emboldened by the experience, she demonstrated remarkable agency in developing her new learning career, as the school still offered no support (she explains that teachers took no interest in her job in the garage). She passed her GCSE grades and was accepted by her garage as an apprentice. Becoming a mechanic was now within her horizon for action, offering a real prospect of being good at something and being recognised for it.

> I just like the satisfaction of knowing that I've helped someone with their car and I can always- once I've got this … like all the qualifications and the experience, I can always help someone if they need it and I can do people favours and that and it's just nice [yeah] to know that I've got that … I'm capable of being able to look after myself. That's what I like.

The apprenticeship has helped Lisa to consolidate what was a tentative identity as a practical person and thus to confirm her identity as a tomboy. For her, the college element 'puts a downer on it a bit', and she rejects the idea that theory is necessary for being a car mechanic. On the other hand, it is 'a cheeky day off', providing an opportunity to meet up with her (male) classmates, some of whom she has become close to, and to partake in a learning culture which almost celebrates the rejection of theory. During the classroom observation she chatted to Alex almost throughout Alan's lesson, who, as seen in Chapter 5, as a former technician struggled to get the respect of students. During the question and answer session, Lisa and her mates had a laugh guessing some of the answers before engaging again in conversation.

Lisa's story thus vividly illustrates that English vocational education and training, and particularly the assessment regime, do nothing to stimulate learning. Lisa explained that college had been 'boring for ages' as students had been working on their folders and were now doing the Phase Tests.

> We've just been doing them all day, which is really crap [laughs] because we're- we was meant to be given them, like … throughout the term … They've left them to the last minute … so we've lit- literally been sitting there all day doing these exams, it's like so … like, just so draining, so boring, it's like urgh, [laughs] like we've- like … 'cos we've finished our

folders and now I'm waiting for mine to be marked, that's all we've got to be getting on with.

In the workplace, a small garage with three mechanics and two apprentices, Lisa can for the most part confirm her identity. Her skills are acknowledged and she does some of the routine maintenance work by herself. Equally, participation in banter with male colleagues reinforces her tomboy identity, drawing on female stereotypes (such as the idea that 'women can't drive'), while positioning herself in opposition to these. However, as for Erika, the workplace also bears a threat to her new learner identity. Early on she became frustrated with having to ask male colleagues for help, revealing the difficulties of being a female apprentice in a male-dominated occupation.

> … like changing a tyre, I always used to struggle, erm … and I'd always want to- want to do it and be able to do it right on my own, but I'd always have to ask for help, and when someone else would come along and do it so easily … it used to really, like … really, like, like break you down inside … but after a while- it's just experience. That's what I found, and being- like keep trying to just keep going, like keep going no matter what.

Also, Lisa is unhappy about what she perceives as her lack of progress due to having to do a lot of menial work and not being allowed to do certain jobs. The garage positions the apprentices as learners. Similar to German workplaces, there is a strict hierarchy and the apprentices are expected to clear up and assist senior mechanics in more complex work. Lisa has a strong sense that other apprentices at her level are given much greater responsibility, an idea which is likely to have arisen from interaction with other apprentices at college, notably Alex, who is a close friend of hers. She is unsure as to the reasons for what she perceives as an unusual status, which is again a threat to her tomboy identity.

At the same time, Lisa has persevered and has grown in confidence in her own ability. She was certain to pass her Level 2 ('you get help with it … they make you pass') and go on to Level 3 and she continues to be agentic in forging her learning career. She hopes to be taken on by her employer and to find 'her place' in the garage as the electrician. Her plans are encouraged by her father who has been taking her on weekend jobs doing up the electricity in people's houses, which she feels has been like a 'mini-apprenticeship', which she hopes will enable her to get on an electronics course on completing the apprenticeship. Her alternative options include becoming a mechanic with the Army or in Formula One—both powerful symbols of masculinity.

Summary Pair Four

For both Erika and Lisa the apprenticeship has particular meaning as it has enabled them to negotiate not only their practical learner but crucially also their tomboy identities. Erika, for example, can realise her tomboydom in the male-dominated environments of the classroom and the workplace without the risk of being marginalised. The differences in the transition again arise from the differential contexts. Both develop confident learner identities and actively shape their learning careers, but for Lisa this is a more difficult process. While both are constructed as 'apprentice as learner', Lisa aspires to be an 'apprentice as worker' in line with her image of the (male) English motor vehicle maintenance trainee.

Chapter 8

A new conceptual and methodological framework for the study of learner identities and school-to-work transitions

Introduction

In this chapter I begin by revisiting and discussing some of the key findings of the study. First, I explore the construction of learning cultures based on my participant observation in the colleges. These serve as examples on the basis of which I draw attention once more to the ways in which particular identities are constituted through the discursive frameworks of institutional settings. Following this, I show how the analysis of young people's biographies reveals a more nuanced picture of identity construction. In a subsequent section I return to the discussions of Chapters 6 and 7 and summarise the most important findings while drawing out the differences between the English and German contexts. A further section draws out the implications for policy. Finally, I conclude by revisiting the literature and outlining my contributions to knowledge. In summary, the findings are:

+   Young people form learner identities through specific experiences of learning. They do so by interpreting situations through their biographical knowledge, of which the unreflected *habitus* is but one part. All young people are capable of reflexively shaping their learning careers and of challenging established dispositions, something which is promoted through experiences that instil a sense of purpose. Social identities (those associated with the occupation and those available in wider society) play a critical role in the process of identity formation, as young people perform identities as they strive for social recognition.

+   The concept of learning culture provides a lens onto the construction of identities within a particular context. Learning cultures are underpinned by discursive frameworks governing the value and status of particular forms of knowledge, learning and assessment, and are co-constructed by the social actors within them. Thus, young people's learner identities are constituted within particular contexts of learning and may vary in different settings.

+   The meaning young people attach to apprenticeship is unique and can only be fully understood within the contexts of their biographical pasts. These reveal the complexity of identity formation as young people move between multiple social contexts. Thus, for some, meanings may be bound up with a personal project such as shoring up battered self-esteem, or it may be closely intertwined with gender identities.

The cross-national comparison brings to the fore the different national contexts and how they impact on young people's identity formation. These concern in particular the ways in which the two different systems construct the social identities of occupations and of apprenticeships, how they facilitate (or not) the transition to vocational education, and how they promote particular learner identities.

Learning cultures

In Chapter 5, I explored the institutional context, the content and structure of apprenticeships, and the learning cultures of the different learning sites. As a participant observer, I experienced first-hand the powerful nature of these learning cultures, the discursive frameworks of the colleges and the matrix of discourses evident in the college classrooms. I could sense a distinct pressure to conform if one wanted to be accepted by the other actors in these learning environments.

In each case, the learning culture was the result of the co-construction of learning opportunities, that is, the interaction of tutors and students, and of apprentices and their co-workers, in an institutional space defined by the rules and regulations, the norms and values of various 'layers of context' (Blommaert, 2006) at the meso and macro levels of society, and, notably by the social identity of the occupation. Thus, while their interpretations and expectations of learning opportunities may vary within a given national context, with its defined social strata and institutionalised pathways, the actors in these social spaces may share a certain social background, have particular dispositions to knowledge and to learning, and thus interpret and act upon the existing learning culture in certain ways, as in the English motor vehicle maintenance classes. In any case, the resulting learning cultures and discursive frames meant that only certain identities were possible in order for the young people to be recognised subjects. It is through these learning cultures, co-constructed by the interactions of social actors within an institutionally defined learning environment, that learner identities are constituted.

The cases of the English and German motor vehicle maintenance classes are pertinent examples. In the English case, as a result of policy considerations concerned with promoting post-compulsory participation in education and accessibility of qualifications, the content of today's apprenticeship is dominated by a cumbersome and arduous process of assessment, which prioritises practice and procedural knowledge, based on long lists of detailed tasks, at the expense of a more meaningful theoretical content and integration of theory and practice. Policy-makers and practitioners make assumptions about the kinds of learners in terms of what they are able to achieve and what their interests are.

The learning culture in the English classes certainly seemed to uphold motor vehicle maintenance predominantly as a practice. The main tutor stressed that he was 'from the trade' and this allowed him to forge trusting relationships with the students. He seemed right in this assumption. The young people in turn valued his practical expertise while they scorned the theoretical approach of the new tutor and sought to undermine his authority.

The tutors' assumptions of the young people's abilities and learning dispositions chimed with those of popular and policy discourse. They saw them as non-academic and capable of learning only by doing. Their expectations of the students' achievement were moderate; they did not expect them to revise or do homework and there was a sense that they created comfort zones (Ecclestone, 2007) within which the priority was to get students through the assessment process.

On the other hand, the dominance of assessment was bemoaned by the tutors, who saw it as inhibiting a better integration of theory and practice. The students on their part, through their disruptive behaviour and open rejection of theory, made it clear that they did not value the college element. They appeared to take a highly instrumental approach, focused on passing the various elements of assessment, although the 'folder work' was perceived as tedium. In terms of their expertise as car mechanics, they saw college as largely an irrelevance, a hurdle to climb to obtain the qualification, which they accepted they needed for their employment.

The learning culture in England contrasted sharply with that in one of the motor vehicle classes in Germany. Here, the apprenticeship of mechatronics was constituted as pivoting on a substantial body of theory and the integration of theory and practice. Tutors were all university educated. The main tutor insisted that the breadth and depth of theoretical knowledge, together with particular teaching and learning arrangements designed to integrate theory and practice, were crucial in terms of the students' competence to keep abreast of the rapid technological development. Thus, the apprenticeship was regarded as challenging, which essentially contributed to its high status, and which in turn motivated the young people to do well in college.

Although the level of attainment was variable (much more so than in the English classes), the learning culture was in sharp contrast to that in the English college. All students were, on the whole, attentive in lessons, some of which were essentially theory-focused. What is more, this was not procedural knowledge but concerned with the underlying laws of physics (such as qualities of types of thread). While the students may not have all appreciated this approach to the same extent, there was a sense that they accepted it as an essential element of the apprenticeship.

In both cases, the students' learner identities were constituted through the broader context of vocational education, apprenticeship and the social identity of the occupations, on the one hand, and through the particular discursive frameworks of the colleges, on the other. In each case, only certain identities were possible. Thus, for example, in Steve's class in the English college, what constituted a good student may, to some extent, be compatible with the rejection of theoretical knowledge, as well as with a certain level of banter and 'laddish' behaviour. By contrast, in Mr. Christen's class in Germany, what counted as a good student was one who was well behaved and diligent and any deviations from this expectation, even minor disruptions, were immediately rebuked, not only by the tutor, but also by other students. In both cases, students performed the dominant identities of the mechanic: as predominantly a practical trade in England, as an occupation based on the integration of theory and practice in Germany.

On the other hand, in German retail, in those classes, where there was considerable variability of attainment and a very noticeable level of disaffection amongst many students, there was also a tangible sub-cultural element. In these classes the 'disaffected' students were concerned with gaining the recognition of their sub-cultural peers rather than of their tutor, and they took an instrumental approach to learning while engaging mostly in interaction with each other. It is possible that these students failed to be attracted by the social identity of the retail occupation, that it was not their first choice, having been unable to obtain a place on their preferred programme, thus reflecting the stratifying nature of German vocational education. On the other hand, many students did seem engaged and motivated. It was interesting that, in a rather 'relaxed' atmosphere with tutors empathising with students whom they perceived as being exploited, what constituted a good student was entirely compatible with being a good classmate. That is, it was possible for students to be popular and engage in interaction with both, tutors and peers from the sub-culture.

In each of these cases, students are constituted as certain types of learners. It is important to understand that these young people are not 'naturally' good or bad students, or practical or theoretical learners, but are constituted as such by the dominant discursive frameworks and the learning cultures which they co-construct. Thus, in the case of some, or possibly most, of the English motor vehicle maintenance apprentices, the students may have been constituted as 'non-academic' at school, something which was subsequently reinforced at college. They come to perceive themselves as 'non-academic' and perform the social identity of the mechanic based on practical know-how as a powerful alternative identity to that of academic learning, which may have denied them a sense of purpose and achievement. In doing so, they draw on and reinforce the discourse of the dichotomy between academic and vocational learning so prevalent in England. Thus, while to the participant observer it appears that the young people celebrate the rejection of theory (which they may well do as it is a strong element in their construction of identity), it is vital not to portray these young people as naturally anti-theory and non-academic, just as their German counterparts do not naturally value theory. Equally, it is crucial not to view them as a homogenous group of disaffected learners.

Learner biographies

As I sought to demonstrate in this book, in order to shed light on and understand young people's identity constructions we need to explore their biographies. In what follows, I draw once more on the biographical interviews so as to revisit and draw out the major themes that emerged when the interviews were analysed in the light of the learning cultures in the different learning sites.

First, while there may be certain dominant learner identities in any one learning environment, it is clear that others co-exist and it is important not to regard groups of young people as homogenous wholes. For example, in the English motor vehicle maintenance class, while one could have been tempted to conclude that all the young people rejected the learning of theory, this was clearly not the case for Nathan. However, it was only through the biographical interview that it became clear that his learner identity sharply contrasted with stereotypical beliefs about young people in vocational education. Through travelling with his army father, he had been brought up in multicultural environments and did not identify with some of the male working class values displayed by his classmates. Also, because of his experience as a successful grammar school pupil and his interest in science from an early age, the apprenticeship for him was a way of integrating practical know-how and theoretical knowledge. Because of his experiences, he did not construct his identity through the practical trade (as an expression of the rejection of academic learning), nor did he seek recognition by his classmates. In a way, therefore, it could be argued that he subverted the identity of an English motor vehicle maintenance apprentice.

Second, young people's learner identities are not simply one-dimensional. Indeed, it became evident that young people are made up of many facets as they interact with multiple social contexts, each with their own discursive frameworks. This relates back to the issue of identities being constituted in certain contexts. For example, Alex, again in the English motor vehicle maintenance class, constructs himself as a practical learner who is 'not good at written work', who does not feel that he can learn from books, and who rejects the value of theory to becoming a good mechanic. On the other hand, in the interview he revealed that one of his main spare time activities is reading from his large collection of travel books motivated by his dream to go travelling in Latin America. It indicates that in the domain of formal learning, once constructed as 'non-academic', young people may draw on the academic-vocational divide to construct practical learner identities. This may then be reinforced in learning cultures in vocational education, which pivot on this divide. However, in other life domains, they may construct their learner identities quite differently.

Third, and importantly, the biographical interviews revealed that young people are not naturally constructing themselves as practical learners, rejecting classroom or academic learning. Indeed, they are not naturally anything, nor is it helpful to explain their learning dispositions by referring to processes of socialisation. Their dispositions are formed through specific experiences of learning in particular learning environments, each with their own discursive framework and expectations of what and how students should learn. In addition, young people at school or during the apprenticeship may have had to deal with personal difficulties, such as low self-esteem, which prevented them from engaging with the learning environment.

A good example is Robert on the English retail apprenticeship, who, by the end of school, had come to fiercely reject any form of classroom learning, something which even prevented him from considering options that otherwise attracted him (such as carpentry). He first started withdrawing from school because of major discontinuities experienced in his family life. Because of his at times disruptive behaviour he was constituted as an unacceptable student. Robert was unable to develop a sense of purpose and decided that school was not for him. However, it is clear from the biographical interview that not only was he good at English and maths, he actually enjoyed these subjects, particularly creative writing. In Robert's case, it appears that by constructing himself as a practical learner, which in England is constituted in opposition to academic learning, he was able to distance himself from what was an overall negative school experience.

Robert's story also draws our attention to the idea that young people in apprenticeships may not reject academic learning *per se*, but merely particular types of teaching and learning arrangements. Indeed most of the young people in the study told of positive experiences at school, in particular subjects or lessons where they found they were able to express their own ideas and views in more interactive teaching and learning arrangements that allowed for the creative interpretation of knowledge. Conversely, many spoke of subjects that did not appeal to them because they required them to learn 'facts', allowed only one answer, and which they perceived as irrelevant. In conventional directive teaching and learning arrangements which require the passive intake of knowledge, these young people may be constituted as bad students, which in turn prompts them to seek alternative routes for identity construction. However, learning dispositions can change, something which will be discussed below.

Fourth, the meaning that individual young people attach to learning needs to be understood in the context of their biographical experience as a whole. Martin and Robert are both cases in point. As described in Chapter 5, observing Martin in his workplace environment of the German supermarket, it appeared that he was enthusiastically performing the identity of the German retail assistant. There was a slight sense of insecurity, a certain naivety about him as he was serving customers, which one could have attributed to the fact that he was in his first year of the apprenticeship and only starting to build up confidence (although it contrasted with Jeanette, who seemed much more detached).

The particular meaning Martin attached to the apprenticeship only emerged from the interview. For him, as for Robert, the apprenticeship was a way to 'prove' himself and to overcome rejection in the context of a difficult learning career at school and low self-esteem due to a disruptive childhood. Similarly, for Stephanie and Mia on the English retail apprenticeship, this was a means to regain confidence in their own learning and to compensate for a school career that, through no fault of their own, had left them with few qualifications. On the other hand, for Erika and Lisa on the motor vehicle apprenticeship, the apprenticeship provided a way to consolidate their tomboy identities. The individual meanings young people attach to apprenticeships are not easily 'observable' and can be understood only through a reconstruction of the apprentices' biographical life experience within the ethnography as a whole.

Finally, while young people perform identities by 'compulsively citing' the norms and values associated with occupations as a critical means for identity construction and because they strive for social recognition, they do not just blindly conform, but rather interpret learning opportunities according to their biographical past. This came out most clearly in the cases of Leena and Claudia on the German retail apprenticeship. While Leena showed a great deal of initiative, took pleasure in advising customers in great detail, and had her own ideas about how to arrange the lay-out, which at times put her on a collision course with the head assistant, Claudia seemed content to work with her manager, whose instructions she followed closely. Both performed the identity of the retail assistant, but their understanding of this varied as they interpreted it in line with their learning dispositions, their anticipation of the future and the broader context of identity formation.

Thus, for Leena, the apprenticeship was a way to consolidate her broader gender identity and identification with fashion. The retail occupation for her was an end in itself, something which had only relatively recently become part of her horizon for action. By contrast, for Claudia, the apprenticeship was a stepping stone on the way to a number of opportunities she was considering.

Thus, it seems that young people do not merely conform to or subvert social identities, but interpret them in more creative ways than foreseen in Butler's (1990) theory of performativity. Here, Ricoeur's (1992) work may be better suited to understanding young people's formation of identity because of the significance of individuals' past. Young people make sense of new experiences in the light of their biographical past and in anticipation of what they are becoming. This understanding throws light on how and why young people draw on different discourses, rather than that they cite or do not cite certain social identities.

Learner biographies and learning cultures in the English and German contexts

In this section I discuss some of the main findings in Chapters 6 and 7, drawing out the structural differences in England and Germany and their impact on young people's transitions and identity formation.

In Chapter 6, we saw that the German apprenticeship offers opportunities for constructing secure identities through the comprehensive nature of the programme, notably its concept of *Handlungskompetenz* based on the development of the whole person, and the social recognition and future perspectives it provides. It illustrated the close intertwining of competence and identity formation and highlighted the powerful role an occupation may have in guiding school-to-work transition, both over time (in Martin's case from a very young age) and in the different learning environments during the apprenticeship.

Thus, for Leena, Martin, and, to some extent, Jeanette, becoming competent, skilled retail assistants was a major motivating force guiding their transitions. The development of competence was promoted in expansive workplaces which afforded them a certain autonomy and level of responsibility, underpinned by company-based training programmes in addition to the college element. The analysis demonstrated that even where young people had experienced disruptive childhoods (Martin) or negative school experiences (Leena), they were still able to construct secure identities through the retail apprenticeship.

By contrast, this was far less possible for the apprentices on the English retail programme, which is based on a narrow set of fragmented skills and little underpinning knowledge and lacks a notion of competence development. Because of its low status and association with low-skilled, low-paid work, the social identity of the retail occupation played little or no role in the young people's decision-making. Rather, taking a job in retail was an option of last resort, and at the time of joining Taurus, they had not heard of the retail apprenticeships. However, once they were given the opportunity to become apprentices, they welcomed it as a way of gaining a qualification, which was hitherto denied them due to disruptive school careers (except for Anita, for whom it was one option within a broader horizon for action).

In this sense, the retail apprenticeships played a critical role. While the apprenticeships were largely of instrumental value, they nevertheless served to restore confidence in the young people's learning. This seemed to have been the result of achieving a qualification and the prospect of progression, but also the more formalised, systematic learning through reflection, as well as project-based learning. Together, these aspects combined to facilitate the development of a certain level of competence and identification with the occupation. Nevertheless, this competence was restricted to routine work processes and circumscribed by standard procedures. It appeared that three of the apprentices had become disillusioned once they had obtained their qualifications. In the absence of any long-term perspectives, they were unable to construct secure identities through the apprenticeships. On the other hand, the apprenticeship had broadened their horizons for action so that, with their confidence restored, they were able to consider other options.

In relation to motor vehicle maintenance discussed in Chapter 7, it was striking that all English and German apprentices identified first and foremost with the practical know-how associated with the occupation. This in itself seemed to provide the basis for constructing secure identities. However, the value of the apprenticeship itself varied between the two groups. Three of the English apprentices identified with the social identity of the occupation as a practical trade. They took an instrumental approach towards the apprenticeship, which they regarded as a necessary evil and a qualification they needed to get in order to work as mechanics. They afforded little importance to the college element, which they did not think was necessary in order to become skilled workers.

By contrast, the German young people all valued the apprenticeship in its own right. The German apprentices constructed themselves as learners, accepting their position in strongly hierarchical environments, their developing competence being based on the systematic integration of theory and practice taught in the various learning sites of the dual system. In comparison, two of their English counterparts constituted themselves as 'workers' (and, in the case of Lisa, aspired to be a worker), working with a high level of autonomy and dismissing the value of college. The different forms of identity construction reflect the contrasting contexts of vocational education in England and Germany, how the apprenticeships are organised, their social value and status, and how the different systems facilitate school-to-work transition and the formation of identity.

It was striking that most of the young people on retail and motor vehicle maintenance apprenticeships, both in England and Germany, had negative school experiences and, as a result, developed a sense that academic learning was not for them (although, as we have seen, this may have been due to a particular form of conventional academic learning rather than academic learning *per se*). All of them believed that they were practical learners, better at doing things 'with their hands' than at reading and writing. Herein lies one of the most important distinctions between the English and German transition systems.

In England, these young people are classed as 'disaffected'. They are judged as rejecting all classroom learning and, if they opt for vocational pathways, are seen as 'second chance' learners. Because of the relatively low status of vocational education, the transition from school to vocational schemes is not facilitated. It is weakly regulated and there is little institutional advice and guidance available. As a result, many of the English young people in the study experienced disrupted transitions, such as Alex and Nathan. Through the strength of the social identity of motor vehicle maintenance based on practical know-how as well as the relatively high level of autonomy in the workplace, these apprentices were though still able to construct secure identities, unlike their counterparts on the English retail apprenticeships.

In comparison, in Germany, the high status and highly regulated dual system of apprenticeship facilitates the school-to-work transition for learners who prefer experiential learning. As we have seen, the apprenticeships constitute a major motivating force, as they provide high-status qualifications and recognised social positions. The dual system provides a highly prestigious route which values and promotes practical know-how, but which is based on the integration of theory and practice, and includes the development of the person. Thus, the young people's construction of identity was based on a broader notion of competence and the valuing of both, theory and practice.

Policy implications

As discussed in this and the previous chapters, many of the young people, on their basis of general schooling, developed learner identities which included rejecting a particular style of academic learning, in directive teaching and learning arrangements. At the same time, in England, where the education system is predicated on prioritising academic education while marginalising vocational education, little value is attached to experiential learning. Instead, young people's rejection of academic learning is commonly equated with a rejection of all learning, and certainly of theoretical knowledge.

This conception is reinforced by the current structure and content of many apprenticeship programmes, including the two which are the subject of this study, which neglect educational development and learning while stressing assessment of narrowly defined tasks. Echoing previous research (for example, Torrance et al., 2005), the concern with testing through a rigid and time consuming assessment regime seems to counter any possibility of engaging young people by arousing their curiosity, and promotes an instrumental approach to the qualification. Other, equally crucial, issues are the low theoretical content, the conceptualisation of knowledge as largely procedural, limited to a minimal underpinning deemed necessary to carry out the tasks, and the lack of integration of theory and practice. It appears that through the current structure of apprenticeships the rejection of theoretical learning by apprentices becomes a self-fulfilling prophecy. All eight apprentices spoke of the tedium and boredom posed by the bureaucracy of 'doing folder work'. In addition, all of the motor vehicle maintenance apprentices understood theory as 'knowing how', which they all felt they would learn better in the workplace.

There are important imperatives to improve the status and quality of apprenticeships. One concerns the issue of social justice, pinpointed by the guiding question in the Nuffield Review of 14-19 education and training (Pring et al., 2009)—'What counts as an educated nineteen-year old in this day and age?'. Apprenticeships should comprise broad occupational profiles, supported by a body of theory as well as general education to enable occupational as well as personal development. As others have pointed out (Avis, 2004), all young people should have access to knowledge that allows them to reflect on and criticise established practice (Engeström, 2004), to transcend contexts so as to enable occupational mobility, and to have long-term perspectives through vocational education and training that include progression to higher education.

Currently, the two apprenticeship programmes studied seem to be pitched so as to enable so-called 'low achievers' to enter them. The above changes (which would require a far more robust statutory framework) would help to establish apprenticeship as a high-status, quality route, which would attract school leavers at all levels as an alternative to academic study. Thus while young people with low school attainment (such as Ollie) may be able to construct an identity as 'apprentice as worker' through the current apprenticeship programme, this should not serve as a justification for keeping standards low. A more imaginative integration of theory and practice could improve the relevance of theoretical knowledge to young people and serve as a motivating force (Aarkrog, 2008).

Much more needs to be done to support the school-to-work transition of young people who choose vocational routes, such as the provision of advice and guidance in schools. All the young people in this study who chose not to stay in education post-16 experienced some disruption. Furthermore, the experiences of the young people in this study suggest the need for different forms of teaching and learning arrangements at school, notably those that provide for more interactive, student-centred learning, acknowledging that people have different learning dispositions (although, as we have seen, these are never one-dimensional and can change over time), as is already the trend in university teaching in order to accommodate an increasingly diverse student population.

However, despite the rhetoric of conceiving apprenticeships as an alternative to higher education in the context of high youth unemployment, fewer university places and higher fees, current government policies, such as the abolition of the Education Maintenance Allowance[5] and the closure of the Connexions[6] service, serve to make it more difficult for young people to access vocational education, particularly for those from disadvantaged backgrounds. Furthermore, a romanticised notion of practical skills as put forward by the Education Secretary (Gove, 2010), if not backed up by a robust body of knowledge as outlined above and as called for in the Wolf Review (2011), is unhelpful to improving the status of vocational education. Nor is giving vocational pathways (such as the Special Diplomas) the 'veneer' of academic education (Unwin, 2009) conducive to establishing apprenticeship as a valuable route in its own right. Both will reinforce the academic-vocational divide, with the former regarded as the gold standard. Practical know-how, so vastly underrated in academic and policy discourse, should be regarded as a valuable skill in its own right, though not without integrating it with a body of theory.

As we saw in the biographies, many young people enjoyed experiences of academic learning where this involved a more creative approach—practical and more abstract forms of knowledge is not a question of either or. As they were constituted as 'non-academic' in particular discursive frameworks that prioritised certain forms of academic learning, the young people constructed identities that centred on practical learning. However, one important finding in this study is that learner identities can change. A case in point is Stefan, who was 'disaffected' at grammar school, but developed a learner identity based on the integration of theory and practice through project-based learning at intermediate school and subsequently through the dual system apprenticeship.

It is tempting to regard the German dual system as the panacea for ensuring smooth transitions. However, on the one hand, a straightforward transfer to other countries, such as England, is hardly possible due to the very distinct governance and labour market systems in these countries (see for example, Brown, Green and Lauder, 2001). In addition, as discussed in Chapter 2, the dual system is not without its shortcomings. This concerns primarily the segregated

5   The EMA was a financial scheme to encourage 19-19-year-olds from low-income households to stay on in education past the compulsory leaving age.
6   The Connexions Agency is a careers service for 13-19 year olds delivered by local authorities. Following spending cuts it has closed in many areas.

nature with a hierarchy of occupations. Related to this, there are concerns over a large group of disadvantaged school leavers who are deemed to lack the required 'maturity' (*Ausbildungsreife*) for entering the dual system and who are left to join the stigmatised 'transition system' (Schmidt, 2010; Büchel, 2002), an issue which goes beyond the scope of this book. In the study, this was apparent in the number of young people in the retail classes for whom retail seemed a second choice. The segregation is also evident in 'second rate' apprenticeships such as that of car service mechanic, through which Aazim was unable to obtain a recognised social position.

Answers seem to lie partly in addressing problems embedded in general education, such as the tripartite school system. This has been acknowledged and many Länder are now abolishing general secondary schools. Other measures would include making the dual system more flexible, for example by allowing for lateral entry. Some moderate initiatives, safeguarding the notion of the *Beruf*, are underway (Hanf, 2011; Pilz, 2009).

Revisiting the literature

The review of the literature in Chapter 3 revealed that studies on school-to-work transitions, including those that examined learning cultures in specific learning environments (for example, Banks et al., 1992; Hodkinson, Sparkes and Hodkinson, 1996; Ball, Maguire and Macrae, 2000a; James and Biesta, 2007; Hodkinson, Biesta and James, 2007, 2008; Colley et al., 2003), lacked a proper conceptualisation of identity formation and relied on theories of social reproduction, socialisation and individualisation. Many studies have suggested a passive socialisation, whereby young people from working class backgrounds come to accept 'working class', or what are perceived as low skilled jobs, suggesting relatively smooth transitions and abiding identities (for example, Bates, 1993; Colley et al., 2003; Lehmann, 2005; Shildrick and Macdonald, 2007). I argued that this analysis reflects these researchers' own negative perceptions of vocational education which dismisses these pathways as positive choices. In addition, the idea that young people on the basis of their upbringing reject school, as so often put forward in transition studies, constitutes these young people as having enduring 'anti-learning' identities.

The problem lies in part with the methodological approach. These studies' analyses are often based on survey data around outcome indicators or semi-structured interviews that neglect young people's biographies. Crucially, researchers commonly seem to take at face value young people's assertions, obtained from semi-structured interviews, that they are 'not good' at or reject academic learning.

As Hollway and Jefferson (2000) have suggested, these assertions and utterances may be an outcome of semi-structured interviews themselves. These amplify the power relationship between researcher and informant, and questions (derived from the researcher's own frame of references) may prompt a response from the 'defended self', whereby young people draw on certain discourses to regain some control. Furthermore, data gathered through participant observation may lead researchers to regard young people as homogenous as they conform to prevalent learning cultures and social identities.

As outlined in Chapter 4, and demonstrated throughout this book, when used appropriately, participant observation is a valuable tool, not only for exploring the learning culture as a context within which learner identities are formed, but also for generating opportunities for the co-construction of meanings between researcher and informant. Nevertheless, ethnographic studies need to be integrated with biographical interviews as identity construction is a highly individuated process.

Through the particular multi-method ethnographic approach of this study, I have been able to show that identities develop on the basis of concrete learning experiences and are often constituted in institutional settings with discursive frameworks that prioritise particular forms of knowledge. While Bourdieu's (1985) theory of social reproduction and the *habitus* concept are useful in drawing our attention to the continued impact of structural factors, notably social background, and the way this shapes young people's decision-making and horizons for action, they are less suitable to account for and explain change, for example in young people's learner identities. Furthermore, by relying on outcome indicators and on data based on semi-structured interviews, researchers neglect the complex processes of identity formation.

Here, the work of Judith Butler (1990) and, in particular, Deborah Youdell (2006) in her research on identities in schools, has offered a valuable framework for understanding identities as discursively constructed. This work draws attention to the power of social norms and identities which young people perform in order to be recognised social subjects. It leaves scope for agency as individuals have to continually cite these norms to construct their identities again and again, making sense of each new situation, while refuting the idea of enduring identities which people enact as in a theatrical performance.

I have shown that a suitable conceptual framework needs to combine the theory of performativity with biographical approaches (Ricoeur, 1992; Alheit, 2002, 2003), as young people make decisions and act upon present situations in the light of their past experiences and their anticipation of the future. Of value here is Alheit's notion of biographical knowledge (2002, 2003) as the total of accumulated experience as a resource. This includes *habitus* but also encompasses the potential for change, or unlived potential: knowledge of alternative options that individuals know exist but have not, as yet, explored, which may be described as latent horizons for action. Examples in this book are young people's informal learning experiences which they later come to draw upon, such as Alex's experience as a Saturday boy or Mia's desire to become a security guard.

While young people developed certain, often negative, learner identities in formal settings, crucially, these were subject to change. They constructed alternative identities, commonly through experiences of informal learning, that conferred on them a sense that they can succeed in and through learning, instilling a sense of purpose (Erikson, 1968).

It is through this rise in confidence and sense of purpose that all young people in the study showed the capacity for biographicity (Alheit, 2003) as the ability to actively and reflexively shape their learning careers in a way as to consolidate their emerging learner identities in anticipation of the future. It is in this sense that learning is transformative (Lave and Wenger, 1991) as new experiences led to emergent identities and broadened horizons for action. And it is also through these experiences that for most of the young people in this study, the apprenticeships constituted a positive choice.

The analysis found that the capacity for biographicity is promoted through social and institutional support and in this confirms the findings of previous research. Many young people relied on the availability of supportive parents in the transition process. Parents assisted with, for example, negotiating placements (Erika) and work experience (Lisa), obtaining a place at college (Nathan), or simply by supporting their children in their decisions.

Most notably it was the institutional support provided by the German dual system that facilitated the German apprentices' transitions, again confirming the findings of previous studies (Evans and Heinz, 1991, 1994a, b). Crucially, as an established route that centres on practical know-how based on the integration of theory and practice, this system served to consolidate the young people's emergent learner identities which they were negotiating based on experiences of largely informal learning. Nevertheless, while their transitions were often less smooth, the English apprentices were equally able to reflexively shape their identities based on experiences which had led to a rise in self-confidence.

Most importantly, the particular meaning that individual young people attach to apprenticeships can be understood only through their biographical past, by exploring their experiences in and out of formal settings of learning on the basis of which they construct their learner identities. Only by reconstructing their learner biographies can we come to understand the processes through which identities are formed, how young people make sense of and take up learning opportunities, why they engage in or disengage from types of teaching and learning, why apprenticeships are of intrinsic or instrumental value, how their learning careers are intertwined with other identities such as gender, or with life projects such as increasing self-esteem. The cross-national comparison serves to bring to light the structural relations and the ways in which these shape, facilitate or hinder young people's transitions, or promote certain learner identities. Only when we understand that young people are not naturally anything, that learner identities are discursively constituted and are fluid and changeable, can we begin to design (vocational) education programmes that are motivating and engaging, that take account of young people's varied past experiences, learner dispositions and identities, without undermining principles of social justice. This study has sought to go somewhere towards addressing this goal.

References

Aarkrog, V. (2008) Convergence of general theory and practice in VET: Five theses about the students' motivation for general subjects in VET, in V. Aarkrog & C. H. Jørgensen (eds) *Divergence and convergence in education and work*. Bern: Peter Lang: 239-259.

Ainley, P. and Rainbird, H. (eds.) (1999) *Apprenticeship—Towards a New Paradigm of Learning*, London: Kogan Page.

Alheit, P. (1994) *Taking the Knocks: Youth Unemployment and Biography—A Qualitative Analysis*, London: Cassell.

Alheit, P. (2002) Identität oder Biographizität?—Beiträge der neueren sozial- und erziehung swissenschaftlichen Biographieforschung zu einem Konzept der Identitätsentwicklung, *Integrative Therapie* 3-4: 190-209.

Alheit, P. (2003) Biographizität als Schlüsselqualifikation—Plädoyer für transitorische Bildungsprozesse, *QUEM-report—Schriften zur beruflichen Weiterbildung* 78: 7-21.

Alvesson, M. and Willmott, H. (2002) Identity Regulation as Organizational Control: Producing the Appropriate Individual, *Journal of Management Studies* 39(5): 619-644.

Archer, L. and Yamashita, H. (2003) 'Knowing their limits'? Identities, inequalities and inner city school leavers' post-16 aspirations, *Journal of Education Policy* 18(1): 53-69.

Ashton, D. N. and Field, D. (1976) *Young Workers*. London: Hutchinson.

Atkinson, P. and Hammersley, M. (1998) Ethnography and participant observation, in N. K. Denzin & Y. S. Lincoln (eds) *Strategies of Qualitative Inquiry*. Thousand Oaks, London, New Delhi: Sage: 110-136.

Avis, J. (2004) Work-based learning and social justice: 'learning to labour' and the new vocationalism in England, *Journal of Education and Work* 17(2): 197-217.

Ball, S. J., Maguire, M. and Macrae, S. (2000a) *Choice, Pathways and Transitions Post-16: New youth, new economies in the global city*. London: Routledge Falmer.

Ball, S. J., Maguire, M. and Macrae, S. (2000b) Space, work and the 'new urban economies', *Journal of Youth Studies* 3(3): 279.

Bandura, A. (1997) *Self-Efficacy: The Exercise of Control*. New York: W.H. Freeman and Company.

Banks, M., Bates, I., Breakwell, G., Bynner, J., Emler, N., Jamieson, L. and Roberts, K. (1992) *Careers and Identities*. Buckingham: Open University Press.

Bates, I. (1993) A job which 'right for me'? in I. Bates and G. Riseborough (eds) *Youth and Inequality*. Buckingham: Open University Press.

Bates, I. and Riseborough, G. (eds.) (1993a) *Youth and Inequality*. Buckingham: Open University Press.

Bates, I. and Riseborough, G. (1993b) Deepening divisions, fading solutions, in I. Bates and G. Riseborough (eds) *Youth and Inequality*. Buckingham: Open University Press.

Beck, U. (1992) *Risk Society: Towards a new Modernity*. New Delhi: Sage.

Beck, V., Fuller, A. and Unwin, L. (2006) Increasing risk in the 'scary' world of work? Male and femail resistance to crossing gender lines in apprenticeships in England and Wales, *Journal of Education and Work* 19(3): 271-289.

Behrens, M. and Evans, K. (2002) Taking control of their lives? A comparison of the experiences of unemployed young adults (18-25) in England and Germany, *Comparative Education* 38(1): 17-37.

Behrens, M., Pilz, M. and Greuling, O. (2008) Taking a straightforward detour: learning and labour market participation in the German apprenticeship system, *Journal of Vocational Education and Training* 60(1): 93-104.

Beicht, U., Friedrich, M. and Ulrich, J.G. (2007a) Steiniger Weg in die Berufsausbildung—Werdegang von Jugendlichen nach Beendigung der allgemeinbildenden Schule, *Berufsbildung in Wissenschaft und Praxis, Zeitschrift des Bundesinstituts für Berufssbildung (BIBB)* 2: 5-9.

Beicht, U., Friedrich, M. and Ulrich, J.G. (2007b) Deutlich längere Dauer bis zum Ausbildungseinstieg, *Berufsbildung in Wissenschaft und Praxis, Zeitschrift des Bundesinstituts für Berufssbildung (BIBB)* 2: 1-10.

BIBB (2009) *Database of Trainees*. Online: www.bibb.de. Accessed:10.7.2011.

Blommaert, J. (2006) *Ethnographic Fieldwork: A Beginner's Guide*. London, Institute of Education. Unpublished. November 2006 draft.

Bloomer, M. (1997) *Curriculum Making in Post-16 Education*. London: Routledge.

Bloomer, M. and Hodkinson, P. (1997) *Moving in FE: the voice of the learner*. London: Further Education Development Agency (FEDA).

Bloomer, M. and Hodkinson, P. (2000a) The complexity and unpredictability of young people's learning careers, *Education + Training* 42(2): 68-74.

Bloomer, M. and Hodkinson, P. (2000b) Learning careers: continuity and change in young people's dispositions to learning, *British Educational Research Journal* 26(5): 583-597.

Bourdieu, P. (1985) The genesis of the concepts of *habitus* and of *field*, *Sociocriticism* 2(2): 11-24.

Bourdieu, P. (1993) *Sociology in Question*. London: Sage.

Brockmann, M. (2011) Problematising short-term participant observation and multi-method ethnographic studies, *Ethnography and Education* 6(2): 229-243.

Brockmann, M. (2012) Learning cultures in retail: apprenticeship, identity and emotional work in England and Germany, *Journal of Education and Work*.

Brown, P., Green, A. and Lauder, H. (2001) *High Skills: Globalisation, Competitiveness and Skill Formation*. Oxford: Oxford University Press.

Büchel, F. (2002) Successful apprenticeship-to-work transitions, *International Journal of Manpower* 23(5): 394-410.

Butler, J. (1988) Performative acts and gender constitution: An essay in phenomenology and feminist theory, *Theatre Journal* 40(4): 519-531.

Butler, J. (1990) *Gender Trouble: Feminism and the Subversion of Identity*. New York: Routledge.

Butler, J. (1993) *Bodies that Matter: On the Discursive Limits of "Sex"*. New York and London: Routledge.

Butler, J. (1997) *Excitable Speech: A Politics of the Performative*. New York and London: Routledge.

Bynner, J. and Roberts, K. (eds.) (1991) *Youth and Work: Transition to Employment in England and Germany*. London: Anglo-German Foundation.

Canning, R. (2007) Reconceptualising core skills, *Journal of Education and Work* 20(1): 17-26.

Chamberlayne, P. and Spanò, A. (2000) Modernisation as lived experience—Contrasting case studies from the SOSTRIS project, in P. Chamberlayne, J. Bornat & T. Wengraf (eds) *The Turn to Biographical Methods in Social Science*. London: Routledge.

Clarke, L. (1999) The changing structure and significance of apprenticeship with special reference to construction, in P. Ainley and H. Rainbird (eds) *Apprenticeship—Towards a New Paradigm of Learning*. London: Kogan Page: 25-40.

Clarke, L. and Winch, C. (2004) Apprenticeship and applied theoretical knowledge, *Educational Philosophy and Theory* 36(5): 509-521.

Clifford, J. (1983) On Ethnographic Authority, *Representations* 2: 118-146.

Clifford, J. (1986) Introduction: Partial truths, in J. Clifford & G. Marcus (eds) *Writing Culture. The Poetics and Politics of Ethnography*. Berkeley, Los Angeles, London: University of California Press: 1-26.

Cohen, P. and Ainley, P. (2000) In the country of the blind? Youth studies and cultural studies in Britain, *Journal of Youth Studies* 3(1): 79-95.

Colley, H., James, D., Tedder, M. and Diment, K. (2003) Learning as becoming in vocational education and training: class, gender and the role of vocational habitus, *Journal of Vocational Education and Training* 55(4): 471-497.

Colley, H. and Jarvis, J. (2007) Formality and informality in the summative assessment of motor vehicle apprentices: a case study, *Assessment in Education* 14(3): 295-314.

Crompton, R. (2001) Gender, comparative research and biographical matching, *European Societies* 3(2): 167-190.

Crossan, B., Field, J., Gallacher, J. and Merrill, B. (2003) Understanding participation in learning for non-traditional adult learners: learning careers and the construction of learning identities, *British Journal of Sociology of Education* 24(1): 55-67.

Dausien, B. (1998) Geschlecht als biographische Konstruktion, in K. Weber (eds) *Life History, Gender and Experience: Theoretical Approaches to Adult Life and Learning. Papers presented at the Conference on Life History, Gender and Experience 1997*. Roskilde: Adult Education Research Group, Roskilde University.

Davies, J. and Biesta, G. (2007) Coming to college or getting out of school? The experience of vocational learning of 14- to 16-year-olds in a further education college, *Research Papers in Education* 22(1): 23-41.

Deissinger, T. (2008) Cultural patterns underlying apprenticeship: Germany and the Uk, in V. Aarkrog and C. H. Jorgensen (eds) *Divergence and Convergence in Education and Work*. Bern: Peter Lang.

Denzin, N. K. and Lincoln, Y. S. (1998) Introduction: Entering the field of qualitative research, in N. K. Denzin & Y. S. Lincoln (eds) *The Landscape of Qualitative Research*. Thousand Oaks, London, New Delhi: Sage.

Deuer, E. (2007) Nachwuchs im Einzelhandel schwer zu rekrutieren?, *Berufsbildung in Wissenschaft und Praxis, Zeitschrift des Bundesinstituts für Berufssbildung (BIBB)* 5: 54-55.

du Bois Reymond, M. (1998) "I don't want to commit myself yet": young people's life concepts, *Journal of Youth Studies* 1(1): 63-79.

Eberhard, V., Krewerth, A. and Ulrich, J.G. (2005) 'Man muss geradezu perfekt sein, um eine Ausbildungsstelle zu bekommen' — Die Situation aus Sicht der Lehrstellenbewerber, *Berufsbildung in Wissenschaft und Praxis, Zeitschrift des Bundesinstituts für Berufssbildung (BIBB)* 3: 10-13.

Ecclestone, K. (2002) *Learning autonomy in post-compulsory education: the politics and practice of formative assessment*. London: Routledge Falmer.

Ecclestone, K. (2004) Learning in a comfort zone: cultural and social capital inside an outcomes-based assessment regime, *Assessment in Education* 11(1): 29-47.

Ecclestone, K. (2007) Commitment, compliance and comfort zones: the effects of formative assessment on vocational education students' learning careers, *Assessment in Education* 14(3): 315-333.

Ecclestone, K., Biesta, G. and Hughes, M. (eds.) (2010) *Transitions and Learning through the Lifecourse*. London and New Yorrk: Routledge.

Educational Reporting Consortium (2010) *Bildung in Deutschland 2010—Ein indikatorengestützter Bericht mit einer Analyse zu Perspektiven des Bildungswesens im demografischen Wandel*, Online: www.bildungsbericht.de/daten2010/bb_2010.pdf. Accessed 7.7.2011.

Elder, G. H. (1985) Perspectives on the life course, in G. H. E. Jr (eds) *Life Course Dynamics: Trajectories and Transitions 1968-1980*. New York: Cornell University Press.

Elder, G. H. J., Kirkpatrick Johnson, M. and Crosnoe, R. (2003) The emergence and development of life course theory, in J. T. Mortimer & M. J. Shanahan (eds) *Handbook of the Life Course*. Dordrecht: Springer.

Engeström, Y. (2001) Expansive learning at work: toward an activity theoretical reconceptualisation, *Journal of Education and Work* 14(1): 133-156.

Engeström, Y. (2004) New forms of learning in co-configuration work, *Journal of Workplace Learning* 16(1/2): 11-21.

Erikson, E. H. (1968) *Identity, Youth and Crisis*. London: faber and faber.

Erpenbeck, J. (2005) *Positionspapier für BIBB Workshop zum 1. EQF Entwurf vom 16.11.2005*.

Esping-Andersen, G. (1990) *The Three Worlds of Welfare Capitalism*. Cambridge: Polity Press.

Evans, K. (2002) Taking control of their lives? Agency in young adult transitions in England and the New Germany, *Journal of Youth Studies* 5(3): 245-269.

Evans, K. (2007) Concepts of bounded agency in education, work, and the personal lives of young adults, *International Journal of Psychology* 42(2): 85-93.

Evans, K. and Furlong, A. (1997) Metaphors of youth transitions: niches, pathways, trajectories or navigations, in J. Bynner, L. Chisholm & A. Furlong (eds) *Youth, Citizenship and Social Change in a European Context*. Aldershot: Ashgate: 17-41.

Evans, K. M. and Heinz, W. R. (1991) Career trajectories in Britain and Germany, in J. Bynner & K. Roberts (eds) *Youth and Work: Transition to Employment in England and Germany*. London: Anglo-German Foundation.

Evans, K. M. and Heinz, W. R. (eds.) (1994a) *Becoming Adults in England and Germany*. London: Anglo-German Foundation.

Evans, K. M. and Heinz, W. R. (1994b) 'Transitions, careers and destinations' in K. M. Evans and W. R. Heinz (eds) *Becoming Adults in England and Germany*. London: Anglo-German Foundation.

Evans, K. Hodkinson, P., Rainbird, H., Unwin, L. (2006) *Improving Workplace Learning*. London and New York: Routledge.

Evans, K., Kersh, N. and Kontiainen, S. (2004) Recognition of tacit skills: sustaining learning outcomes in adult learning and work re-entry, *International Journal of Training and Development* 8(1): 54-72.

Evans, K., Rudd, P.W., Behrens, M., Kaluza, J. and Woolley, C. (2001) *Taking Control? Agency in Young Adult Transitions in England and the New Germany. End of Award Report for ESRC*. London: Institute of Education.

Foskett, N. and Hemsley-Brown, J. (2001) *Choosing Futures—Young people's decision-making in education, training and careers markets*. London: RoutledgeFalmer.

Foucault, M. (1991) *Discipline and Punish: The Birth of the Prison.* London: Penguin.

Fuller, A. (2004) *Expecting too much? Modern Apprenticeship: purposes, participation and attainment.* Nuffield Review of 14-19 Education and Training Working Paper 10. Online: www.nuffi eld14-19review.org.uk/fi les/documents17-1.pdf. Accessed 3.5.2008.

Fuller, A., Beck, V. and Unwin, L. (2005) The gendered nature of apprenticeship—Employers' and young people's perspectives, *Education + Training* 47(4/5): 298-311.

Fuller, A. and Unwin, L. (1998) Reconceptualising apprenticeship: exploring the relationship between work and learning, *Journal of Vocational Education and Training* 50(2): 153-173.

Fuller, A. and Unwin, L. (2003a) Creating a 'Modern Apprenticeship': a critique of the UK's multi-sector, social inclusion approach, *Journal of Education and Work* 16(1): 5-25.

Fuller, A. and Unwin, L. (2003b) Learning as apprentices in the contemporary UK workplace: creating and managing expansive and restrictive participation, *Journal of Education and Work* 16(4): 407-426.

Fuller, A. and Unwin, L. (2007) What counts as good practice in contemporary apprenticeships?, *Education + Training* 49(6): 447-458.

Fuller, A. and Unwin, L. (2008) *Towards Expansive Apprenticeships: A Commentary by the Teaching and Learning Research Programme.* London: TLRP.

Fuller, A. and Unwin, L. (2009) Change and continuity in apprenticeship: the resilience of a model of learning, *Journal of Education and Work* 22(5): 405-416.

Furlong, A. (2004) *Cultural dimensions of decisions about educational participation among 14-19 year olds.* Nuffield Review Working Paper 26. Online: www.nuffield14-19review.org.uk. Accessed 3.5.2008.

Furlong, A. (2009) Revisiting transitional metaphors: reproducing social inequalities under the conditions of late modernity, *Journal of Education and Work* 22(5): 343-353.

Furlong, A. and Cartmel, F. (2007) *Young People and Social Change: New Perspectives.* Maidenhead: Open University Press.

Furlong, A., Cartmel, F., Biggart, A., Sweeting, H. and West, P. (2003) *Reconceptualising Youth Transitions: Patterns of Vulnerability and Processes of Social Exclusion,* Edinburgh: Scottish Executive.

Gibson, P. (2004) Life and learning in further education: constructing the circumstantial curriculum, *Journal of Further and Higher Education* 28(3): 333-346.

Giddens, A. (1991) *Modernity and Self Identity. Self and Society and the Late Modern Age.* Cambridge: Polity Press.

Goffman, E. (1968a) *Stigma—Notes on the Management of Spoiled Identity.* New Jersey: Pelican Books.

Goffman, E. (1968b) *Asylum: Essays on the Social Situation of Mental Patients and Other Inmates.* Harmondsworth: Penguin.

Goffman, E. (1969) *The Presentation of Self in Everyday Life.* London: The Penguin Press.

Goffman, E. (1971) *Relations in Public.* New York: Penguin.

Goffman, E. (1972) *Interaction Ritual—Essays on Face-to-Face Behaviour.* London: The Penguin Press.

Goodwin, J. and O'Connor, H. (2003) Entering work in the 1960s: reflections and expectations, *Education + Training* 45(1): 13-21.

Goodwin, J. and O'Connor, H. (2005) Engineer, mechanic or carpenter? Boys' transition to work in the 1960s, *Journal of Education and Work* 18(4): 451-471.

Goodwin, J. and O'Connor, H. (2007) Continuity and change in the experiences of transition from school to work, *International Journal of Lifelong Education* 26(5): 555-572.

Gove, M. (2010) *It's not simply an academic question – why we need radical reform of vocational education*. Speech to the Edge Foundation, 9.9.2010: Online: www. education.gov.uk/inthenews/speeches/a0064364/michael-gove-to-the-edge-foundation. Accessed 6.7.2011.

Green, A. (1998) Core skills, key skills and general culture: in search of the common foundation in vocational education, *Evaluation and Research in Education* 12(1): 23-43.

Greinert, W.-D. (2007) The German Philosophy of Vocational Education, in L. Clarke & C. Winch (eds) *Vocational Education: International Approaches, Developments and Systems*. London: Routledge.

Hammersley, M. and Atkinson, P. (2007) *Ethnography: Principles in Practice*. London: Routledge.

Handley, K., Clark, T., Fincham, R. and Sturdy, A. (2007) Researching situated learning— Participation, identity and practices in client-consultant relationships, *Management learning* 38(2): 173-191.

Hanf, G. (2010) *Personal communication by Email*. M. Brockmann. London.

Hanf, G. (2011) The changing relevance of the *Beruf*, in M. Brockmann, L. Clarke & C. Winch (eds) *Knowledge, Skills and Competence in the European Labour Market: What's in a vocational qualification?* Abingdon: Routledge.

Harney, K. (1998) Beruf ist Lebensperspektive, *Der berufliche Bildungsweg* 3: 2-4.

Heckhausen, J. and Tomasik, M.J. (2002) Get an apprenticeship before school is out: How German adolescents adjust vocational aspirations when getting close to a developmental deadline, *Journal of Vocational Behavior* 60: 199-219.

Heinz, W. R. (1995) *Arbeit, Beruf und Lebenslauf—Eine Einführung in die berufliche Sozialisation*. Weinheim und München: Juventa Verlag.

Heinz, W. R. (2002) Transition discontinuities and the biographical shaping of early work careers, *Journal of Vocational Behavior* 60: 220-240.

Heinz, W. R. (2009) Structure and agency in transition research, *Journal of Education and Work* 22(5): 391-404.

Heinz, W. R. and Krüger, H. (2001) Life course: Innovations and challenges for social research, *Current Sociology* 49(2): 29-45.

Heinz, W. R. and Taylor, A. (2005) Learning and work transition policies in a comparative perspective: Canada and Germany, in N. Bascia, A. Cumming, A. Datnow, K. Leithwood & D. Livingstone (eds) *International Handbook of Educational Policy— Part Two*. Dordrecht: Springer: 847-864.

Hemsley-Brown, J. (1999) College Choice: Perceptions and Priorities, *Educational Management & Administration* 27(1): 85-98.

Hochschild, A. R. (1983) *The Managed Heart—Commercialisation of Human Feeling*. Berkeley and Los Angeles, CA: University of California Press.

Hodkinson, P., Biesta, G. and James, D. (2007) Understanding learning cultures, *Educational Review* 59(4): 415-427.

Hodkinson, P., Biesta, G. and James, D. (2008) Understanding learning culturally: overcoming the dualism between school and individual views of learning, *Vocations and Learning* 1: 27-47.

Hodkinson, P. and Hodkinson, H. (2003) Individuals, communities of practice and the policy context: school-teachers learning in their workplace, *Studies in Continuing Education* 25(1): 3-21.

Hodkinson, P., Sparkes, A.C. and Hodkinson, H. (1996) *Triumphs and Tears: Young People, Markets and the Transition from School to Work*. London: David Fulton Publishers.

Hollway, W. and Jefferson, T. (2000) *Doing Qualitative Research Differently: Free Association, Narrative and the Interview Method*. London: Sage.

Holstein, J. A. and Gubrium, J. F. (1995) *The Active Interview*. Thousand Oaks, CA: Sage.

House of Lords (2007) *Apprenticeship: A Key Route to Skill*. London: The Stationery Office Limited.

Irwin, S. (1995) *Rights of Passage—Social change and the transition from youth to adulthood*. London: UCL Press.

James, D. and Biesta, G. (2007) *Improving Learning Cultures in Further Education*. Abingdon: Routledge.

James, D., Davies, J. and Biesta, G. (2007) The learning of practices and the practices of learning, in D. James & G. Biesta (eds) *Improving Learning Cultures in Further Education*. Abingdon: Routledge.

Jephcote, M. and Abbott, I. (2005) Tinkering and tailoring: the reform of 14-19 education in England, *Journal of Vocational Education and Training* 57(2): 181-202.

Johnston, L. MacDonald, R., Mason, P., Ridley, L. and Webster, C. (2000) *Snakes & Ladders: Young People, Transitions and Social Exclusion*. Bristol: Policy Press.

KMK (Standing Conference of the Ministers of Education and Cultural Affairs) (2003) '*Framework Curriculum (Rahmenlehrplan) for the occupation of motor vehicle mechatronic.* ' Online: www.kmk.org/fileadmin/pdf/Bildung/BeruflicheBildung/rlp/ KfZMechatroniker.pdf. Accessed 3.4.2008

Knoppik, S. (2009) *Licht und Schatten: Ausbildung beim Discounter*. Kiel: Norddeutsche Rundschau.24.10.2009.

Krakau, U. and Rickes, M. (2007) Förderung selbst regulierten Lernens in Fachklassen des dualen Systems—Rahmenbedingungen, Umsetzung und Evaluation, *Berufs- und Wirtschaftspädagogik* 13: 1-16.

Kutscha, G. (2007) *Was Ausbildungsnovizen im Einzelhandel können sollen, aber nicht wissen können*. 5. BIBB Fachkongress, Düsseldorf.

Lave, J. (1991) Situating learning in communities of practice, in L. B. Resnick, J. M. Levine & S. D. Teasley (eds) *Perspectives on Socially Shared Cognition*. Washington: American Psychological Association: 63-82.

Lave, J. and Wenger, E. (1991) *Situated Learning—Legitimate Peripheral Participation*. New York: Cambridge University Press.

Lawy, R. (2006) Connective learning: young people's identity and knowledge-making in work and non-work contexts, *British Journal of Sociology of Education* 27(3): 325-340.

Lehmann, W. (2005) Choosing to labour: structure and agency in school-to-work transitions, *Canadian Journal of Sociology* 30(3): 325-350.

Lempert, W. (2006) *Berufliche Sozialisation—Persönlichkeitsentwicklung in der betrieblichen Ausbildung und Arbeit*. Baltmannsweiler: Schneider Verlag Hohengehren.

Lewis, P., Ryan, P. and Gospel, H. (2008) A hard sell? The prospects for apprenticeship in British retailing, *Human Resource Management Journal* 18(1): 3-19.

186   *Learner biographies and learning cultures*

286

MacDonald, R. and Marsh, J. (2005) *Disconnected Youth? Growing up in Britain's Poor Neighbourhoods*. Basingstoke: Palgrave Macmillan.
Maguire, M., Ball, S.J. and Macrae, S. (2001) Post-adolescence, dependence and the refusal of adulthood, *Discourse: Studies in the Cultural Politics of Education* 22(2): 197-211.
Marcus, G. E. (1998) *Ethnography through Thick & Thin*. Princeton, NJ: Princeton University Press.
Marsden, D. (2007) Labour market segmentation in Britain: the decline of occupational labour markets and the spread of 'entry tournaments', *Socio-Économie du travail, Économies et Sociétés* AB(28): 965-998.
Mason, G., Osborne, M. and Voss-Dahm, D. (2008) *Labour market outcomes in different national settings: UK-German comparisons in retailing*. London: National Institute of Economic and Social Research. Unpublished draft.
Mayhew, K., Deer, C. and Dua, M. (2004) The move to mass higher education in the UK: many questions and some answers, *Oxford Review of Education* 30(1): 65-82.
McNay, L. (1999) Subject, Psyche and Agency: The Work of Judith Butler', in V. Bell (ed) *Performativity & Belonging*. London: Sage: 175-193.
Miller, L. (2005) Addressing gender segregation in apprenticeships in England, *Education + Training* 47(4/5): 283-297.
Ministry of Education and Research (2008) *Berufsbildungsbericht (Report on Vocational Education) 2008* Online: www.bmbf.de/pub/bbb_08.pdf. Accessed 10.7.2011.
MSC (Manpower Services Commission) (1981) *A New Training Initiative: A Programme for Action*. London: HMSO.
Mulder, R. and Sloane, P. (2004) *New Approaches to Vocational Education in Europe*. Oxford: Symposium Books.
Müller, W. and Gangl, M. (eds.) (2003) *Transitions from Education to Work in Europe: The integration of youth into EU labour markets*. Oxford: Oxford University Press.
Murray, J. (2011) Do an apprenticeship: bags of money and no graduate debt. *The Guardian*. London. 7.2.2011.
Musekamp, F. Spöttl, G. and Becker, M. (2008) *Kurzbericht zum Kfz-Servicemechaniker-Projekt*. Bremen: ITB, University of Bremen.
Nagel, U. and Wallace, C. (1997) Participation and identification in risk societies: European perspectives, in J. Bynner, L. Chisholm and A. Furlong (eds) *Youth, Citizenship and Social Change in a European Context*. Aldershot: Ashgate: 42-55.
Nayak, A. and Kehily, M. J. (2008) *Gender, Youth and Culture—Young Masculinities and Feminities*. Basingstoke: Palgrave Macmillan.
Nickolaus, R., Riedl, A. and Schelten, A. (2005) Ergebnisse und Desiderata zur Lehr-Lernforschung in der gewerblich-technischen Berufsausbildung, *Zeitschrift für Berufs- und Wirtschaftspädagogik* 101(4): 507-532.
Nickolaus, R. Knöll, B. and Gschwendter, T. (2006) Methodische Präferenzen und ihre Effekte auf die Kompetenz- und Motivationsentwicklung—Ergebnisse aus Studien in anforderungsdifferenten elektrotechnischen Ausbildungsberufen in der Grundbildung, *Zeitschrift für Berufs- und Wirtschaftspädagogik* 102(4): 552-577.
O'Connor, H. and Goodwin, J. (2004) 'She wants to be like her mum?' Girls' experience of the school-to-work transition in the 1960s, *Journal of Education and Work* 17(1): 95-118.
Paechter, C. (2006) Reconceptualising the gendered body: learning and constructing masculinities and feminities in school, *Gender and Education* 18(2): 121-135.

Paechter, C. (2010) Tomboys and girly-girls: embodied femininities in primary schools, *Discourse: Studies in the Cultural Politics of Education* 31(2): 221-235.

Paechter, C. and Clark, S. (2007) Learning gender in primary school playgrounds: findings from the Tomboy Identities Study, *Pedagogy, Culture & Society* 15(3): 317-331.

Parker, A. (2006) Lifelong learning to labour: apprenticeship, masculinity and communities of practice, *British Educational Research Journal* 32(5): 687-701.

Paulini-Schlottau, H. (2006) Verbesserte Chancen für Frauen durch die Neuordnung der Einzelhandelsberufe, in M. Granato & U. Degen (eds) *Berufliche Bildung von Frauen.* Bonn, Bundesinstitut für Berufsbildung: 61-72.

Paulini-Schlottau, H. (2007) Modernisierte Aus- und Fortbildung im Einzelhandel, in BIBB (eds) *Ausbilder-Handbuch.* Bonn: BIBB.

Pilz, M. (2009) *Modularisierungsansätze in der Berufsbildung.* Bielefeld: Bertelsmann Verlag.

Pollard, A. and Filer, A. (1999) *The Social World of Pupil Career—Strategic Biographies through Primary School.* London: Cassell.

Pollard, A. and Filer, A. (2007) Learning, differentiation and strategic action in secondary education: analyses from the Identity and Learning Programme, *British Journal of Sociology of Education* 28(4): 441-458.

Pring, R. (1995) *Closing the Gap: Liberal Education and Vocational Preparation.* London: Hodder & Stoughton.

Pring, R., Hayward, G., Hodgson, A., Johnson, J., Keep, E., Oancea, A., Rees, G., Spours, K. and Wilde, S. (2009) *Education for All—The Future of Education and Training for 14-19 Year-Olds.* London: Routledge.

Puhlmann, A. (2006) Welche Rolle spielt das Geschlecht bei der Berufswahl?, in M. Granato & U. Degen (eds) *Berufliche Bildung von Frauen.* Bonn: Bundesinstitut für Berufsbildung: 28-36.

Raffe, D. (1994) Compulsory education and what then? Signals, choices, pathways, in OECD *Vocational Education and Training for Youth: Towards Coherent Policy and Practice.* Paris, OECD.

Raffe, D. (2008) The concept of transition system, *Journal of Education and Work* 21(4): 277-296.

Rattansi, A. and Phoenix, A. (1997) Rethinking youth identities: modernist and postmodernist frameworks, in J. Bynner, L. Chisholm & A. Furlong (eds) *Youth, Citizenship and Social Change in a European Context.* Aldershot: Ashgate: 121-150.

Rauner, F. (2007) Vocational education and training—A European perspective, in A. Brown, S. Kirpal & F. Rauner (eds) *Identities at Work.* Dordrecht: Springer: 115-144.

Reissig, B. and Gaupp, N. (2007) Hauptschüler: Schwierige Übergänge von der Schule in den Beruf, *Aus Politik und Zeitgeschichte* 28: 10-17.

Renold, E. (2005) *Girls, Boys and Junior Sexualities.* London and New York: Routledge Falmer.

Richardson, W. (1998) Work-based learning for young people: national policy 1994-1997, *Journal of Vocational Education and Training* 50(2): 225-249.

Ricoeur, P. (1992) *Oneself as Another.* Chicago and London: The University of Chicago Press.

Roberts, K. (2004) School-to-work transitions: why the United Kingdom's educational ladders always fail to connect, *International Studies of Education* 14(3): 203-215.

Roberts, K. (2009) Opportunity structures then and now, *Journal of Education and Work* 22(5): 355-368.

Roberts, K., Clarke, S.C. and Wallace, G. (1994) Flexibility and individualisation: a comparison of transitions into employment in England and Germany, *Sociology* 28(1): 31-54.

Rosenthal, G. (2004) Biographical research, in C. Seale, G. Gobo, J. Gubrium, & D. Silverman (eds) *Qualitative Research Practice*. London: Sage.

Rosenthal, G., Köttig, M., Witte, N. and Blezinger, A. (2006) *Biographisch-narrative Gespräche mit Jugendlichen—Chancen für das Selbst- und Fremdverstehen*. Opladen: Barbara Budrich.

Rudd, P. W. and Evans, K. (1998) Structure and agency in youth transitions: student experiences of vocational further education, *Journal of Youth Studies* 1(1): 39-62.

Ryan, P. (1999) The embedding of apprenticeship in industrial relations: British engineering, 1925-65, in P. Ainley & H. Rainbird (eds) *Apprenticeship—Towards a New Paradigm of Learning*. London: Kogan Page.

Ryan, P., Gospel, H. and Lewis, P. (2006) Educational and contractual attributes of the apprenticeship programmes of large employers in Britain, *Journal of Vocational Education and Training* 58(3): 359-383.

Ryan, P. and Unwin, L. (2001) Apprenticeship in the British 'training market', *National Institute Economic Review* 178(1): 99-114.

Scherr, A. (1995) *Soziale Identitäten Jugendlicher—Politische und berufsbiographische Orientierungen von Auszubildenden und Studenten*. Opladen: Leske + Budrich.

Schittenhelm, K. (2005) *Soziale Lagen im Übergang—Junge Migrantinnen und Einheimische zwischen Schule und Berufsausbildung*. Wiesbaden: VS Verlag für Sozialwissenschaften.

Schmidt, C. (2010) Vocational education and training (VET) for youths with low levels of qualification in Germany, *Education + Training* 52(5): 381-390.

Schollweck, S. (2007) *Lernprozesse in einem Handlungsorientierten Beruflichen Unterricht aus Sicht der Schueler*. Frankfurt a. M.: Peter Lang.

Schoon, I. and Parsons, S. (2002) Teenage aspirations for future careers and occupational outcomes, *Journal of Vocational Behavior* 60: 262-288.

Sembill, D., Schumacher, L., Wolf, K. D., Santjer, I. and Pasch, H.-J. (2000) Prozessanalysen selbstorganisierten Lernens—Ein komplexes Lehr-Lern-Arrangement zur Verbesserung der Problemlösefähigkeit, in K. Beck (eds) *Lehr-Lern Prozesse in der kaufmännischen Erstausbildung*. Landau: Verlag Empirische Pädagogik.

Shepherd, J. (2010) *Ministers urges unsuccessful university applicants to reapply*. The Guardian. London. 20.7.2010.

Shildrick, T. and MacDonald, R. (2007) Biographies of exclusion: poor work and poor transitions, *International Journal of Lifelong Education* 26(5): 589-604.

Skeggs, B. (1997) *Formations of Class & Gender*. London: Sage.

Skillsmart Retail (2008) *Retail Apprenticeship/Retail Advanced Apprenticeship, Framework Issue Number: Issue 5 V3*. London: Skillsmart Retail.

Skocpol, T. and Somers, M. (1980) The uses of comparative history in macrosocial inquiry, *Comparative Studies in Society and History* 22(2): 174-197.

Smith, D. I. (2009) Changes in transitions: the role of mobility, class and gender, *Journal of Education and Work* 22(5): 369-390.

SOSTRIS (1999) *Social Strategies in Risk Societies—Case Study Materials: Unqualified Youth*. London.

Spielhofer, T. and Sims, D. (2004) Modern apprenticeships in the retail sector: stresses, strains and support, *Journal of Vocational Education and Training* 56(4): 539-557.

Stake, R. E. (1998) Case studies, in N. K. Denzin & Y. S. Lincoln (eds) *Strategies of Qualitative Inquiry.* Thousand Oaks, London, New Delhi: Sage: 86-109.

Stake, R. E. (2000) The case study method in social inquiry in R. Gomm, M. Hammersley & P. Foster (eds) *Case Study Method.* London: Sage: 19-26.

Stauber, B. (2006) Biography and Gender in Youth Transitions, *New Directions for Child and Adolescent Development*(113): 63-75.

Stauber, B. (2007) Motivation in transition, *Young—Nordic Journal of Youth Research* 15(1): 31-47.

Stauber, B., Pohl, A. and Walther, A. (2007) *Subjektorientierte Übergangsforschung: Rekonstruktion und Unterstützung biografischer Übergänge junger Erwachsener.* Weinheim und München: Juventa Verlag.

Steedman, H. (2010) *The State of Apprenticeship in 2010—International Comparisons.* A report for the Apprenticeship Ambassadors Network. London: London School of Economics and Political Science.

Stender, J. (2006) *Berufsbildung in der Bundesrepublik Deutschland, Teil 1: Strukturprobleme und Ordnungsprinzipien des dualen Systems.* Stuttgart: S.Hirzel Verlag.

Strauss, A. L. and Corbin, J. (1990) *Basics of Qualitative Research: Grounded Theory Procedures and Techniques.* Newbury Park, CA: Sage.

Streeck, W. (1996) Comment on Ronald Dore's Unions Between Class and Enterprise, *Industrielle Beziehungen,* 3(2): 187-196.

Taylor, A. (2010) The contradictory location of high school apprenticeship in Canada, *Journal of Education Policy* 25(4): 503-517.

The Data Service (2011) *Quarterly Statistical First Release.* Online: www.thedataservice. org.uk/NR/rdonlyres/19409349-6523-4244-9F5F-AB56C59E3DBC/0/SFR_June11_ Published.pdf. Accessed 30.7.2011.

The Institute of the Motor Industry (IMI) (2011) *Standards and Qualifications—Vehicle Maintenance and Repair.* Online: www.motor.org.uk/standards-and-qualifications/ vehicle-maintenance-and-repair-ma-n-i.html. Accessed 2.2.2011.

Torrance, H. (2007) Assessment *as* learning? How the use of explicit learning objectives, assessment criteria and feedback in post-secondary education and training can come to dominate learning, *Assessment in Education* 14(3): 281-294.

Torrance, H. Colley, H., Garratt, D., Jarvis, J., Piper, H., Ecclestone, K. and James, D. (2005) *The Impact of Different Modes of Assessment on Achievement and Progress in the Learning and Skills Sector.* London: Learning and Skills Research Centre.

Troman, G. (2002) Method in the messiness: Experiencing the ethnographic PhD process in G. Walford (ed) *Doing a Doctorate in Educational Ethnography.* London: JAI Elsevier: 99-118.

Tsolidis, G. (2008) The (im)possibility of poststructuralist ethnography—researching identities in borrowed spaced, *Ethnography and Education* 3(3): 271-281.

Ulrich, J. G. (2006) Berufskonzepte von Mädchen und Jungen, in M. Granato & U. Degen (eds) *Berufliche Bildung von Frauen.* Bonn: Bundesinstitut für Berufsbildung: 37-60.

Ulrich, J. G. and Krekel, E. M. (2007) Zur Situation der Altbewerber in Deutschland. Ergebnisse der BA/BIBB-Bewerberumfrage 2006, *Berufsbildung in Wissenschaft und Praxis, Zeitschrift des Bundesinstituts für Berufssbildung (BIBB)* 1: 1-7.

Unger, T. (2008) Wissensstrukturen beruflicher Identität, in *Entwicklung eines Leistungspunktesystems in der beruflichen Bildung.* Conference Proceedings. Berlin,

19-20 February 2008. Bonn: Bundesministerium für Bildung und Forschung: 41-52.

Unwin, L. (2004) Growing beans with Thoreau: rescuing skills and vocational education from the UK's deficit approach, *Oxford Review of Education* 30(1): 147-160.

Unwin, L. (2009) *Sensuality, sustainability and social justice—Vocational education in changing times.* London: Institute of Education.

Unwin, L., Fuller, A., Bishop, D., Felstead, A., Jewson, N. and Kakavelakis, K. (2008) *Exploring the Dangers and Benefits of the UK's Permissive Competence-Based Approach: The Use of Vocational Qualifications as Learning Artefacts and Tools for Measurement in the Automotive Sector.* London: Institute of Education.

Unwin, L. Fuller, A., Turbin, J. and Young, M. (2004) *The Impact of Vocational Qualifications.* Research Report 522, Nottingham: Department for Education and Skills.

Unwin, L. and Wellington, J. (2001) *Young People's Perspectives on Education, Training and Employment—Realising their potential.* London: Kogan Page.

Vaughan, K. and Roberts, J. (2007) Developing a 'productive' account of young people's transition perspectives, *Journal of Education and Work* 20(2): 91-105.

Vickerstaff, S. A. (2003) Apprenticeship in the 'golden age': were youth transitions really smooth and unproblematic back then?, *Work, employment and society* 17(2): 269-287.

Vocational Training Act (*Berufsbildungsgesetz*) (as of 23 March 2005) *Federal Law Gazette [BGB1]*

Walford, G. (2009) For ethnography, *Ethnography and Education* 4(3): 271-282.

Walther, A. (2006) Regimes of youth transitions—Choice, flexibility and security in young people's experiences across different European contexts, *Young—Nordic Journal of Youth Research* 14(2): 119-139.

Wengraf, T. (1998) *Representation of interpreted biographies in contexts: general concepts and unique cases.* London: Middlesex University.

Wengraf, T. (2001) *Qualitative Research Interviewing.* London: Sage.

Wengraf, T. (2008) *The Biographic-Narrative Interpretive Method (BNIM)—A Guide.* London, unpublished.

Willis, P. (1977) *Learning to Labour: How Working Class Kids Get Working Class Jobs.* London: Saxon House.

Winch, C. (2006) Georg Kerschensteiner—founding the dual system in Germany, *Oxford Review of Education* 32(3): 381-396.

Witzel, A. and Kühn, T. (1999) *Berufsbiographische Gestaltungsmodi—Eine Typologie der Orientierungen und Handlungen beim Übergang in das Erwerbsleben.* Bremen: ITB.

Wolf, A. (1995) *Competence-based Assessment.* Buckingham: Open University Press.

Wolf, A. (2011) *Review of Vocational Education—The Wolf Report.* London: Department for Education.

Wyn, J. and Dwyer, P. (1999) New directions in research on youth in transition, *Journal of Youth Studies* 2(1): 5-21.

Youdell, D. (2006) Impossible Bodies, *Impossible Selves: Exclusions and Student Subjectivities.* Dordrecht: Springer.

www.ingramcontent.com/pod-product-compliance
Lightning Source LLC
Chambersburg PA
CBHW070915270326
41927CB00011B/2584